# DARING TO RESIST

## Jewish Defiance in the Holocaust

# DARING TO RESIST

## Jewish Defiance in the Holocaust

*Essays*

David Engel

Yitzchak Mais

Eva Fogelman

*Editor* Yitzchak Mais
*Associate Editor* Bonnie Gurewitsch
*Managing Editor* Barbara Lovenheim

MUSEUM OF JEWISH HERITAGE | A LIVING MEMORIAL TO THE HOLOCAUST

Produced and published on the occasion of the exhibition
*Daring to Resist: Jewish Defiance in the Holocaust*
by the Museum of Jewish Heritage – A Living Memorial to the Holocaust,
New York, NY, April 2007 – July 2008
36 Battery Place
New York, NY 10280
www.mjhnyc.org

Major funding for the exhibition was provided by: the Conference on
Jewish Material Claims Against Germany, the Elizabeth Meyer Lorentz Fund
of The New York Community Trust, the Edmond J. Safra Philanthropic
Foundation, and the National Endowment for the Humanities*

NATIONAL
ENDOWMENT
FOR THE
HUMANITIES

*Any views, findings, conclusions, or recommendations expressed in this publication
do not necessarily reflect those of the National Endowment for the Humanities.

Project Director: Dr. Louis D. Levine
Project Coordinator: Ilona Moradof
Designer: Susan Huyser

"Resisting in Jewish Time" © 2007 by David Engel
"Jewish Life in the Shadow of Destruction" © 2007 by Yitzchak Mais
"On Blaming the Victim" © 2007 by Eva Fogelman

Library of Congress Control Number: 2006939551
ISBN 0-9716859-2-4

Cover photo: Cover of *Yugnt Shtime (The Voice of Youth)*, underground newspaper
published in Yiddish by the Bund youth movement, Warsaw, January – February, 1941.
The caption under the image reads: FASCISM MUST BE SMASHED!
YIVO Institute for Jewish Research

Printed by Phoenix Design Aid, Denmark
www.phoenixdesignaid.dk

Rachel Posner, the wife of Rabbi Akiva Posner, the last rabbi in prewar Kiel, Germany, took this photo in their home on Hanukkah,1932. On the back of the photograph she wrote: "'Death to Judah,' the flag says; 'Judah will live forever,' the light answers."

# Table of Contents

Jewish partisan unit in the Rudnicki Forest, Poland, c. 1944.
Many of these partisans had been active in the Kovno Ghetto resistance.

# FOREWORD

A project such as *Daring to Resist: Jewish Defiance in the Holocaust* is the kind of undertaking that is so central to our identity as an institution—our mission, our constituents, our history—that it seems to have grown organically out of our Core Exhibition. The Museum was unique when it was opened in 1997 and remains so precisely because it tells the story of 20th century Jewish history and the Holocaust from the point of view of those who lived it. First person narrative is the hallmark of our institution. In all of the exhibitions we have mounted, oral histories, diaries, memoirs, and other first person accounts have guided the stories we have told. The voice in the current exhibition, *Daring to Resist*, like the voice in its award-winning predecessor, *Ours to Fight For: American Jews in the Second World War*, is that of dignity—bold and courageous—in the face of considerable obstacles.

With *Daring to Resist*, my admiration for the achievements of the leadership and staff of the Museum is unsurpassed. I thank Judah Gribetz, along with the Museum's Collections and Exhibitions Committee, which he leads, for their thoughtful oversight of this endeavor. Shalom Yoran, a Holocaust survivor, partisan, and Museum trustee, urged us to think about this project years ago. He insisted that the world must know how Jews fought—with the little they had—for the survival of the Jewish people, and he insisted that it be done while survivors were still here to tell their stories and to be heard by subsequent generations. As the first donors to this exhibition, Shalom and his wife Varda were vital to its development; their support and interest in it have never wavered. The staff, led by our extraordinary director David Marwell, has once again set its sights on a complex and nuanced topic and has done an exemplary job making it accessible to a broad public. The exhibition team, led by Dr. Louis D. Levine, Yitzchak Mais, and Bonnie Gurewitsch, has done an impressive job.

*Daring to Resist* makes important contributions to scholarship, public history, and Jewish pride. The generous and early support from the National Endowment for the Humanities (NEH), which understood and appreciated the national significance of this project, has been extremely gratifying to all of us. In addition to the NEH, this milestone accomplishment would never have come to fruition had it not been for the leadership gifts of the Elizabeth Meyer Lorentz Fund of The New York Community Trust, which supported the excellent films in the exhibition, the Conference on Jewish Material Claims Against Germany, which is the standard-bearer for protecting the memory of those who perished and honoring those who survived, and the Edmond J. Safra Philanthropic Foundation, whose ongoing support has been crucial to the success of the Museum.

We are also grateful for the support of The David Berg Foundation, Robert I. Goldman Foundation, The Blanche and Irving Laurie Foundation, the Nash Family Foundation, Righteous Persons Foundation, L'Oréal USA, and a number of trustees and individuals, many of whom—in addition to Shalom and Varda Yoran—have a deep personal connection to this history, including Frank and Cesia Blaichman, Patti Askwith Kenner and Family, George and Adele Klein, Ingeborg and Ira Leon Rennert, Nancy Fisher, and Gil and Claire (Israelit) Zweig. To all of them, and to the many others who have helped in ways big and small, our sincerest thanks.

Robert M. Morgenthau
*Chairman*

# PREFACE AND ACKNOWLEDGEMENTS

As a historian, I am fond of saying, "context is everything." In trying to understand Jewish resistance during the Holocaust, this dictum becomes especially critical. If the reader has any doubts, he or she need only think about the oft-repeated question, "Why did the Jews go like sheep to the slaughter?"

This question, in and of itself, is evidence that the public, including many Jews, has confused Jewish powerlessness during the Holocaust with passivity. People conclude, wrongly, that, because Jews were not able to mount significant, sustained, and effective opposition to Nazi persecution, they did not resist at all. The question, based as it is on a false premise, requires an answer that calls for layers of understanding and, yes, an appreciation of context.

The answer involves understanding the context in which Jews found themselves, the inconceivable choices they were forced to make, the limited options that were available to them, the incredible isolation of their communities, the lack of knowledge of their true situation, and the overwhelming strength and ruthlessness of their enemy. The answer also requires knowledge of the many ways that Jews tried to maintain their dignity, to spread the word of their fate, to ensure that their stories would be known, and to save fellow Jews.

The myth that all Jews went passively to their deaths persists, in part, because there has been little effective public education that relates to this very complex issue with an appropriate context and perspective.

I am immensely proud of the work the Museum's leadership and staff have done to remedy this deficit through this special exhibition, *Daring to Resist: Jewish Defiance in the Holocaust*. Not only have we communicated this vital story of Jewish resistance through an engaging and visually striking exhibition; we have further elaborated upon that bold statement with this eloquent volume which, in and of itself, is an enormous contribution to the field.

Our sincerest thanks go to Barbara Lovenheim, who not only supported the book financially, but served lovingly as its managing editor. Yitzchak Mais and Bonnie Gurewitsch are the godparents of this volume and of the exhibition. As editor and associate editor, they shepherded the book and, as curator and associate curator, nurtured the exhibition—from broadest concept to smallest detail. Dr. Louis D. Levine, Director of Collections and Exhibitions, kept the project on track and supervised its most complicated technical details. Ilona Moradof, assistant curator, was the core around which the constituent parts of this project revolved, guided by her steady hand. Igor Kotler, our staff historian, contributed his considerable research skills. In addition, the following individuals made important research, curatorial, registrarial, and organizational contributions to the project: Esther Brumberg, Alana Cole-Faber, Rachel Hapoienu, Bryan Kessler, Indra Mahabir, Matthew Peverly, Andrew Piedelato, Adam Rosenthal, Irene Lehrer-Sandalow, Michael Spielholz, Anna Thomas, Frieda Wald, and Rebecca Wolinsky.

Almost every other person on the Museum staff contributed to this project in some way, so I ask their forgiveness as I am able to single out only a few: Nili Isenberg, Paul Radensky and the rest of the Education department, under the direction of Elizabeth Edelstein have prepared our Gallery Educators, teachers in public and private schools, along with curriculum materials, tours, and outreach so that tens of thousands of students will benefit from the exhibition; Elissa Schein and her staff have organized symposia, music, and film programs that will enrich our understanding of resistance; Abby Spilka and her staff in Communications have been the public face of the exhibition; Felica Kobylanski, Jilian Cahan Gersten, and Sharon Steinbach have helped to raise the funds that have made the exhibition and its attendant programs possible.

The staff was joined by some incredibly talented

people who were integral to this project's success. The exhibition found its visual expression through the skill and dedication of Mike Lesperance and Lonny Schwartz of The Design Minds. The exhibition was fabricated and mounted by a team of master craftspeople and specialists from 1220 Exhibits, led by Craig Dunn and Lisa Hardin. Our boundless admiration to the brilliant filmmakers—Bestor Cram, Anne Marie Stein, Beth Sternheimer of Northern Light—the results speak eloquently. Our sincerest appreciation goes to Paul Rosenthal, who tirelessly honed our language and helped with a variety of interpretive tasks with his usual dexterity and flair.

The considerable talents of the staff and consultants brought this challenging project to fruition through the dedicated efforts of project director Dr. Louis D. Levine and Ivy L. Barsky, deputy director of the Museum.

The muscular essays by David Engel, Yitzchak Mais, and Eva Fogelman are complemented by Bonnie Gurewitsch's informative chapter introductions. David Engel's discussion of "Jewish time" in history, while specific to our purposes of exploring Jewish resistance, holds lessons for anyone interested in Jewish history, and, in fact, for anyone interested in writing and documenting history in general. Eva Fogelman broaches a singularly difficult subject—blaming the victim—with a psychologist's sensitivity and expertise. Yitzchak Mais's passionate prose reflects his zeal for this subject matter and his dedication to setting the record straight—from a Jewish perspective.

The exhibition was strengthened by the rigorous academic scrutiny of extraordinary and generous scholars. Two teams of prominent scholars met with our curatorial staff, in Israel and in New York, and assisted with conceptual development and issues of contents.

Our admiration and appreciation go to Professors Randolph Braham, Deborah Dwork, David Engel, Yisrael Gutman, Marion Kaplan, Samuel Kassow, Michael Marrus, Robert Shapiro, Nechama Tec, and Susan Zucotti. We also assembled a group of Holocaust survivors, who served as lay advisors. The exhibition reflects this very important input in significant ways.

We would like to thank our colleagues at sister institutions who generously shared expertise, artifacts, documents, and photographs, which enabled *Daring to Resist* to reflect a broad spectrum of materials and ideas. In particular, we thank our institutional partner, Ghetto Fighters' House, led by its extraordinary director, Simcha Stein, and his colleagues, Yossi Shavit, Zvi Oren, and Judy Grossman.

Special thanks to Yad Vashem, Avner Shalev, Yehudit Inbar, Nomi Halperin, Cecilia Haddad, and Elana Weiser. Our thanks also go to Eleonora Bergman, Jewish Historical Institute, Warsaw; Miriam Intrator and Michael Simonson, Leo Baeck Institute, New York; Fruma Mohrer, Marek Web, Gunnar Berg, Leo Greenbaum, and Jesse Cohen, YIVO Institute for Jewish Research; Susan Goldstein Snyder, United States Holocaust Memorial Museum; Ilya Altman, Russian Research and Educational Holocaust Center; Graciela Ben-Dror, Yehoshua Buechler, and Roni Kochavi, Moreshet Archives; Anita Tarsi, Beit Theresienstadt Museum; Mitch Braff, Jewish Partisan Educational Foundation; and Kenneth M. Mandel, Great Projects Film Co., Inc.

Many thanks to the following who assisted the project with their research and expertise: Shoshana Barri, Sara Bender, Suzy Bock, Gila Fatran, Ariel Hurwitz, Mark Kuperwaser, Chaim Schatzker, Barbara Snow, Yonat Rotbein, Danny Wool, and Mark Wygoda.

Finally, to the many survivors and their families who gave of their precious legacy—artifacts, testimony, memories—our sincerest gratitude and admiration.

David G. Marwell, Ph.D.
*Director*

# Resisting in Jewish Time

*David Engel*

More than a century has passed since Albert Einstein proved that time is relative. Einstein showed how two observers traveling in different directions would perceive time differently, yet both would be correct—no person's perception of time is any more valid than that of anyone else. Similarly, since a people's actions are intimately connected to their perception of time, their actions and choices may be strongly affected by their personal circumstances—the directions in which they are traveling, to use Einstein's illustration as a metaphor.

Likewise, historical periods have no independent existence outside of how they are conceived by people. Imagine, for example, that we could each visit the past in our own time machines. As we travel back from the modern era, through the Middle Ages, to ancient times, there would be no signposts along the way to announce the end—or start—of a particular era; instead we would have to decide for ourselves not only how to define and label particular periods of time but whether it would be useful to mark them at all. Our decisions would depend heavily upon how each of our particular journeys unfolded and what we were able to see en route. Moreover, since each of us would be looking from our own unique perspective, we might well disagree over precisely how far we had come. In fact, we might not even be able to tell in which direction we were traveling.

If this thought experiment seems too fanciful, it might help to consider our own personal life histories.

When we reflect on our lives, we often think of them as divided into clear phases. However, these phases may not be obvious to others, who encounter us at different times. For example, some of us may consider that the phases of our lives are clearly defined by significant milestones—the moment we left our parents' homes, when we got married, or when we became parents. On the other hand, when colleagues at work think about us, they may try to understand us by employing a different perspective—one that is defined by our professional environment. To them, our jobs and their particular histories are likely to provide more useful points of reference, and from their point of view they will not be wrong. It might even happen that, although they will analyze their lives according to their family status, they will still try to understand our experiences based primarily on what they see when they meet us in the workplace. They will measure our journey through life using one time scale, we another.

In the same way, the periods into which we conventionally divide history, where we place the divisions, and the direction of movement we ascribe to them, do not always correspond to the periods that others identify in their own particular histories. For example, Americans and Japanese may define what they call the Second World War as the period from December 7, 1941, when Japanese forces attacked Pearl Harbor, to September 2, 1945, when General MacArthur accepted Japan's surrender on the deck of the battleship *Missouri*. Europeans, on the other hand, are more likely to place the war's beginning on the day between

September 1, 1939 and June 22, 1941, when their countries were either invaded by Germany or joined the military struggle, and the war's end, when German forces departed their territory, or when Germany surrendered in May 1945.

In other words, conventional periodization reflects only one possible way of looking at an era. It adopts the perspective of one observer to the exclusion of all others, even though others may measure the same intervals in different but equally appropriate ways. We should do well to keep these ideas in mind when thinking about any historical episode. When thinking about the horrific encounter between Nazi Germany and the Jews of Europe, and particularly about the behavior of Jews during that encounter, they bear special emphasis. We have become accustomed to identifying the entire period of Nazi rule in Germany, from January 30, 1933 to May 8, 1945, with a set of events we call the Holocaust, by which we commonly mean the destruction and catastrophic loss of life incurred by the Jews of Europe at the hands of the Nazis and their collaborators.

It has also become customary to regard Jewish losses as unfolding in discrete stages, as the perpetrators of the Holocaust sought to identify Jews, isolate them from the surrounding society and weaken them physically and spiritually before proceeding to mass murder. As a result, each stage is defined by actions taken by Germans: the anti-Jewish boycott of April 1, 1933; the enactment of the Nuremberg Laws in September 1935; the violence of *Kristallnacht* in November 1938; the secret order of Reinhard Heydrich on September 21, 1939, mandating the establishment of ghettos and Jewish Councils in occupied Poland; the mass shootings of Jews following Germany's invasion of the Soviet Union on June 22, 1941; the Wannsee Conference in January 1942; the mass deportation of Jews from Warsaw during the summer of 1942; and the dispatch of Adolf Eichmann to Budapest to organize the murder of Hungarian Jewry in March 1944.

Each of these events is conventionally taken as the beginning of a new chapter in the destruction of the Jews. In other words, we have learned to measure the Holocaust according to the actions of the perpetrators—in German time.

But if time and its divisions are fundamentally subjective, then we should be able to measure and analyze the Holocaust differently. Surely there must also be a victims' time—a Jewish time—in which the period of Nazi rule is divided and analyzed in a decidedly different manner than that which we have been accustomed to imagine.

What might it mean to measure the Holocaust in Jewish time?

Jewish time differed from German time first of all in the direction in which Jews and Germans thought they were moving through it. Shortly after the Nazi takeover, Germany's new propaganda minister, Joseph Goebbels, announced triumphantly over the radio: "the year 1789 is stricken from history."[1] He meant that the liberal political and social arrangements inaugurated by the French Revolution, epitomized by the values of liberty, equality, and fraternity, would be replaced by a totally "new order," one that (as Hitler himself promised in a speech in Breslau in March 1933) would "liquidate traditions and memories," so that "new thoughts, new conceptions, and new realities" could lead the way to innovation and progress. "All of us," Hitler declared, "have surely come to the conclusion that we stand on the threshold of a new age."[2] The Nazi revolution thus seemed to its leaders to be propelling them rapidly forward through time, away from any place they had ever been, constantly crossing new frontiers with such force that they could continue indefinitely.

To be sure, German Jews also sensed from Goebbels's proclamation that an era in their own history had expired. For them, the French Revolution, which the Nazi minister had consigned to the unrecoverable past, had ushered in an age of emancipation, culminating in 1871 when Jews became equal citizens of the newly unified German state. Now, they understood that, as Heinz Kellermann, a Jewish youth leader, put it in August 1933, "our external emancipation, in the sense of legal, economic, and social equality, has come to an end."[3] However, instead of looking forward, as the Nazis did, to a future entirely unencumbered by older political models, many Jews saw a return to days of yore. "Jewish history has begun all over again," proclaimed a Berlin rabbi in his first Passover sermon of the Nazi years.[4] Similarly, Jacob Marcus, an American rabbi and scholar who had studied in Germany during the 1920's, observed in 1934 that, with the Nazi rise to power, "the Jew was driven back...to complete medieval darkness."[5] Jews now saw themselves traveling through time as if they were attached to a pendulum, which, having reached the end of its period in one direction, had been drawn inexorably backward, retracing its path along points well known from earlier ages.

"For a long time the Jewish people has been living through a process of continuous oscillation...between the poles of emancipation and ghettoization," Kellermann observed. In fact, he explained, anyone familiar with Jewish history could not help but understand Nazi anti-Jewish actions as simply "a new variation on the same theme."[6]

Much of how Jews, both in Germany and throughout the area of eventual German domination, acted in the face of the Hitler regime was predicated upon this interpretation of Nazi Jewish policy as a regression to an earlier age. In particular, many of their ideas about what resisting their oppressors might mean seem to have been formed out of this mindset. On the most basic level, openly expressing the notion that the Nazis were treading familiar ground may itself have been a way for Jews to display a defiant attitude toward the regime, as if no ruler could visit any punishments upon them that they had not withstood successfully before. Indeed, the version of Jewish history most familiar to German Jews at the time taught that throughout seventeen centuries of "unprecedented suffering and constant martyrdom in which each century brought new depths of abuse and humiliation," Jews had continuously demonstrated "a great, noble pride in bearing a teaching that reflects eternity"— a teaching that allowed Jews to outlive all their oppressors without "sinking to the level of brutal vagrants."[7] Hence for many Jews the association of Nazism with the Middle Ages not only heralded a renewed era of misfortune; it also pointed the way to withstanding any conceivable abuse. Jews needed to recapture as best they could what they took to be their ancestors' authentic Jewish way of life.

Defying the Nazis by becoming more authentic meant in the first instance learning about the Jewish heritage that was supposed to have shielded their ancestors from the blows of a hostile surrounding society. For many German Jews who had adopted the ethos and modes of behavior of the surrounding society during the era of emancipation, this heritage felt unfamiliar. Hence teaching Judaism and Jewish history to children and adults became a prime focus of collective Jewish activity.

One of the first projects undertaken by the groundbreaking umbrella organization, Reichsvertretung der Deutschen Juden (the Reich Representation of German Jews), formed in 1933, was to open a Center for Adult Jewish Education. As its director, the philosopher Martin Buber, explained, the purpose was "to shape a society that can hold fast, overcome, and preserve the spark [of Jewishness]."[8]

Similar attitudes prevailed among Jews in all countries that fell into the Nazi orbit: educational and cultural activities aimed at endowing Jews of all ages with the spiritual power of perseverance were a communal priority even where, unlike in Germany, they had to operate underground. In Poland in 1940 the Zionist youth movement Dror (Freedom), which until then had denigrated the educational value of traditional, diaspora-based Jewish culture, secretly published an anthology of Jewish texts from the First Crusade and the Cossack massacres of the seventeenth century, emphasizing that the experience of earlier Jewish generations would "strengthen in us the urge to live and the will to carry on in our own difficult times."[9]

One of the models Jews believed they could find in the Jewish past was that of a community that knew how to look after its own members in both the social and political spheres. "The path of German Jewry in the last century," proclaimed the editor of the Jewish monthly *Der Morgen* in January 1934, has been a "path of individuals," one that placed personal achievement above collective responsibility. That path, the editor continued, "has been a mistake." Now, he declared, all must realize that "being Jewish. means commitment and obligation" to the entire community, for "it is inconsistent with the times to think that people can separate their personal fate from that of German Jewry" as a whole.[10]

The Nuremberg Laws, which according to German commentators constituted the Jews as a legally autonomous national minority dependent entirely upon its own resources, reinforced regard for the

# Analyzing the Holocaust in Jewish time means identifying the stages through which Jews came to dismiss their initial sense that under Nazi rule they were reliving their past.

community as an indispensable intermediary between Jews and the state. Similarly, the *Judenräte* (Jewish Councils) established in other countries after the German conquest appeared to many Jews, initially at least, a vital instrument of survival, an intercessor and a buffer between them and their new rulers.[11] Councils had been a paramount function of the Jewish community in medieval times; in the new incarnation of the Middle Ages, it seemed appropriate, even necessary, that Jews conduct their internal and external affairs within an autonomous communal framework.

In other words, what Nazis perceived as innovations marking new stages in their relationship with the Jews of Europe did not, to most Jews, signal anything new at all. Quite the contrary: The revocation of citizenship, the strict regulation and restriction of economic activity, the summoning of the *Judenräte*, the establishment of ghettos, the imposition of the yellow star—all of these were implicit in the fundamental notion that the Third Reich had reversed the Jews' forward progress through time and propelled them back into their own past. In 1933, Heinz Kellermann (and many other Jews) labeled the direction of the pendulum in which Jews had begun to swing through time as "ghettoization."

Thus when the first Polish Jews were enclosed in actual physical ghettos in October 1939, they saw little remarkable in the situation. In fact, whenever the Nazis resurrected an anti-Jewish practice from an earlier era, Jews could feel increasingly certain that their assessment of the direction in which they were moving through time was accurate.

Analyzing the Holocaust in Jewish time thus means identifying the stages that marked the process through which Jews lost their initial sense that under Nazi rule they were reliving their past. The key questions are: What, if anything, did Jews see as new in their unfolding experience; when, if ever, did they see it; and how, if at all, did what they see affect how they behaved?

No single, simple answer to these questions will suffice for all Jews within the Nazi orbit, if only because Jews experienced German rule for different durations and during different intervals on the road to the Final Solution.[12] As a result, there is not one way to measure the Holocaust in Jewish time but many. Nevertheless, Jews in different places did experience certain situations under Nazi rule that the medieval paradigm could not easily explain.

First, during the Middle Ages, violence against Jews was more often than not perpetrated by mobs acting on their own, or, at most, with the sanction of local leaders. Territorial rulers, on the other hand, tended to discourage such violence—not out of regard for the Jews' welfare but because mobs challenged the social discipline that rulers sought to enforce. In times of physical threat, then, Jews had become accustomed to appeal to rulers for protection; the thought that rulers might make common cause with the mob or become purveyors of violence themselves did not fit in with the Jews' overall experience. In many places, Nazi authorities operated at first along similar lines, using local collaborators as proxies in violent actions, then stepping in ostensibly to restore order as part of a ruse aimed at heightening Jewish dependence upon them. However sooner or later, the official military and police forces of the Third Reich came to attack Jews openly, and when they did, the legacy of the Middle Ages was of little use.

Jews' relations to territorial rulers during the Middle Ages were predicated also upon confidence that the rulers were dealing with them according to universally accepted rules. Although the privilege of living and working in any location and of maintaining a Jewish community there was always granted by an individual king or feudal lord, Jews could assume that wherever they went or whoever governed the territory, conditions of their residence would be more or less the same. Under Nazi rule, that assumption was patently false.

Not only did Jews beyond the Nazi realm live under markedly different conditions than Jews within its boundaries, but, beginning in 1939, other nations went to war against the Third Reich and Jews under Nazi rule could see an alternative to their situation at close hand. As the war against the Third Reich progressed, the fundamental confidence in an Allied victory made it seem that this alternative would materialize in the near future.

Finally, the violence that the Third Reich purveyed was of an incommensurably greater magnitude than any that Jews had experienced in the past. The mass deportations and killing of Jews at the instigation of the German state violated all historical precedent, eliminating any chance that the Nazis had transported Jews back to an earlier time. The Middle Ages were an era of persecution, the Nazi years one of devastation.

These features of the Third Reich initially appeared to Jews as anomalies, inexplicable deviations from their normal worldview and expectations. It took a steady accumulation of such anomalies to persuade Jews that they were not merely occasional or accidental departures from the norm but were an essential part of the norm itself, requiring a new explanation. The earliest articulation of such a new explanation is generally identified with a speech made by Abba Kovner, a 23-year-old poet and leader of the Hashomer Hatza'ir Zionist youth movement in Vilna (p. 108), who announced to his comrades on December 31, 1941, that "we are facing a well-planned system that is hidden from us at the moment," a system designed to bring about "absolute, total annihilation."

At the time, Kovner was well ahead of his fellow Jews in assessing the meaning of the mass shootings of Jews that contradicted the dominant paradigm of a return to the Middle Ages; most Jews required far more evidence before they would accept that their old way of understanding their situation had been mistaken.

"We have no assurance that we are facing the immediate absolute liquidation of the ghetto, its total annihilation," one of Kovner's colleagues admonished. Kovner himself acknowledged that his new paradigm could not explain "why Vilna is bleeding while Bialystok is peaceful and calm;" yet, he insisted, "anyone who observes what is happening around us with a clear mind, an open heart, and mainly with a healthy instinct, cannot but be convinced."[13]

Kovner's instinct was uncommonly keen. Nevertheless, during the ensuing months, an increasing number of Jews observed enough anomalous features of the Third Reich's behavior to comprehend that those features were not anomalous at all. For some, like Kovner, the participation of German soldiers in mass shootings of Jews on the Eastern front during the second half of 1941 provided the necessary trigger. For others, the key turning point came when the Nazi authorities began deporting Jews "to the East"—not banishing them to a place beyond their realm, as rulers sometimes did in medieval times, but forcibly removing them from their homes and communities and relocating them in camps under Nazi authority. Others needed to hear an accumulation of reports about the death camps before they were convinced that the Nazis were a phenomenon unknown in Jewish history.

But once they came to this realization, their perception of the direction in which they were moving through time under Nazi rule changed fundamentally: They could now be compared to the traveler in our thought experiment who had been misled by certain sights they observed from the window of their time machine into thinking that they were visiting the past instead of the future. Now they believed—together with the Nazis—that instead of being transported back into an earlier age, they were hurtling rapidly forward through a totally new era. Unlike the Nazis, though, they saw that this era would soon end, either with Germany's defeat or with the extinction of the Jews of Europe.

Those who wish to measure the Holocaust in Jewish time must first orient themselves along this fundamental axis. The different perceptions that catalyzed that reversal for different groups of Jews—perceptions regarding the meaning of mass shootings, deportations, and the killing centers—mark the principal chronological divisions in the Jews' own lived experience of the Nazi era.

Different perceptions of the meaning of
mass shootings, deportations, and killing centers
mark the principal chronological divisions
in the Jews' experience of the Nazi era.

But what is to be gained by measuring the Holocaust in Jewish time? Was the history of the Holocaust altered in any fundamental way by whether Jews perceived time to be moving forward or back?

To be sure, the outcome of the Holocaust did not depend to any statistically significant extent on the Jews' use of historical paradigms to understand their collective situation; that situation was controlled entirely by the Germans, and Jews were powerless to change it. However, the decisions Jews made individually and collectively about how to confront their situation were surely influenced by whether they thought the Nazis aimed to persecute them or to kill them. Those decisions, in turn, profoundly affected the fate of many individual Jews, the character of collective Jewish life facing death, and the legacy the Holocaust's victims left for future generations.

This is not to say that as long as they viewed their condition as essentially medieval, they felt less urgency to resist their tormentors. The wide scope of communal activities of medieval communities that Jews tried initially to resurrect—in education and culture, social welfare, mutual assistance, health care, gathering and disseminating information, and, whenever necessary, inventing of subterfuges to help Jews avoid the consequences of evil decrees—were doubtless conceived on some significant level as acts of opposition to the regime that had been imposed upon them. The primary aim of such activities, however, was to promote collective endurance over the long term. As German Jewish historian Ismar Elbogen explained in the early days of the Nazi regime, "They can condemn us to hunger, but they cannot condemn us to starvation."[14]

In Eastern Europe Jews spoke of *iberleben*—not merely surviving but outliving the Nazis. They assumed that the backward swing of history's pendulum initiated by the Nazi conquest would one day reach its natural end, after which the course of events would lead again to a regime of greater freedom. It was unclear, however, whether that development would take place within the lifetimes of those who were present when the Nazis took control. It was thus necessary to make sure that both present and future generations possessed the material and spiritual resources that would enable them to persevere, both as individuals and as Jews, under conditions of great hardship until the hardship abated. Achieving that goal embodied a collective effort to thwart the oppressors' evil designs.

The perception of movement forward through time that gradually replaced the earlier, backward-looking one undermined the basic assumption of the old communal strategy, but it did not suggest an obvious new premise for resistance. Not only did Jews now see themselves in an unprecedented situation, where Jewish history could no longer serve as a guide; they also could not be certain whether they or the Nazis would run out of time first. Some Jewish leaders continued to seek direction from the past—not only the distant Jewish one, in which Jews had outlived their oppressors, but the recent European one as well. During the First World War, Germany had ultimately been defeated by the combined military superiority of the Allies despite stunning initial victories on both the eastern and western fronts. As far as those leaders could ascertain, the factors that had brought the German armies down a quarter century earlier remained present during the current war; hence, they reasoned, it was only a matter of time before the forces of liberation came to the rescue. They could not be certain, however, how much time would pass before the inevitable occurred and whether the Jews for whom they were responsible could hold out until it did. Those questions became subjects of intense debate in Jewish communities throughout Nazi-occupied Europe, and attitudes toward them shaped many features of Jewish behavior as the Final Solution reached its apogee.

For those who held out hope that the Nazi-propelled phase of their journey through time would end while they remained alive, active overt and hostile defiance of the regime, through public acts of disobedience, mass escapes, or armed revolt, appeared potentially self-defeating. They likened their situation to that of hostages, who are conventionally advised to wait calmly to be rescued, all the while doing what they can to assuage their captors' wrath. Some were even prepared to hand over a portion of their charges for deportation to be killed in the hope of sating the appetite of the Nazi beast long enough to keep it from consuming the rest before rescue arrived.

For those to whom such hope seemed illusory— mostly young people who had no personal memories of the First World War—all that could be salvaged was the spiritual legacy the victims left to future generations—not only the legacy of Jews whose good fortune placed them beyond the Nazis' reach but of humanity as a whole. Hence they directed their efforts toward two types of projects—documenting the last days of their communities and the way in which they were destroyed, (in the manner of Emanuel Ringelblum's clandestine archive of the Warsaw Ghetto, Oyneg Shabbes, p. 52), so that the memory of those who perished might be preserved and the destroyers punished when liberation came, and taking arms in hand for one great physical confrontation with the enemy so that the murderers would pay an immediate price for their actions. And, more importantly, for those who took this course, as one of them, Rózka Korczak of Vilna, put it—"to infuse our history with a new sound, a new content: not only tragedy but...heroic struggle, self-defense, a fight for life...and death with honor."[15]

Dolek Liebeskind, a member of the Jewish Fighting Organization in the Krakow Ghetto, put it another way: "We are fighting for three lines in history"—lines that needed to be written before Jewish time ran out.[16]

Ironically, those who turned to armed revolt out of a sense that Jewish time was running out found themselves in conflict with another community whose perception of time differed from their own. For the Polish resistance movement, to whom the ghetto fighters frequently turned for support (including weapons), any armed uprising against the Nazi occupiers before the Allies were actually knocking on the gates of victory was premature. Some Polish underground leaders feared that revolts in the ghettos would invite German reprisals against Poles. Some hoped to dissuade Jews from taking up arms, not realizing that Jews were subject to a time schedule radically different from theirs. In this fashion the subjectivity of time complicated the story of Jewish resistance.

But how can Jewish time claim equal validity with German time as a way of measuring the Holocaust? Were not Jews' assessments of their direction in time overwhelmingly wrong? Einstein notwithstanding, it hardly seems that Jews and Germans marked the stages between the rise of the Third Reich and the destruction of European Jewry with the same degree of accuracy. Perhaps in this case what is true of the physical world is not true of history after all.

But the objection misses the point. We who observe the events we call the Holocaust from chronological distance do not need to decide which of the groups that lived through those events understood the moments they occupied in time with greater accuracy. We do, however, need to be aware that we can observe those events today only vicariously, by retracing the paths that the different participants in them traveled and seeing them through their eyes.

German and Jewish participants moved through those events along different paths; hence their perceptions of time as they traveled them were necessarily different as well. If we follow the path that German perpetrators traveled, we shall see the Holocaust in German time; but if we wish to walk together with Jewish victims, to understand how they lived in the shadow of death, we can use only Jewish time to mark changes along the way.

Surely the victims are every bit as reliable and worthy guides to their encounter with the Third Reich as those who ended their lives.

THREESOME (oil on canvas) painted by Felix Nussbaum
while he was in hiding in Belgium, January 1944.

# Jewish Life in the Shadow of Destruction

*Yitzchak Mais*

Current awareness of the Holocaust stands in marked contrast to that of the early postwar decades, which witnessed—with some notable exceptions—a "strange silence" shrouding the Holocaust, in both Jewish communities and the academic world.[1] In the last three decades, however, in addition to the creation of Holocaust museums and memorials around the world, there has been an unparalleled explosion of creative and intellectual activity aimed at dealing with this unique catastrophe. These activities range from popular TV dramas, movies, plays, and fiction to art exhibitions and concerts, along with an expanding body of scholarly research and publications in such diverse fields as history, literature, philosophy, and psychology. Six decades after the end of World War II, the Holocaust is recognized as a watershed event with ramifications of critical significance for Jews and non-Jews alike.

Unfortunately, both popular and scholarly works dealing with the Holocaust routinely highlight the Nazi process of persecution that ultimately ended in the brutal murder of the Jews. Scant attention is paid to Jewish life in Europe before the Nazi assault. Thus we know the Jews primarily as victims, with little knowledge of who they were. We learn little about their family life, their communities, their languages, and their views of their world and future before the war. Nor do we know how they responded to the unimaginable assault on their lives and their families. Regrettably, Jews under German domination are often depicted as passive objects—faceless extras in the drama of their own destruction.[2]

A disturbing consequence of this lack of knowledge is that often, in very subtle ways, Jews themselves are blamed for being victims.[3] The questions people ask often imply guilt. The Holocaust author and survivor Primo Levi observed: "Among the questions that are put to us [survivors] there is one that is never absent: Indeed, as the years go by, it is formulated with ever increasing persistence, and with an ever less hidden accent of accusation. More than a single question, it is a family of questions. 'Why did you not escape? Why did you not rebel? Why did you not avoid capture beforehand?'"[4] These queries imply that the victims could have acted differently, and that by not doing so, they were somehow "wrong," or even worse, might be somehow responsible for their own demise.[5]

This widespread depiction of Jews as innocent but passive victims presents a fundamentally skewed picture of what was a far more complex and nuanced situation, and prevents people from viewing the behavior of Jews during the Holocaust in a positive light.

There is a need, therefore, to present the often-ignored Jewish dimension of the Holocaust. Doing so will help audiences get inside the heads of the threatened Jews, so they can understand not only how Jews perceived and reacted to changing Nazi policies but how they understood the implications of these policies. A more complete perspective will reveal that Jews were not passive victims, but active agents who responded with a surprisingly wide range of resourceful actions. Such a presentation is the objective of both this volume and the exhibition that inspired it.

The presentation of the Jewish perspective, as opposed to the Nazi perspective, requires us to suspend our historical hindsight. Although we know that the Nazis carried out a systematic assault on the Jews that culminated in mass murder, Jews at the time did not know this. The unprecedented nature of the murderous anti-Jewish policies made it nearly impossible for Jews to understand their impending destruction.

Visitors to our exhibition will be challenged to re-evaluate their understanding of what constitutes resistance. While we consciously offer no rigid definition of what comprises Jewish resistance, we have organized our presentation around four categories of responses that reflect the intentions—and often the results—of the actions of a multitude of Jews who attempted to defy the Nazis. These four types of resistance occurred in all areas of Nazi domination and are an adaptation of the categories suggested by the Swiss historian, Werner Rings, in his important research on how European peoples responded to German occupation.[6]

Rings' four categories are Symbolic and Personal Resistance— attempts to preserve individual dignity, Jewish identity, and Jewish continuity; Polemic Resistance—attempts to compile and spread the news of Nazi brutalities to Jews in occupied Europe and also the free world; Defensive Resistance—attempts to aid and protect Jews; and Offensive and Armed Resistance, spontaneous acts of revenge and organized armed efforts against the Nazis and their collaborators.

Our goal is to demonstrate that there was no single response but rather a *multitude* of reactions intended to defy German plans to dehumanize Jews and destroy Judaism. Our "typology of resistance" outlines the diverse Jewish responses, but importantly, without establishing a hierarchy of merit.

Although most Jews fell victim to Nazi brutality, they did, not, as a rule, give in to demoralization or moral collapse, thus refuting the prevalent stereotype: True the Jews were slaughtered, but clearly not like sheep! The tragic fate of the Jews demands empathy and commemoration; the dignity and strength exhibited by both victims and survivors in the face of unprecedented violence requires recognition and demands respect. For Jewish audiences, there is a particular need to understand the diversity of Jewish defiance.

Yehuda Bauer, the noted Israeli Holocaust historian, highlighted this relevancy: "A Jew seeking to understand what his Jewishness means must take into account his people's greatest catastrophe. He must ask himself, for example: How did the values and attitudes to which I am heir stand up under the most terrible test in history? If Jews were able to face the Nazi terror in one way or another, is it because something in their tradition, culture or history helped them, or did their particular tradition have nothing to do with it? Is there something that I as a Jew should remember and which I should warn Jews and others, lest a similar fate befall them?"[7]

## A JEWISH PERSPECTIVE ON THE HOLOCAUST

**D**avid Engel's essay "Resisting in Jewish Time" (p. 10) argues that a Jewish perspective on the periodization of the Holocaust will complement the traditional approach that divides the Holocaust into stages using milestones defined by the actions of the Nazis.[8] A central theme in our Jewish-centered narrative is the evolution of Jewish responses to the various Nazi policies devised against them. To illustrate this evolution we have developed four thematic periods: **Responding to the Nazi Rise to Power; Resisting Occupation; Resisting Deportation;** and **Resisting Mass Murder.**

**Responding to the Nazi Rise to Power**
In general, the initial Jewish reaction to Nazi anti-Jewish measures, on both the individual and communal level, was an attempt to lead normal lives. This striving for normalcy can be seen in numerous initiatives undertaken by leaders of the Jewish community, by Jewish organizations, and by individual Jews, all of whom responded to what they believed was a brutal—but temporary—situation. This range of activities addressed the material and spiritual needs of the persecuted Jews, reflecting the resourcefulness and vitality of the Jewish community as well as its desire to frustrate the aims of the Nazis and their collaborators.

This active opposition to an increasingly hostile environment began in Germany in 1933 shortly after Hitler's rise to power. It included creating alternative activities and organizations for Jews to replace those from which they were excluded. A major achievement was uniting the often-conflicting ideological groups under a single umbrella organization, Reichsvertretung der Deutschen Juden (Reich Representation of German Jews). Led by Rabbi Leo Baeck, this official representative body was formed in September 1933 and served as a much-needed liaison with the hostile Nazi government as well as a source of material aid, education, and emigration assistance for its Jewish constituents.

That same year also witnessed the creation of the Kulturbund (Cultural Union of German Jews), which allowed Jewish artists and audiences, who had been excluded from public cultural life, to continue their cultural activities in newly organized theaters and orchestras throughout Germany. As a reaction to their exclusion from the general Winter Relief programs in 1935, Jews established their own Winterhilfe (Winter Relief), which aided and supported many impoverished Jews who, for the first time, needed to receive welfare. Finally, throughout this period, the Jewish community initiated practical alternatives for banned Jews in a variety of disciplines (medicine, law, education, sports), allowing them—at least for a time—to pursue their interests and their profession after being "legally" excluded by the regime.

There were also a number of attempts to confront and reduce Nazi persecution and discrimination. Jews undertook legal actions in the courts, and attempted to sway public opinion. An extraordinary legal initiative was the Bernheim Petition, which challenged the legality of Nazi anti-Jewish laws within the areas of former Poland that had been annexed to Germany. Backed by Jewish organizations, Franz Bernheim filed a complaint against the German government in the League of Nations (the predecessor to the UN) in May 1933. Remarkably, the League, which supervised this area, upheld the grievance. Germany was forced to retract its laws and, until 1937, stop discriminating against Jews in Upper Silesia.

Clandestine political groups opposing the Nazi regime counted among their members an unusually high number of Jewish activists, including those who

## Jews were not passive victims, but active agents who responded with a surprisingly wide range of resourceful actions.

made up the Jewish-organized Baum Group. Jewish political activity dramatically increased, especially among the various Zionist movements, which escalated their social, educational, and political activities, allowing desperate Jewish youth an opportunity for positive self-expression, and sustaining their hopes for emigration to Palestine.

Jewish religious institutions became a haven for those rejected by German society by intensifying their educational and outreach programs to all members of the Jewish community. The law banning *shechitah* (kosher butchering) in April 1933 was successfully evaded by a few dedicated individuals, who continued to perform kosher slaughtering clandestinely throughout the 1930's despite the threat of severe punishment.[9]

Jews were forced to decide whether to stay and "ride out the storm" or to leave. But options for those who wanted to leave were limited, since countries like the United States, Great Britain, and British-controlled Palestine refused to revise their strict quota system to admit more Jewish refugees. Many Jews had to rely on their ingenuity and courage. The fact that thousands escaped to Shanghai, the Dominican Republic, and other countries with unfamiliar cultures indicates their determination and desperation. We can empathize with parents who were faced with the choice of letting their children go on their own to Palestine, via Youth Aliyah or, after *Kristallnacht*, on *Kindertransports* to England. Parents had to struggle with their deepest fears of never seeing their children again.

Avraham Barkai, a noted researcher, observed that the manifold initiatives undertaken by the German Jewish community were "an important expression of its solidarity, cohesiveness, and the collective will to resist the ever more hostile environment."[10]

## Resisting Occupation

It can be said that individuals and communities base their expectations for the future on their experience of the past. In many lands occupied by the Nazis—Poland, Lithuania, and the Ukraine in particular—many Jews were influenced (and tragically misled) by memories of the benevolent German occupation of World War I, considered a vast improvement over life under the brutal Czarist regime that it replaced. Although Jews in Western Europe feared a German invasion, they were confident that their generally successful integration into society would result in their protection by local authorities. Moreover, they believed that their non-Jewish neighbors would not abandon them.

Occupation occurred in different countries at different times between 1939 and 1944 [11] and had different effects. The attempt to isolate Jews was universal, but isolation could range from discriminatory laws to the requirement for Jews to wear the yellow star to forced concentration in sealed ghettos. For the most part, Jews recognized the occupation as a difficult but not unusual hardship of a wartime regime.

This resigned recognition was especially true among Jews who confronted hellish conditions in the ghettos of Eastern Europe. It is important to understand life in the ghetto the way imprisoned Jews experienced it, and crucial to consider it from their perspective and within the context of their understanding of the future. Unaware of their impending fate, Jews approached life in the ghettos on its own terms and not simply, as it is generally perceived today, as a way station to the death camps.

Almost without exception, we note that Jews in sealed ghettos, as well as those living throughout occupied Europe, strongly believed that the forces of good would ultimately triumph over the forces of evil, and that the Allies would eventually defeat Germany and her collaborators. Hence, Jews developed the deep conviction that, just as they had repeatedly been saved from enemies who sought to destroy them throughout their long history, so would they ultimately be rescued from the Nazis. Although large numbers of Jews would surely perish, the majority optimistically believed that it was possible for many, especially the productive, to hold out and survive their oppressors—a conviction known in Yiddish as *iberleben* (to survive and outlast).

Jews, therefore, viewed occupation as an existential challenge that required them to look to their long tradition of autonomous Jewish communal life and to

Jews Defeat Nazis in an International Court of Law: The Bernheim Petition engage in activities to confront and frustrate their tormentors. They provided services that were normally supplied by municipal authorities and now were administered by the Jewish Councils, such as housing allocations, food distribution, employment, sanitation, health services, refugee shelters, schools, and religious services. Other organizations, like the House Committees in Warsaw, which often operated in opposition to the Jewish Councils, instituted a wide range of voluntary welfare and social services to combat starvation, demoralization, and rampant epidemics.

A particular challenge facing the Jews was the need to maintain morale in the ghettos. Social and cultural activities were initiated by prewar political parties like the Bund, the Zionists, and the Socialists. The various Zionist youth movements played an especially critical role in sustaining and nurturing ghetto youth, both physically through their soup kitchens and spiritually through their educational and social initiatives (p.80). Rabbis led religious activities, often clandestinely. The numerous cultural activities, which ranged from theater productions and concerts to art exhibitions and literary evenings, were clear evidence of an untrammeled spirit and the desire to live in the fullest sense of the word.

There were also many examples of underground activities, including the daring work of the women couriers, who risked their lives disseminating and receiving information from the isolated Jewish communities throughout Europe; the publication and distribution of illegal underground newspapers to inform the population of the true nature of German policies; the establishment of clandestine archives to document the events for posterity; and the extremely dangerous acts of smuggling food into the ghetto by children.

Lucy Dawidowicz, the historian, provides a moving summary of Jewish defiance in the ghettos: "Despite the attempts by the Germans to impose a state of barbarism upon them, the Jews persisted in maintaining or in re-creating their organized society and their culture. The milieu in which the Germans confined them was a state of war or condition of insecurity…. Nevertheless, in nearly all the ghettos, the Jews conspired against the Germans to provide themselves with arts, letters, and society—above all, with the protection of the community against man's solitariness and brutishness. Never was human life suspended."[12]

## Resisting Deportation

In considering the Jewish responses to mass deportations, one thing must be remembered: Although we know today that Nazi trains led to Auschwitz and other killing sites, Jews, at the time, did not. It is important to distinguish between the early deportations of Jews from their towns to larger cities, other provinces and even other countries, which resulted in actual resettlement, not murder, and the later deportations of Jews to the death camps. The precedent of the early deportations made Jews more susceptible to deceptive tactics later when the Final Solution was actually implemented.[13] Most Jews were taken in by Nazi deceptions, and accepted the claim of "resettlement in the East" as "reasonable" and consistent with the Nazi policy of forced population transfers. Many Jews were disarmed by the German use of terror and deception, as well as by their own inability to imagine what was truly unimaginable.

Following the German invasion of the Soviet Union in June 1941, ghettos were established in some of the major Jewish population centers in the German-occupied Soviet territories. These included Vilna, Kovno, Riga, and Lvov. In contrast to those established in Poland prior to June 1941, these ghettos were created in the wake of the mass shootings carried out by mobile killing units and local collaborators. Jewish responses in these new ghettos were similar to the acts of defiance that took place in the Polish ghettos, as we have described previously. Life continued, but under the heavy shadow cast by mass shootings and accompanied by an intensifying sense of isolation. Menacing rumors of deportations added to the burden of a constantly deteriorating situation in which life was impossibly hard and fraught with hunger, disease, and the imminent prospect of death.

Some Jews, particularly those active in the Bundist and Zionist youth movements, as well as a few political activists in the ghettos, began to perceive the possibility of a shift in anti-Jewish policies. The omens of a radical new reality—seen in random mass shootings and deportations—led to a deepening sense of vulnerability and uncertainty.

But new questions and options also arose: How does one evaluate Nazi occupation, now compounded with random mass shootings? Is cooperation or defiance the best way to ensure survival of the community and

# The public will be challenged to reevaluate their understanding of what constitutes resistance.

individuals? Should Jews obey orders for "resettlement in the East," or should they try to go into hiding, or escape to the forests? When childbearing is banned, is it better to try and perpetuate the Jewish community—or is it wrong to bring a child into the world? How can your contact with the outside world—the need for spreading the news, getting the news, and seeking aid—be maintained, and will the world respond? Is it better to work for the Nazis and survive by being useful, or is it wrong to aid the enemy?

In the variety of responses taken by the desperate Jews, one finds no single answer, no single reaction—only "choiceless choices." Jews everywhere confronted impossible dilemmas and obstacles without being certain that the course of action they chose would ultimately result in saving their lives. Yet, even in this context, they acted.

Women couriers smuggled clandestine reports of massacres in the recently occupied former Soviet territories. These reports reached various political movements in the Polish ghettos and were disseminated via underground press to ghetto inhabitants. But the overwhelming majority refused to believe that *all* Jews were slated to be killed. Their continuing belief in *iberleben*—that rescue and survival were still possible for many Jews—prompted them to vehemently oppose the idea of armed resistance.

While small groups of young people began planning for armed activities against the Nazis, the majority of Jews in ghettos continued their previous patterns of confronting Nazi persecution. In Warsaw, only toward the conclusion of mass deportations and near decimation of the ghetto in the fall of 1942, did the few remaining Jews accept the option of armed revolt and support the young activists. In Vilna, on the other hand, the underground never received the support of the ghetto population and was forced to escape to the forests to carry out armed resistance (p. 108).

The onset of deportations from Western Europe to the "East" in the spring and summer of 1942 also raised deep concerns about the appropriate response to the Nazi onslaught. There was an urgency to identify options for survival: Some Jews, like the family of Anne Frank, went into hiding; some were smuggled from France into neutral countries. But only a limited number of Jews had the contacts and financial means to either hide or escape.

In Eastern and Western Europe, the option of armed resistance was often dependent on the ability of Jews to receive material support from national underground movements. But members of these movements operated from a different perspective and timetable. Non-Jewish resisters wanted to delay their armed uprisings until the German forces were seriously weakened. Jews did not have the luxury of waiting while the killing process intensified and their communities were threatened with imminent annihilation.

Yet in Belgium the circumstances demanded independent Jewish armed action. On July 31, 1942, an underground Jewish group destroyed files from Belgium's Jewish Council in order to sabotage deportations and, on April 19, 1943, resistance fighters in Tirlemont stopped a deportation train headed for Auschwitz and freed 200 Jews (p.124). In Eastern Europe, ghetto underground groups were determined to fight with arms despite the lack of material support from national underground movements.

New and daunting choices and challenges presented themselves as the uncertain threat of mass deportations grew. Should they report for deportation or try to hide? Which neighbors could be trusted to supply food and shelter? Hide the entire family or just the children? Should parents arrange to have their children hidden with non-Jewish families or in convents?

Since German policy punished the entire Jewish community for illegal acts of individuals, there was constant tension about the decision to engage in acts of sabotage, escape, or armed resistance. The decision to escape to the forest often pitted individual survival against survival of the family, since partisan units would accept individuals but not entire families. There were also other critical issues: If you wanted to take up arms, did you want to be part of a distinctly Jewish resistance, remaining to fight in the ghetto as a Jew among Jews? Or should you escape to the forest to join the universal struggle to defeat the Nazis?

The variety of Jewish responses makes it clear that there was no one answer or reaction: Individuals interpreted events differently, saw different consequences, and argued with great intensity about which path of action was more likely to save lives and communities.

### Resisting Mass Murder

By the time that most Jews began to comprehend and internalize the reality of Nazi mass murder—often only after their arrival at a death camp—they had long been cut off from the outside world and they were in a dreadfully weakened physical and mental state. They had few, if any, resources to call upon.

It seems, however, that humans, by nature, resist acknowledging absolute helplessness. This resistance to hopelessness is a major factor in understanding how Jews responded during the Holocaust; it explains why those who eventually took up arms or supported armed resistance did so only after finally losing hope of a better outcome, or realizing that no amount of productive work, cooperation, or bargaining could save them. They also knew that their actions would pose no threat to the survival of the already doomed—or destroyed—community.

It is remarkable that, in the face of these grim realizations, and after years of physical and mental stress and deprivation, so many Jews still had the fortitude and will to try to take control of their lives. Many determined to die with dignity, others decided to die fighting, still others held fast to their beliefs and identity, trying to preserve their values and faith.

While the general public knows of the heroic revolt in the Warsaw Ghetto in April 1943, it is often considered an isolated occurrence. In fact, armed underground groups operated in more than ninety ghettos throughout Eastern Europe. As stated previously, most Jews opposed armed uprisings because they felt that they would hasten the total destruction of the ghetto. Because of this opposition from fellow Jews, many members of the underground decided to escape the ghetto

and join the partisans. Nonetheless, armed uprisings broke out in the ghettos of Bialystok, Bedzin, Krakow, Czestochowa, Lachwa, and Tyczyn.[14]

Large numbers of Jews also participated in partisan and underground movements throughout Europe, in countries such as Belgium, France, Greece, Holland, Italy, Slovakia, the Soviet Union, and Yugoslavia. Remarkable manifestations of Jewish resistance were the unprecedented armed revolts in three of the six death camps. Fully realizing that few would actually survive the revolt or the ensuing escape to the forests, Jewish prisoners planned and carried out uprisings in Treblinka, Sobibor, and Auschwitz-Birkenau (p. 130).

But it is important to stress that armed resistance was not the only form of Jewish defiance. Other forms of resistance manifested themselves wherever Jews were. These other forms of resistance carried out by Jews in death camps included escapes to inform the outside world about the system of industrialized mass murder; the struggle by many to preserve communal values and humanity through religious observances or mutual aid; and, finally, the awe-inspiring example of those Jews, who, upon realizing that death was imminent and unavoidable, chose to set an example by the way they died.

Some left behind ethical wills, imploring their families to remember the tragedy, avenge their deaths, and continue to live as good Jews. There are examples of Jews chanting prayers or singing national or Zionist anthems as they were led into the gas chambers.[15] These desperate but heroic last acts were a clear defiance of Nazi attempts to dehumanize them and an absolute expression of symbolic resistance.

Understanding the Holocaust from a Jewish perspective allows one to acquire a deeper awareness of the obstacles and dilemmas that Jews confronted and promotes a respect for the varieties of Jewish defiance. As one resister reflected, the miracle was not that Jews could occasionally take up arms, but rather that such diverse forms of resistance existed at all.

Ultimately, in this book and exhibition, we have sought to change the widely held perception that Jews, by and large, failed to resist. The question is not, as some would pose it, Why did Jews fail to mount cohesive and effective resistance to the Nazis, but rather, how was it possible that so many Jews resisted at all?

Hanukkah in the
Westerbork Transit Camp,
Holland, 1943.

# Sanctifying Life and God's Name

*Bonnie Gurewitsch*

**D**uring the Holocaust Jews responded to gradually intensifying attacks from the Nazi regime that began with Nazi propaganda, continued with destructive edicts, and ended in genocide. German Jews, well-integrated and often totally assimilated into German life, were shocked first by the Nazi dissemination of vicious lies and stereotypes about them, and then by the passage of anti-Semitic laws designed to separate, isolate, and disenfranchise them. Their new status as legal pariahs cast doubt on their self-image as worthy German citizens.

The Reichsvertretung [German Jewish community leadership] realized that Jews needed tools to combat Nazi propaganda. Led by Rabbi Leo Baeck, the Reichsvertretung set up various Jewish educational, vocational, and cultural programs for children and adults, serving individuals and the larger Jewish community. Fidelity to Jewish beliefs and values was stressed in prayers and messages sent to synagogues.

The German Jewish philosopher Martin Buber, director of the Center for Adult Jewish Education, urged Jews to "draw on their inner strength to overcome the dangers of their position" and aspire to the image of "the conquering Jew who stands his ground."[1] Jewish leaders felt that if German Jews could stand fast, they would have the moral and physical strength to withstand and outlast Nazi persecution.

In November 1938, however, after the savage attacks during *Kristallnacht*, all German Jews saw large-scale emigration as a solution. In spite of restrictive immigration policies and the financial penalties of leaving Germany, more than sixty percent of German Jews were able to leave Germany before the outbreak of World War II. For those who remained, communal activities were increasingly restricted and Jewish life became gradually reduced to the personal sphere.

Resisting physical and psychological isolation, Zionist leaders conducted youth activities in secret. The symbolic nature of this activity was recognized at a meeting of Zionist leadership in November 1941, where metal chains were distributed, symbols of the "continuity of [their] activities, until the bitter end (p. 30)."

Jews in Germany became subject to curfews, travel was restricted, meetings were forbidden, food rations were severely limited, and forced labor was imposed on them. By 1942 deportations to Poland were well underway. In March 1943 Jizchak Schwersenz, a former teacher of the Youth Aliyah School in Berlin, and his colleague, Edith "Ewo" Wolff, created the Chug Chalutzi (Zionist Circle), to provide hiding places and spiritual guidance for many of his remaining students. They met secretly, in private homes or in the forest near Berlin, to study Jewish texts, conduct religious and cultural activities, and maintain Zionist ideals. Ewo helped find hiding places for Schwersenz and other members evading deportation, hoping to smuggle them to safety in Switzerland, so they could eventually reach Palestine.

In occupied countries, where Jews were denied basic human freedoms, countless Jews kept diaries, in which they felt free to express their individual identities, ideals, and hopes for the future. Tragically, only a few of these diaries survived.

On November 12, 1942, Yitzchok Rudashevski, a fifteen-year-old boy in the Vilna Ghetto, wrote an optimistic entry in his diary: "The ghetto resounds with good news…the Germans have suffered a defeat at Stalingrad." In April 1943, however, after hearing news of continued deportations and mass murder, he concluded: "We must not trust nor believe anything. We may be fated for the worst." Yet he did not despair. His diary reflects how he resisted the demoralization and dehumanization of ghetto circumstances, retaining his value system and his hopes for a future in a better world.

Sixteen-year-old Moshe Flinker and his family evaded deportation from Holland by escaping to occupied Belgium, where they lived illegally. In his diary he grapples with the classic questions of reward and punishment, and rails against the injustice in the degree of Jewish suffering. He affirms his Jewish identity by continuing to pray and study Jewish texts, and finds some consolation in the religious promise of "the end of our suffering in exile." Like the Zionists of the Chug Chalutzi, he sees a solution to Jewish suffering in the establishment of a Jewish homeland in the Land of Israel.

While writing a diary is a personal expression of symbolic resistance, Friedl Dicker Brandeis and Adela Bay were involved in symbolic resistance on a community level, using their skills to instill a sense of dignity, humanity, and even joy in others. Brandeis, a renowned artist from Vienna, reached out to children in the Terezin Ghetto/Camp, teaching them to express themselves artistically, thereby releasing their imaginations from the cage imprisoning their bodies.

The pianist Adela Bay, and other artists in ghettos and in slave labor camps, used their talents to sustain hope and meaning. Defying hunger, misery, and forced labor, Bay and others used their inner resources to maintain their humanity and their identity. They "wrote" poetry without pen and ink, created musical performances, and fashioned puppets or gifts of friendship out of scraps of stolen materials. Others used satire, humor, or prayer as symbolic weapons to defy their German oppressors, knowing that if they were caught they could be beaten or killed. When Adela Bay played the piano after years of persecution, her colleagues marveled at her moral strength: "What is in her head, nobody could take away."

In the desperate conditions of the Warsaw Ghetto, Rabbi Yitzchak Nissenbaum is said to have declared: "This is a time for *Kiddush Hahayim* (sanctification of life), and not for *Kiddush Hashem* (martyrdom) through death."[2] Rabbi Nissenbaum encouraged Jews to transform their instinctive urge to sustain physical life into an effort to infuse their lives with meaning.

This directive is exemplified in the life of Dr. Janusz Korczak, director of the orphanage in the Warsaw Ghetto that became an island of peace, morality, and security in a chaotic and dangerous ghetto environment. Two hundred children learned, performed, and governed themselves in the protected world that Korczak and his devoted assistants created for them. In a final act of loyalty, Korczak, his assistant Stefania Wilczyńska, and their staff accompanied their children to their deaths in Treblinka, fulfilling Korczak's promise that he would not abandon them. Their dignified march to the deportation train is a symbol of the moral defiance of evil.

Like Korzcak's march to the deportation train, death with dignity took many forms during the Holocaust. When Jews realized that they were doomed, many chose to confront death as Jews who still controlled their own actions. Many saw their deaths in the context of Jewish martyrdom, *Kiddush Hashem*, part of Jewish historical memory that expresses itself in ritualized prayers and defiant actions. Survivor testimonies tell of Jews comforting children, speaking defiantly to their executioners, reciting *Viddui* prayers (confession of sins), singing *Hatikvah* or other national anthems, and publicly affirming their faith prior to being murdered.

Other Jews, such as Rabbi Leib Geliebter, realizing that their deaths were imminent, left written testimonies, letters, or messages to future generations. These messages were hidden or buried in the hope that survivors would find them and remember the martyrs, study Jewish texts in their memories, and avenge their deaths. These testaments reaffirm the covenantal relationships between Jews and God, faith in a surviving remnant, and the continuity of the Jewish people.

When Hitler came to power in 1933, German Jews did not have an overall representative body. They established the Reichsvertretung der Deutschen Juden (Reich Representation of German Jews) to insure the internal unity of German Jewry and represent it before the German authorities. Rabbi Leo Baeck (1873-1956), a distinguished Berlin theologian, became its president. Even as the situation of the Jews in Germany deteriorated and Rabbi Baeck's own safety was threatened, he refused opportunities to emigrate, preferring to remain at the head of the German Jewish community. He promoted a dual plan: emigration for young people and preservation of the cultural and spiritual life for the remaining Jewish community. "The Nazis could take our property," he said, "but not our spirit. So far as possible we wanted the individual Jew, when exposed to persecution, to feel that he could find refuge in the protective mantle of the Jewish community."[1] At the beginning of 1943 Rabbi Baeck was deported to the Terezin Ghetto/Camp, where he continued to teach and lead by example. Baeck survived the war and settled in London.

# Rabbi Leo Baeck: "Honor and Inner Strength"

## Words of Consolation

*A*t the beginning of August 1935 the Reichsvertretung sent out a call to all Jewish communities of Germany with the request to read the following message during the service on Shabbat Nachamu, the Sabbath of Consolation that follows Tisha B'Av. Although Leo Baeck did not sign his name to the call, his style is clearly noticeable. The prayer shows Jews how to confront the rising tide of anti-Semitism in Germany, by strengthening Jewish pride, honor, and inner strength. This symbolic resistance to Nazi persecution reinforces Jewish individual and communal identity.

"Be comforted, be comforted, my people" today's Shabbat calls out to us. Out of what in these days, when we must pass through a tide of insults, can comfort arise for us? It arises from the answer that our faith, our honor, our youth give to us. Against all defamations we set the sovereignty of our religion, against all offenses, our constant effort to walk in the path of our Judaism, to follow His commandments.

True honor [is what] everyone gives to himself; he gives it to himself through a life that is inviolable and pure, simple and upright; also through a life of restraint. That is the indication of inner strength. Our honor is our honor before God; it alone will exist. Do our youth not give us an example of unpretentiousness and courage to master this difficult life in new ways?

Let us, parents and teachers, raise a generation, strict and demanding of themselves, helpful to everybody else, with a strong body and fresh spirit, religious and deeply rooted in Judaism. Do not let yourself be pushed down and do not let yourself become embittered. Trust Him, to whom time belongs.

## Yom Kippur Prayer

*Shortly after the enactment of the Nuremberg Laws in September 1935, Rabbi Leo Baeck wrote a message titled "The Reichsvertretung Speaks to Us," to be read in synagogues at the beginning of Yom Kippur. The message directly challenged the anti-Semitic ideology of the Nazis, calling it a lie and slander. When the Gestapo discovered the message, it forced the Reichsvertretung to send telegrams to synagogues, forbidding the prayer to be read. Rabbi Baeck was subsequently arrested for a few days.*

In this hour the whole House of Israel stands before its God, the God of Justice and the God of Mercy. We shall all examine our path before Him. We shall examine what we have done and what we have failed to do. We shall examine where we have gone and where we have failed to go. Wherever we have sinned, we will confess it freely. We will say, "We have sinned" and, with fervent resolve to repent before God, we will pray that God may forgive us.

We stand before our God. With the same strength with which we have acknowledged our sins, the sins of the individual and the sins of the community, we shall express our abhorrence of the lie directed against us and of the slander of our faith and its expressions. This slander is far beneath us. We believe in our faith and our future.

We stand before our God. Our strength is in Him. It is in Him that our history finds its truth and its honor. He is the source of our survival through every change, of our fortitude in all our trials. Our history is the history of spiritual greatness, spiritual dignity. We turn to it when attack and insult are directed against us, when need and suffering press in upon us. God led our fathers from generation to generation. He will continue to lead us and our children through our days.

We stand before our God. His commandments that we fulfill give us strength so that we bow before Him and stand straight before other men. We serve Him and we remain steadfast in all the changes and the happenings of the world. Humbly, we place our trust in Him. Our path lies clearly before us and we see our future.

Mourning and pain fill our hearts. Through moments of silence before our God, we want to give expression to that which fills our souls. More forcefully than any words could ever do, this silent prayer will speak.

Rabbi Leo Baeck, standing, addresses a meeting of the Reichsvertretung. Photographed by the noted Jewish photographer Abraham Pisarek, who documented the widespread activities of German Jews. Berlin c. 1934.

"In times of distress the community must grow anew, gain life, and existence. It is from the community that the individual must draw the strength to live and be active."

After the events of *Kristallnacht* in November 1938, organized Jewish educational activities in Germany gradually became restricted, and finally illegal. When Jewish schools were closed, active Zionist youth movements in Berlin went underground. Meeting in small groups in various apartments, maintaining clandestine contacts with the Zionist movement in Switzerland, they focused on eluding deportation, smuggling young men and women out of Germany, and sustaining the spirits of those who remained.

Jizchak Schwersenz, a former teacher at the Youth Aliyah School in Berlin and a leader of a religious Zionist youth group, continued teaching and giving moral support to young people who remained. He worked with Edith Wolff ["Ewo"], a child of a mixed marriage who had converted to Judaism. She used her contacts with Christians to provide Jews who were evading deportation with false documents, food ration stamps, and shelter. In March 1943 Schwersenz and Wolff formed the Chug Chalutzi (Zionist Circle), a resistance group composed of twenty to forty members. The group lasted until the end of the war and succeeded in saving many of its members.

# Zionism Underground in Berlin

From the memoir of Jizchak Schwersenz, published in Israel in 1969

One day in November 1941, Alfred Selbiger [a Zionist leader in Berlin] invited me and ten other key leaders to his office. There he gave each one of us a metal chain and said, "We are now forbidden to wear the symbols of our movement [Hechalutz Zionist youth movement]. Therefore I am giving you each this chain, which you should wear instead of our symbol. The chain will symbolize our organization and witness the continuity of our activities until the bitter end. And if one of us will be privileged to reach freedom sometime, this chain will be a memento of this difficult period that we are now experiencing. The chain will remind us of our great goal, which we must transmit to future generations." Overcome with emotion, agitated, we parted and went our separate ways.

In the last months of 1941 frightening rumors started reaching us about the true intentions of the Nazis—to totally destroy European Jews in all occupied countries. At the end of the year, after Ewo's return from an intelligence mission to Vienna, she told me that we must find ways of escaping deportations. At the beginning of 1942 Ewo laid out her plan for going underground, with the expectation of an end to the Third Reich. At first I rejected her plan categorically. As a Jew who had been educated in Prussian principles, I couldn't imagine walking around with false papers, a precondition for a life underground. But Ewo stuck stubbornly to her recommendation, claiming that every Jew was morally obligated to save his or her life for the goal of building the Jewish homeland after the war, and for the sake of Jewish continuity in general. Jews must not go meekly to slaughter like animals.

*On February 27, 1943, a massive Factory* Aktion *took place in Germany to deport Jewish slave laborers to Auschwitz-Birkenau. Some 4,000 Jews escaped. The round-up prompted Schwersenz and Wolff to form the Chug Chalutzi. Wolff would find hiding places for Jews; Schwersenz would provide spiritual guidance.*[1]

When the illegal youth group was organized in March 1943 in Ewo's apartment by a handful of comrades, who remained the pillar of the group until the end, I charted as our goal to concern ourselves not only with the physical existence of our members, but to take care of their spiritual and humanistic development as well. We saw as a primary goal to fortify their awareness of being an integral part of the Jewish people. We were forced to realize that our small but cohesive group, by virtue of its dedicated and persistent action, would change the negative value of Jewish fate—the cruel persecutions and the anguished cry of the Jewish people that cut our hearts—to a positive value, by choosing to identify with this fate and doing our part in restructuring it, so that these persecutions and these sufferings would never occur again.

What good would it have done for our commonly held goals of Zionism and pioneering life if we had succeeded in surviving until the storm passed without simultaneously steeling our character, broadening our horizons, and strengthening our Jewish consciousness? In the isolation of our illegal existence, cut off from the world, we were impelled to tighten the ties in our minds and souls to the Jewish people and to the Land of Israel.

Many of our members had just lost their parents and siblings to the Nazis and had no idea how to find a roof over their heads. The group became the core of our lives and charged us all with courage, activism, youthful exuberance, and values to live by. We would gather in the Grunewald forest [disguising the meetings as picnics] and sit there together to study the Bible, Jewish history, and the Land of Israel, our so-distant homeland. We would sit and revel in the classics of world literature, and try to learn Hebrew, our people's language. We learned and learned, without stopping, and without tiring.

*The Chug Chalutzi continued to meet secretly in the homes of Jewish sympathizers, where members prayed and studied. They were assigned different overnight shelters, sometimes for each day of the week, since it was necessary to change lodgings frequently to escape notice from neighbors. Ration cards and false documents were distributed at these meetings.*

One day in April 1943, Alfred-Avraham Bernstein asked to be accepted into the group. His parents had already been deported to the East. Avraham, who was only fourteen, succeeded in escaping and saving his

Jizchak Schwersenz (standing, left end of second row), with his students from the Youth Aliyah School, where he taught. Berlin, 1940.

"The goal was to direct people towards Jewish values and to fill their lives with spiritual values and emotional content based in Judaism."

The Chug Chalutzi symbol drawn by Manfred Lewin. At the top are the mountains of Galilee and the rising sun of freedom containing the Tablets of the Law. In the center is the shore of Palestine. The watch-tower symbolizes the will to defend, in accord with the group's motto, "in spite of everything." A fence separates the Chug Chalutzi from freedom; a Hebrew letter in the form of a sword cuts the fence, allowing Jews to enter Palestine.

nine-year-old sister Lottchen. Since he had been a member of our youth movement, and a student at the Youth Aliyah School, accepting him was not problematic. Accepting Lottchen was different. Since she was only nine, if she were arrested, she might endanger the entire group; we could not expect her to be capable of lying wisely to her interrogators and fooling them. Lottchen was a sweet child and very quiet, but wise for her age.

After discussing the matter at length, we decided to accept the risk and take her into our group. We taught her what to say in the event of arrest and what she must answer to strangers in general. She was to say that her home had been bombed, her parents had been killed, and she did not know where she belonged. We also gave her an assumed name. Ewo volunteered to care for Lottchen, with the devoted assistance of Heinz Linke, a *mischling* (a person of mixed "Aryan" and Jewish origins) and a member of our original Zionist youth group. He was living in hiding with his Jewish mother when he joined us. At the age of twenty-two he was the oldest member of the group.

After Ewo was arrested [in June 1943] Heinz volunteered to bear the burden of looking after Lottchen. As fate would have it, not Lottchen but her brother Avraham was arrested, deported, and subsequently murdered in one of the death camps. But Lottchen survived all dangers intact and ten years later she married

Heinz. Another invaluable member was Eva-Chava Fleischmann. She joined the Chug Chalutzi after the tragic deportation of her parents. Her courage, her fortitude in the face of every trial and challenge, her calm and considered judgment, and even the deep piety that she inherited from her parents served as an inspiring example to us all. Chava's fine qualities were especially prominent after the arrest of Ewo. With motherly concern, she looked after the day-to-day needs of our group.

In July 1943 we received a short letter from Auschwitz-Birkenau from Karla Wagenberg, a member of our movement, who was deported from Berlin at the age of seventeen. During a work commando outside the camp, she managed to give the letter to a German, who mailed it. We didn't fully understand the details of the letter. But the mention of the word "oven," in Hebrew letters, was a clear hint. The addition of the message, "many of us are already with Alfred," who had been shot to death in November 1942, was unmistakable.

One day a member of our group asked to meet me. He had fallen in love with a student from the Youth Aliyah School and now his girlfriend was pregnant. The birth was expected shortly. Needless to say, during this period there was no way to hold a conventional wedding. At most it was possible to hold a secret wedding ceremony in the presence of witnesses, "according to the Law of Moses and the people of Israel." But in this case we had to solve the problem of taking care of both the mother-to-be and the birth under illegal living conditions. Immediately I telephoned Berta Gerhardt, one of our Christian protectors, and she agreed to meet with our comrade. She then took all steps needed to insure that the birth took place under proper conditions. The boy who was born lives today with his parents and sister in freedom as a citizen of the State of Israel—and it was my privilege to prepare him for his **bar mitzvah.**

*In February 1944 Schwersenz, armed with illegal documents, escaped to Switzerland with the help of a refugee assistance group. He tried to smuggle out other members of the group, but was unsuccessful. He lived in Switzerland for ten years before immigrating to Israel. Ewo was arrested and sent to prison for providing a woman with a false food ration card. After liberation in 1945 she immigrated to Palestine. She died in Israel in 1997. Schwersenz died in Germany in 2005.*

*The Jewish scouts in Germany had a tradition of holding an annual Scouts Day on the holiday of Tu B'Shvat. The last celebration took place in a school in Berlin, in February 1942, half a year after the start of deportations from Berlin. Wearing white shirts under their jackets, fifty male and female scouts attended, the remnant of three Berlin Jewish scout troops. The meeting was disguised as an educational lecture with slides, still permitted under Nazi laws, but at this time any meeting of Jews was extremely dangerous. Scout Aryeh Davidowitz's report on the event appears in Schwersenz's memoir.*

YOUNG MACCABI UNION
OF SCOUTS, TROOP EMUNA (FAITH)
BERLIN, MARCH 1942

To Our Members in the Countries of the Diaspora and in the Land of Israel

Even though we do not know whether this letter will ever reach you, we write it hoping that at least one of us will remain alive and hand it over to you some day. Many of our members have already been taken to Poland, where an unknown fate awaits them. But the Jewish Scout is told never to despair, and we were therefore determined to meet this year and honor Scouts Day. Despite the danger involved there was an atmosphere of high spirits and joy in the room. We had gathered together the fifty Jewish scouts who still remained in Berlin. We sat in a big circle, and the room echoed to the sound of our singing "Be Prepared..." and all the other songs. The candles flickered gaily and members looked into the flames.

After that Mary Simon read us a story about trees and plants in our Jewish homeland, which made us forget our dangers and our sorrows. We sang again, and several poems were read.

We then stood to attention to sing the anthem of the [Zionist] Movement. When we unfolded the flag that we had kept with us, we gave the Scouts' salute and sang the song of the flag: "Carry it to Zion, the Banner and the Flag." Then Erwin Tichauer stepped forward and read the names of his group's members who had been deported. As he read each name members replied, "Here," so that even those who were missing were with us, for we are always with them in our thoughts. We ended by singing *Hatikvah* (the Zionist anthem), which gave us courage and confidence in our ability to persevere for the future.

At this difficult time we send our good wishes to all of you. Do not forget us. We will all be united in spirit until the day comes when once more we can all be together. Shalom! Be of good courage!

On June 24, 1941, Germans occupied Vilna, a city in Lithuania with a prewar population of 57,000 Jews. Vilna had been a major center of Jewish religious, cultural, and political activity since the end of the eighteenth century, distinguished by renowned scholars and intellectuals. By the end of 1941 the Nazis had murdered 33,500 Vilna Jews. Most were killed in Ponar, a clearing in a wood outside Vilna with large pits that were used as mass graves. The remaining 20,000 Jews were crowded into a ghetto with narrow streets on the edge of the city. Despite these conditions, culture and education thrived. Ghetto residents attended theater, concerts, literary clubs, and lectures. Children went to school and engaged in sports. Herman Kruk, an historian who lived in the Vilna Ghetto and documented the life of its Jews until his deportation and death in Estonia in 1944, wrote that "as the Vilna Jewish community was for years known as the 'Jerusalem of Lithuania,' so the Vilna Ghetto in respect to its cultural life deserves to be called the 'Jerusalem of the ghettos,' because it was a symbol of Jewish spiritual resistance under the Nazi regime."

# Vilna: Resisting with Music

From the oral history of Adela Bay

When the war broke out in 1939, I was in Vilna and had a job in a music school. When the Germans invaded in 1941 they tortured people in the streets and in their apartments and made them work at forced labor. One day the director of my music school told us no Jewish people could work there anymore.

Lithuanian and Ukrainian soldiers on horses drove us out of our homes and into the old part of the city designated for the ghetto. They boarded up the ghetto and closed it immediately. The conditions were so awful that we didn't think we would survive more than a week or two. Many people went to work for the Germans. I worked in the ghetto for the Jewish Council—the government of the ghetto. But we survived two years, from 1941 to 1943. How? People have a tremendous survival drive. Also organization, mutual assistance and friendship. We organized committees for lost children, for elderly people, and for labor. Everyone worked in different divisions. I worked with my girlfriend, an engineer, in the engineering division.

After a while a young man who eventually didn't survive organized an orchestra. This was a most unusual phenomenon. People who went to work every day at 4 am came in the evening, tired and hungry, to practice. They took their instruments into the basement and, without light, rehearsed. But there was also a protest. I will never forget the first concert because many people were very unhappy—maybe they had just lost their families—and they put announcements in the street that said that a concert must not be held in a graveyard.

But that didn't disturb us because Jacob Gens, the ghetto *forshteyer* (head of the ghetto administration) liked music and gave us money for regular concerts. I played *The Hungarian Fantasy* with the orchestra. In order to do this, I had to go into the city with a policeman to get into my old apartment. There, somewhere in the corner, I found the whole score. I took the score back to the ghetto, and at night, reading with a little candle, I wrote out parts for all the instruments. On other nights I played other pieces. Then they created a magnificent musical theater. Concerts were big events. Afterwards we met in a coffee house. We also opened a regular school for children and a musical school. And so I taught there, too.

Meanwhile there were so many *Selektions* (for deportation) that people who didn't have legitimate papers to survive were simply taken away and killed. But those of us who had a *Schein* (work permit) were not taken away. I had a *Schein* because I worked in the Ghetto *Verwaltung* (administration). I survived this way for two years. Unbelievable when I think about it.

*The work permits deceived Jews into thinking that they would survive if they were working. However, the Germans kept changing the permits and rounding up more Jews for deportation. The ghetto was liquidated on September 23 and 24, 1943. Most survivors were sent to concentration camps. The 27-year-old Adela was sent to a forced labor camp in Kaiserwald, outside of Riga, Latvia, with many female prisoners. Isolated from the outside world, they were underfed, and worked eleven hours a day. The majority were murdered during the liquidation of the camp in September 1944.*

In the factory they didn't make us work on Sunday. So we gathered around a girl laborer, a magnificent girl, so talented. Whatever happened , she wrote a poem. If they shaved our heads, she wrote a poem. We were always looking for a piece of paper and pencil so she could write. I remember her and I'm proud of her.

We also had a so-called "Arts Day." Once we made a puppet show. Believe me, this puppet show could be on Broadway. It was unbelievable. After 8 pm the lights in our rooms went out. So we went into the bathroom and sat there and cut off pieces from our own dresses to make little dresses for the puppets in our show. I remember all the songs in the show and how we made puppets that went to work every day. We sang *"Tsu, Eyns, Tsvey, Dray, Tsu, Eyns, Tsvey, Dray"* (One, two, three, march! One, two, three, march!) and changed the words of the song that we had to sing in the morning when we really went to work. The last stanza said that that one day there won't be work anymore and all the puppets jumped up!

*In the summer of 1944 the Soviets advanced and took Adela Bay and 500 other women to work in a factory in Torun, Poland. They shaved the heads of the women so they would not run away. When the war was almost over the factory manager gave the women food and told them to walk away in the snow. After a terrible battle between the Germans and Soviets, some women found refuge in an empty apartment vacated by Germans. Eventually they jumped on a coal train and jumped off near Lublin.*

I went to the radio station in Lublin and found my old gentile friends and they were of course terrified when they saw my shaved head. But they said, "Don't go anywhere, you will be on the radio again. Tell us if you can play piano." I said, "I don't know, in six years I didn't touch the piano."

So they wheeled in a little piano. I sat down and played *Das Ständchen* by Schubert, whch I had played before the war, and a Debussy prelude. Everybody stayed and cried. The head of the radio station said, "You see, she didn't save anything; even the hair on her head she doesn't have. But what is in her head, nobody could take away."

Adela Bay, New York City, c. 1970. "What is in her head, nobody could take away."

How can I forget that? It was a sensation. After a few months I played a Liszt concerto, with a real orchestra, in Lublin. When I gave a recital in December 1945, my relatives in America heard about me over the radio, because there was a Jewish radio program that mentioned my survival. We started corresponding. Even though I had a very good reception and a job, I decided to leave.

*Bay immigrated to Sweden and then to South America to join her sister. A year later she immigrated to the US and settled in New York City. She earned a degree in musicology at Columbia University, taught piano, and played professionally until she died in 2002.*

A scene from an amateur theater production of David Pinski's play, *The Eternal Jew*, performed in the Vilna Ghetto, c. 1942. Music by Vladimir Durmashkin, directed by Bergolski. "My brother scored the music for the play," recalled Henny Durmashkin Gurko, who also lived in the Vilna Ghetto. "A performance was given for all the young and the teenagers in the ghetto, and it was beautiful. It was very good for us; it gave us a lift."

## FLYING FROM THE CAGE

We had schools for children in the ghetto. We had a choir. We had theater.
We had discussions. We wrote poems and songs. Can you imagine?
The mothers were called to special discussions. I'll never forget what they said,
"Now we are in a cage, but we have to do everything, everything possible
that when the children will come out of the cage, they should be able to fly."
They did everything they could to create a normal atmosphere.

FROM THE ORAL HISTORY OF ZENIA MALECKI, VILNA GHETTO

36

*Rabbi Ephraim Oshry, a prominent authority on Jewish law who was interned in the Kovno Ghetto, Lithuania, was often sought out by ghetto residents to answer questions of Jewish law that arose in the abnormal*

*conditions of the Holocaust.[1] Appointed as custodian of a warehouse containing Nazi-confiscated Jewish books, he had access to Rabbinic texts that were essential to him as sources for his responses. He answered many queries orally and wrote down questions and answers in pencil, using scraps of paper torn from concrete sacks. Eventually he buried these responses in tin cans, hoping that after the war they would be found and serve as testimony of heroic Jewish devotion to the practice of their religion, even in the dreadful circumstances of the Holocaust.*

*While the ghetto was liquidated, Rabbi Oshry hid in a bunker. After Kovno was liberated in August 1944, he retrieved his hidden archive. He settled in New York City and published five volumes,* Responsa From the Holocaust.

*Rabbi Oshry's shofar, shown here, was used in the Kovno Ghetto and is one of many unique artifacts on display in the exhibition,* Daring to Resist.

*The following is a sample of one of Rabbi Oshry's responsa.*

Rabbi Ephraim Oshry in the Kovno Ghetto.

## BLOWING A CRACKED SHOFAR

**Question:** On the day before Rosh Hashanah of 5702 [1942] I was asked on behalf of [Jews in a labor camp] whether, in the absence of any other shofar, they could fulfill the obligation of hearing the shofar on Rosh Hashanah by blowing a slightly cracked shofar.

**Response:** Most [scholars] maintain that if less than half of the shofar is cracked, it may be used. All the more so in this situation, when no other shofar was available. I also considered the fact that these Jews were seeking to fulfill a mitzvah (commandment) while still alive, not knowing what tomorrow will bring.

Moshe Ze'ev Flinker, one of seven children, was born in The Hague, Holland, on October 9, 1926. In July 1942, the Flinkers received a deportation notice and traveled illegally by train to Brussels, where they did not register as Jews. Sixteen-year-old Moshe began his diary in November 1942. In it he tried to reconcile his deeply-held religious beliefs with the massive persecution and deportation of Jews that plagued him. Moshe ends the first notebook of his diary with a verse from *Hatikvah (*the Zionist anthem) indicating that despite his feelings of emptiness and despair, he has not abandoned his Jewish identity or faith. On April 7, 1944, Passover eve, Gestapo agents forced their way into the Flinkers' apartment and saw a supply of *matzoh* (unleavened bread). The Flinkers could not deny their Jewishness. The entire family was arrested and sent to Auschwitz. Moshe and his parents were murdered; his siblings survived and moved to Israel. After liberation, Moshe's sisters returned to Brussels and, in the basement of their family's house, they found three of Moshe's notebooks.

# "We Shall Never Abandon Our Faith"

From *Young Moshe's Diary, The Spiritual Torment of a Jewish Boy in Nazi Europe*

**November 26, 1942**

Today I taught my sisters again, but first I put on my tefillin and said my morning prayers. I didn't do anything at all after teaching my sisters.

We are in a very bad situation. Our sufferings have by far exceeded our wrong-doings. What other purpose could the Lord have in allowing such things to happen? I feel certain that further troubles will not bring any Jew back to the paths of righteousness; on the contrary, I think that upon experiencing such great anguish they will think that there is no God at all in the universe, because had there been a God He would not have let such things happen to His people. I have already heard this said many times. The time has come for our redemption—we are more or less worthy of being redeemed.

**November 30, 1942**

What can God mean by all that is happening and by not preventing it? This raises a further question. Is our distress part of the anguish that has afflicted the Jewish people since the exile? [The first exile began in 586 BCE when Babylonians destroyed Jerusalem and the First Temple.] Or is this different from all that has occurred in the past? I incline to the second answer, for I find it very hard to believe that what we are going through today is only a mere link in a long chain of suffering. In former times the persecutions were always localized [but] today it is quite possible to destroy the entire people of Israel. Why does the Lord not prevent this? Why does He permit our tormentors to persecute us? And what can be the result of these persecutions?

The answer to these questions does not seem difficult to me. We know that we were expelled from our country for our great iniquities; therefore, if we wish to return we must completely repent of our evil ways. Then we shall be able to go back to our Land. We must therefore hope that since most Jews do not dwell where they used to and that since most of us wish to be redeemed, with the Lord's help we shall soon be saved. Perhaps even on the forthcoming feast of Hanukkah.

### December 18, 1942

I have begun to study this language [Arabic] because a large part of the inhabitants of the Land of Israel and the surrounding countries speak it. It is obvious that we shall have to live in peace with our Arab brothers, the sons of Ishmael, who are also Abraham's descendants.

### December 22, 1942

I have studied the Bible each day—but I have found nothing in it. Then I remember the man who used to pick up our laundry in The Hague. One day this man came to fetch the laundry but it was not ready and I asked him to come back later. He said to me: "I really do not have to come back. We have enough customers, but I shall fulfill your request, for after this time anoth-

er period will come." And if he said this of laundry, then it is surely true concerning the words of the Bible.

### December 24, 1942

This morning I felt the cold of winter and I immediately thought about what my brethren [Jewish deportees to the East] will do in this cold. We need supernatural help, if the Lord still wishes to save us. If He will not grant us this miracle of salvation, not many Jews will live to take part in our redemption. But the Lord will not be able to forsake His people. Undoubtedly He will save us. He must save us.

### January 19, 1943

Last Sabbath I was beginning my prayers but I found I could not concentrate and I started to leaf through the prayer book. When I reached the penitential prayers I started to read more closely and I saw there a prayer which made a very strong impression on me. From this I saw again that the troubles of the Middle Ages and our troubles today are identical. And I thought to myself: "But the troubles passing over us today are already the

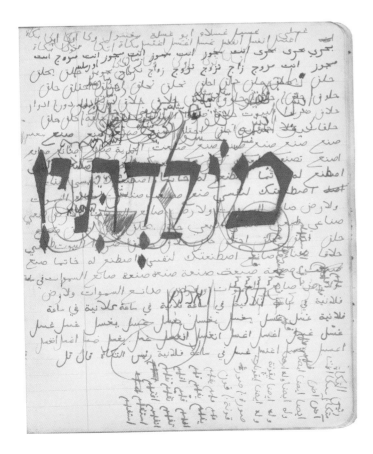

Above: Moshe Flinker.

Left: Page from Moshe Flinker's diary on which he practiced Arabic writing. In the center is the Hebrew word *moladeti*, meaning my homeland. Underneath he wrote: *Chazak Ve'ematz*, be strong and have courage. "I have begun to study Arabic," he wrote in the diary, "we shall have to live in peace with our [Arab] brothers..."

end of our troubles in exile," an idea which I have had in my heart many times.

The Lord knows that I do not rebel against Him nor dare do anything against Him, and He knows how thankful I am to Him that He protects my family, but something devours my heart, a vast yearning to participate with my brothers in all that happens to them. Yet (last year on *Tisha B'Av*) when I thought about the wretched condition of our people, the sorrows that were nearing, the people being deported, I again started to cry. Everything became heavy for me, and I prayed to God with a broken heart to have mercy on His people, to have pity on the remnants of Jacob, to bring us back to Him, to renew our days as of old.

### February 12, 1943

When I pray I feel as if I am praying to the wall and am not heard at all, and there is a voice inside me that says: "Why are you praying? The Lord does not hear you." Yes, I think that the holy spark that I always felt within me has been taken from me, and, here I am, without spirit, without thought, without anything.

Now, when Germany is receiving blow after blow from all sides, and she is compelled to abandon one Russian city after another, they never forget the people they have already so tortured and crushed, nor do they let the slightest opportunity pass to shame or humiliate them. The Propaganda Minister considers it to be the right moment to abuse us and blaspheme against our people even more violently. Whether they believe in all the charges and accusations they have leveled against us or not really doesn't matter; the troubles they have caused us already are so terrible and fiendish that their original motivation is beside the point. But from their actions we see that this war must end with the solution of the Jewish problem (speaking from the Orthodox Jewish point of view, I would say in the redemption of the Jews) because, as far as I know, the hatred of the Jews has never been as widespread or poisonous as it is now.

### March 9, 1943

Even before the war my heart longed for my homeland, the Land of Israel, but now this love and yearning have greatly increased. For it is only now that I feel how much we need a country in which we could live in peace as every people lives in its country. And when I

pray and do not see my beloved country it is as if I had been praying to the wall. O, I love all of it so much! My people and my country do not leave my thoughts for even a moment; all day long they are in my mind. Several times I have asked myself whether I will ever get the chance to stand on its holy earth, if the Lord will permit me to walk about in my Land. Oh, how my soul yearns for you, my homeland, how my eyes crave the sight of you, my country, the Land of Israel.

### May 19, 1943

I thought at one time—that I would be a statesman, a Jewish statesman, and in that way work for my people and my God. When I first got this idea and wrote it in my diary, I tried to do all I could to bring it about. But after some time had passed I saw, and what is more important I felt, that it was all worthless. There is no longer any value to the Arabic I am studying and my activities in this direction would appear to be useless. Thus nearly all the positive content in my life is shown to be pointless, and I am left with almost nothing. My great complaint is against this terrible emptiness. I now understand that ideas and thoughts are worthless if one cannot convert them into action, so now all day long I do nothing but search for some positive content for my life, so as not to be entirely lost.

### May 25, 1943
FAITH

There is no more beautiful thing in the world than to believe with unshaken faith in a sacred ideal, in an ideal you have chosen for the good of the people and the homeland. We carry this faith inside of us and, after our death, it will be received by our descendants to strengthen them, to fulfill our ideals. Faith is the holiest thing in the world; "faith" explains and defines all we ought to be, how we ought to conduct ourselves and what we ought to believe; the abiding faith we have in our people, our eternal people, our unique people, whose great suffering serves only to intensify our determination and courage. The faith we possess in our own land which belonged to us once and will belong to us again, the land which was sanctified through our faith in it, and which grants us new strength each and every day.

We shall never abandon our faith lest we abandon ourselves; our faith will accompany us forever until we shall be granted, with the help of our Lord, the right to return to our Promised Land, where we shall live as one nation in one country, with the one and only God.

Therefore, my Lord, have mercy upon Thy people and have mercy upon me, for otherwise we shall all be lost. Thou knowest we worship only Thee. Have mercy, please, Lord, have mercy.

## May 25, 1943
### THOU HAST CHOSEN US
Yesterday was Shavuot (festival), and so with perhaps a bit more than usual fervor, I said this holiday prayer; and when I reached these words, my head reeled as I thought of how many generations of Jews have said them, in how many times of trouble have we repeated these words, so full of meaning, "Thou hast chosen us." Yes, Thou has chosen us. Then I wondered whether it were really worthwhile to belong to such a "chosen" people; but even as I thought, I realized that such thoughts were useless. Whether it be worthwhile or not, we were chosen once and that is all there is to it.

## July 4, 1943
All I have is hope; my entire being depends on it. And at the same time I have nothing. What will useless hope bring me? I don't know what to do. Everything is becoming hollow. Formerly, when I took up my Bible and read it, it was as if I had returned to life, as if the Lord had taken pity on me; even in my darkest moments I found consolation in Him. Now even this is denied me, all seems lifeless, it does not enthuse me.

## Tisha B'Av 5703, August 10, 1943
Today it is two thousand five hundred and twenty-nine years since the destruction of our first Temple. On this day we recall all our people, from the defenders of the walls of Jerusalem to the victims of the Gestapo, who have fallen in the name of their people and their Lord. On this Tisha B'Av, in these days of incomparable trouble, we are united with all Israel, united in agony and pain. On this Tisha B'Av of the year 5703, our eyes fill with tears but we shall not cast down our heads. On this memorial day we shall lift our heads and straighten our backs, for we most assuredly know that the blood of our people which has run like water will not remain unavenged; vengeance shall certainly be exacted.

## Undated
When I speak of vengeance, I do not wish you to understand by this that every Jew should arise and attack a German to avenge the blood of our brothers and sisters and their endless pain. When one speaks of vengeance of this sort it is always accompanied by a prayer to the Lord that He should execute our vengeance. No, my brothers, I want you to observe only the positive side of vengeance. Our revenge, for our sufferings today and for the sufferings of our long exile, will be the building of our country and the return of our beloved people to their homeland. That will be the greatest revenge that could ever happen. For this vengeance we ask the help of our Lord, the Lord of Israel, who has protected us from annihilation throughout our long exile. He will surely save us and settle us anew in our homeland, our holy land, the Land of Israel.

## September 6, 1943
Now that I have reached the end of the first notebook of my diary, feelings of thankfulness come over me: first to our Lord, the Lord of Israel, who has protected me and my family in such terrible times, and who has given me the privilege of understanding and knowing His divine guidance and heavenly protection. My Lord, so close art Thou to me and yet so far. I search for Thee constantly, my thoughts go out unto Thee, and my acts as well. My Lord, my Lord, do not abandon me.

## Undated
Trouble never ends…. And every time I meet a child of my people I ask myself: "Moshe, what are you doing for him?" I feel responsible for every single pain. I ask myself whether I am still sharing in the troubles of my people, or whether I have withdrawn completely from them.

Some three or four months ago I would have had no trouble at all answering these questions, because then I was attached to my brothers with all the fibers of my heart and soul, but now all has changed. From the moment I became empty, I have felt as if all this no longer concerns me. I feel as if I were dead.

*We have not yet lost our hope*
*The two thousand years' hope*
*Of receiving mercy from our Lord*
*The Lord of Zion and Jerusalem.*

Friedl Dicker Brandeis, born in 1898, was a highly-regarded Viennese artist who studied with Walter Gropius, Paul Klee, and Wassily Kandinsky. In 1934 she fled to Prague where she joined an anti-Fascist Communist group. There she married Pavel Brandeis, her cousin, and taught art to the children of Austrian and German refugees in her home studio. In December 1942 she and Pavel were deported to the Terezin Ghetto/Camp. In Terezin she taught art to over 100 children to help them escape their desolate existence by focusing inwards and releasing their imagination. She believed that children would gain self-esteem by finding life and beauty in their gloomy surroundings. Assuming that her students would survive the war, she thought they would always benefit from the skills she helped them develop. Even so, their isolation, an uncertain future, and the fear of "deportation to the East" strongly influenced the composition of their drawings. When Pavel was deported to Auschwitz in September 1944, Friedl voluntarily took the next transport to be with him. She was killed on October 9, 1944. Pavel survived the war.

# Freeing the Spirit in Terezin

Recollections from the students of Friedl Dicker Brandeis

Friedl said in her lectures at Terezin that it was best for children to work in large groups because they were "cooperative" and not "competitive" units. "They are prepared to overcome difficulties arising from shortages of materials, to help others, and to keep order among themselves," she told teachers in 1943. "The execution of the [artistic] task gives the child pleasure, and the concentration necessary to do this makes him self-disciplined." Students who were less talented were happy to assist with the mixing of paints and the preparation of canvases. Everyone felt needed.

### Helga Kinsky

One morning a small woman with very short hair and big hazel eyes suddenly appeared in our room. The determination of her walk and her energy excited us and introduced a completely different rhythm. We immediately accepted her and gave ourselves up to the will of this new force.

Friedl flew into the room, and of course she talked to us as she was handing out the materials. She was with us the whole time that we worked. The lessons were short. We worked intensively and, as I recall, in silence. She would give us a subject, to stir our imagination...a field with a horse roaming about...or, maybe, she would show us some model or picture. I remember precisely the collage with the horse. Friedl brought us piles of scrap paper and showed us how to make a collage.

She would talk about how to begin a drawing, how to look at things, how to think spatially, how to dream about something, how to do something, how to realize our fantasies. I do not remember that she worked with us one on one, but rather there was contact with the entire group.

We lived on the top floor of the children's home. We would draw from the window—the sky, mountain, nature.... That is probably especially important for prisoners: to see the world on the other side, to know that it exists.

That probably also applied to Friedl. It was important for me to know that she existed, that she was alive.... A force of freedom. In her presence, everything turned out, almost by itself.

### Lily Edna Amit

A person can be defined through their influence on others. Sometimes I had the same sort of feeling you get with a doctor: Friedl herself was the medicine. To this day, the mystery of her sense of freedom remains incomprehensible to me. It flowed from her to us like an electric current.... Once I drew a boat and a candle in darkness, and it did not come out right for me. Friedl said: "Here you need light to define the darkness, and darkness here to define the light."

### Eva Stichova-Beldova

Friedl would assign the children a theme and then let them go on working independently and without any further instructions. I remember how the children drew a paintbrush. She did not show them a paintbrush, but she told them that a paintbrush has bristles. When I collected the drawings, I noticed that every child had drawn the bristles differently.

It was always difficult to get paper, and paints were also in short supply. Friedl did not give much thought to equipment and materials, perhaps because there were so few materials and we did not have much choice anyway. The children would often just draw with a pencil, no matter what the theme was.... The children were not even supposed to think—simply draw, collect themselves, dream, and then draw again, whatever came of it. The goal of these lessons was spontaneous expression, which was supposed to lead to freeing of the spirit.

### Zuzana Podemelová

I worked with children from Germany. Their parents had been shot right in front of their eyes; the children were in a terrible state. Once, these children came running toward me. "There's this wonderful lady," they said. "She lets us draw with paints—anything we want, we draw. We love her."

I met Friedl for ten minutes.... Her eyes told the whole story. They radiated light. I asked her how to help my children. Friedl answered, "Just let them come visit me." For them it was a huge thing—they got pleasure from drawing. Pleasure awakens the thirst for life. Yes, the simple pleasure of drawing.

Above: Friedl Dicker Brandeis, 1936.
Left: *Candle and Ship,* watercolors on paper, 1943/44, by Lily Bobašová (now Lily Edna Amit), one of Friedl's students from Terezin. "Here you need light to define the darkness," said Friedl, "and darkness here to define the light."

Janusz Korczak (pen name of Henryk Goldszmit), born in 1878 or 1879, a renowned Polish-Jewish physician and author, devoted his life to caring for children and developing innovative techniques that urged adults to respect children's autonomy. When Germany occupied Poland, Korczak's orphanage was moved to a smaller house in the Warsaw Ghetto. There the number of orphans doubled from 100 to 200. Korczak and his assistant Stefania Wilczynska struggled to provide them with food and basic necessities, often sacrificing their own well-being to do so. Korczak refused to wear a Star of David and was arrested when he complained to the Gestapo about rotten potatoes. He refused an offer to hide in Warsaw with a false identity; he would not abandon his charges. When his orphans were deported to their deaths in Treblinka on August 5, 1942, Korczak and his staff led them. "I will never forget that picture," wrote observer Nahum Remba. "It was not a march to the trains; it was an organized protest against the brutality of the oppressors. All the children were standing four in a row, Korczak at the head with raised eyes, holding two children by the hand, leading the children into the train."[1]

# "He Loved Every Child"

From the diary of Janus Korczak, *The Ghetto Years, 1939-1942*

People are naïve and good-hearted. And probably unhappy. They have not much of an idea what happiness consists of. Everyone understands it differently. And everyone combats boredom and nostalgia in a different way. The spirit feels a longing inside the narrow cage of the body. Man feels and ponders death as though it were the end, when in fact death is merely the continuation of life, it is another life.

Perhaps it is not safe to tell the general public about this. Anyhow, is my own universe and its fate not related to the fate of my entire generation, from the Australian cannibal islands to the workshop of a poet to a scientist looking through his telescope?

When little Genka coughs during the night, in an altruistic sense I feel pity for her, but egoistically I weigh the disturbance in the night, the concern for her health against: [Is] she contagious; and the expense of extra food, the trouble, and the costs involved in sending her to the country.

I feel sleepy. Before my beehive begins to buzz, I shall try to nap for an hour. I am convinced that in a future rational society the dictatorship of the clock will come to an end. To sleep and eat when you feel like it.

How lucky that the doctors and the police cannot prescribe how many times my heart has the right to beat. I do not like to sleep at night because then I cannot sleep in the daytime. Bread and water taste better at night. It is nonsense to put a child to bed for ten hours of uninterrupted sleep.

For rest and relaxation I moved to the children's hospital. The city is casting children my way, like little seashells—and I am just good to them. I ask neither where they come from, nor for how long or where they are going, for good or evil. The "Old Doctor" doles out candy, tells stories, answers questions. Dear, tranquil year remote from the tawdry marketplace of the world. A book, a visit from a friend—and always some patient who needs particular care.

In a hospital, children recover, or die.

*Froim Erwin Baum, a Korczak child, was outside the ghetto, looking for bread, when Nazis raided the orphanage. Baum survived the war. Below are excerpts from his oral history recalling Korczak.*

I remember my feeling for Dr. Korczak: If God would allow me to give twenty-five or thirty years of my life and get Dr. Korczak back, I would do it gladly because of the person he was. He was everything for every child, a nice, gentle person, his hands were little, like pillows to touch, and loveable. When he walked into a room, the room lit up. The minute he sat down, children were all around him.

He had time for every child. And he loved every child. The child could have been sick or full of pimples. Dr. Korczak took him in and kissed him right away.

We ran a court in the orphanage. If someone did something wrong, one child could sue another child. Dr. Korczak was very strict and the rules had to be obeyed.

When the war started, kids who lost their parents were brought to the orphanage and Dr. Korczak accepted everyone. They put more beds and the place got smaller and more crowded. There were no more rules—the main thing was survival. The orphanage expanded from 107 children to 250 and Dr. Korczak was a father to everyone. We were cramped together and it wasn't nice. But Dr. Korczak gave us inspiration and hope.

If a child had a loose tooth, somehow, without any pain, he got the tooth out and gave fifty cents to the child. He collected all these teeth, and from the teeth of the children he built a little castle. Somehow he had time for every child. And he loved every child.

Food was rationed, two slices of bread per person. Dr. Korczak never ate his two slices but gave them to the children. He ate very little and grew thinner and thinner.

He struggled to survive, but not for himself—for the children. He virtually went out and begged for food for children.

He just would not walk away.

And I came one morning and the house was empty. They were all taken, the children were taken.

Janusz Korczak with children and teachers in front of the *Dom Sierot* orphanage, Warsaw, 1935.

"He had time for every child. And he loved every child.... He struggled to survive, but not for himself—for the children. He virtually went out and begged for food for the children."

The Jewish tradition of leaving a moral testament began with the Biblical patriarchs who summed up their ethical values in instructions to heirs about how to behave. On March 28, 1943, Rabbi Leib Geliebter (1906-1973) wrote an ethical will in Yiddish, in a labor camp in Czestochowa, Poland, as a letter to his brothers-in-law. Geliebter describes the deportations from Czestochowa and what he knew about the fate of deportees from reports of escapees from the killing centers. This documentation reflects his need to preserve the brutal facts for future generations. He also describes specific family members, aiming to preserve family history and to leave a written monument honoring those who perished without proper burial. He enjoins readers to study *Mishnayot* (chapters of oral law) in memory of the deceased and to avenge their deaths, which he characterizes as *Kiddush Hashem* (Jewish martyrdom). By writing an ethical will when the future of Judaism was in jeopardy, Rabbi Geliebter reaffirmed his faith that Judaism would survive and future generations would follow his will and testament.

# "Take Revenge for Our Jewish Blood!"

Letter written by Rabbi Leib Geliebter, Czestochowa, Poland, March 28, 1943

ב"ה

**To my dear brothers-in-law Mr. Arie ג"ר, Mr. Mottel ג"ר, and Mr. Nachum Menashe ג"ר, may they live long!**

I am writing you a letter in the form of a report, not knowing if it will ever reach you, because we have no contact with the outside world. We are fenced in with our wives in a work camp in a corner of the city. My only wish is to let you know what happened to our family, their fate and how they perished, pathetically, sanctifying God's name, just because they carried the name Jew.

I am writing this to make myself feel better, so that the world will know, and to relieve the burden from my heart a little.

You know me as a faithful, devoted husband of your sister Hannah Rivka. Your parents were my parents; your whole family was dear to me. As of today, Hersh and I are living, thank God, in one apartment. I hope that we will live to the moment of salvation, but this is hard to believe, because we are completely powerless; we are being shot daily, without law or trial, like dogs. God have mercy on us! Every moment is a frightening experience. Even writing this letter is dangerous, since we work for the Germans all day, one is not allowed to stay in the apartment.

But I want to make clear to you where the bones of your dear perished ones lay, so that you can take revenge for our young, innocent human blood, spilled just because we carry the name Jew, a true sanctification of God's name.

The sad misfortune of deportation and murdering happened in Poland on the day before Tisha B'Av, [July 22, 1942]. It started in Warsaw. They said that people were being sent East for work. Jews believed this and went like sheep, without resistance. But later we learned their fate because several men were able to escape and revealed the pure truth, the whole secret. Our hair stands up from sorrow. We were cruelly tricked. They were sent to Treblinka, near the city of Malkinia, a station in a forest. There the Jews were let out of the trains and undressed. Completely naked, they were driven with sticks into giant halls marked with signs *"Zur Judenstadt"* (to the Jews' City). This is how the Nazis cynically decorated the building, suggesting that Jews were going to be bathed. Women's hair was cut so it could be used for their purposes. Everyone's clothes and packages were left in the first hall; Jews were driven into a second hall.

After entering the second hall the air was exhausted from the room, gas was let in, the floor was electrified with electric current, and everything was burnt to ashes. Then the floor opened up and automatically disposed of the ashes, which were then buried. People died with *Shema Yisrael* (the prayer said when death approaches) on their lips like true heroes. Within fifteen minutes there was no sign of life.

About one percent of the deportees were left alive to clean up, to sort and straighten out the clothing and to collect the monies—2,000 pounds of gold and sacks of diamonds. Everyone took their valuables on the [deportation] trains because they believed they were going to work. Every garment was screened and examined and all the valuables fell into Nazi hands. All this we learned after the *Aktions* took place.

If the Jews had known that they were being sent to a certain death, no one would have budged from his place. They would have preferred to be shot on the spot instead of being carried away to be burned at the stake in prepared hells.

In Poland there were three such hells: Treblinka, Belzec, and Auschwitz. Jews from all over Europe were brought there—doctors, engineers, lawyers and other educated intellectuals—and killed. They also killed Gypsies in these places. Jews from foreign countries came with full suitcases. Only when they arrived, after a few days of traveling, did they see the disaster. If they had known, they would not have come so well-dressed, like lords. No one wanted to believe that Germans, who came from the nation of culture and civilization, would do such a thing. As long as the world existed such barbarism had not been practiced.

Now I will devote myself to the happenings of our own family. We were in Czestochowa two years. Starting

on September, 28, 1942, the first day of *Chol Hamo'ed Sukkot* 5703, about 5,000 men were packed together daily like animals into cattle cars. With tears in their eyes and hearts full of pain, they said good-bye to their families, doubting if they would ever see each other again. Putting their bags on their shoulders, they were ordered into the streets by the police. There was a great deal of crying and painful sighing. How bitter were our hearts as we were separated from our beloved women, including my dear, devoted and beloved wife, Hannah Rivka, that good soul. She would have sacrificed herself for me, and I for her. How tragic was the parting from one another and from my dear sister, Renia Rachel. Her two-year old son, Yitzhak'l Israelek, was a phenomenon. He would have been a great person in Israel; he had signs of wisdom, talking like a grown up, with an extraordinary vocabulary; he was a gifted child who

Leib Geliebter [left] with Rabbi Shmuel Zusha Rudover, head of the Talmudic academy, Plock, Poland, c. 1935.

Geliebter's young nephew Yitzhak'l Israelek, about two years old, Czestochowa, Poland, c. 1942. He was murdered in Treblinka. "He would have been a great person in Israel; he had signs of wisdom; he was a gifted child..."

already knew the *aleph-bet* (Hebrew alphabet). I regret all our losses very much, but this child was as dear to me as my own. The world would have benefited from such a child; he was one in a thousand. All our dear ones were torn away in the bloom of their lives. Our fathers and mothers, dear sisters and brothers were taken away and robbed from us.

And why? What did we transgress to deserve such an end, may God have mercy on us! The Nazis have abandoned all laws of civilization. Everyone points the gun at us and shoots without mercy.

Now I will tell you what happened to the rest of the family. Our dear mother-in-law and your sister Rose and her young daughter were in Warsaw at the same time, and were sent away from there. Shmuel Simcha, our *mechutan* (in-law) was also sent away. Sala escaped and is now in Krakow. My beloved father, Reb Moshe Mordechai, and mother [Yiska Chaya Rudover] as well as my brother Pinchas, his wife [Leah, née Hershkowitz] and son Abraham Michal, his sister Esther and her husband Hersh Lichtman, and my youngest beloved sister Hannah Anjia were in Przysucha [Poland] until the *Aktion*. They must have suffered the same fate as we did.

Your brother Fishel is in Russia and your sister Blima, her husband Moshe Yitzchak Braun, and your brother-in-law Leib Lichtenstein are in Siberia. Their father-in-law passed away in Skierniewice [Poland] with great honor on 20 Kislev 5701 [December 20, 1940, prior to deportations]. Today this is called dying luxuriously. The ones who are in Russia will surely survive the war.

Therefore, I am turning to you in the name of all who died. In your lifetime, take revenge for our young Jewish blood, young souls that call out to you. Remember and say *Kaddish* (mourner's prayer). See to it that *Mishnayot* are learned, and erect monuments for your parents, sister, brother, and children. Nachum Menashe, you are a hero, you are a determined person. The souls [of the deceased] are crying out: "God take revenge for the spilled blood of your servant" [Psalms 79:10].

It is even a greater heartache since no sign of a grave remains. God have mercy. The dear souls should not be forgotten. The *Yahrzeit* (memorial day) should be every *Hosha'na Rabba*, every year. I write just like Moses, our teacher, of blessed memory, when he

"In the name of all who perished, take revenge for our young Jewish blood, young souls that call out to you."

finished the writing of the *Sefer Torah* (Torah scroll). He wrote with tears when he had to write about himself, in the eyes of all Israel.[1]

Remember us all your lives. To immortalize, say *"Yitgadal v'yitkadash sh'may rabba"* (the *Kaddish*, mourner's prayer).

This is the wish of your brother-in-law, Leibish ben Moshe Mordechai.

*Geliebter omitted his family name from the letter for fear of being identified. Then he buried the letter, family photos, and documents in glass jars, knowing that these would identify him if they were recovered after the war. Miraculously, Geliebter survived and retrieved the letter and photos. He settled in New York and died in 1973. Sala and the others mentioned in the letter died, except for those who may have survived in the Soviet Union.*

Clandestine drawing by
Peter Loewenstein of prisoners
in Terezin Ghetto, 1944.

## DOCUMENTING THE UNIMAGINABLE
# Recording the Truth, Telling the World

*Bonnie Gurewitsch*

t is told that as the historian, Simon Dubnow, was taken to his death in Riga, he turned to his fellow Jews and urged them: "Write and record!" (*schreibt un farschreibt!*) This message resonates within a strong Jewish tradition of recording history for posterity, its urgency highlighted by the German policy of secrecy and deception.

The Germans conducted their war against the Jews in secret, inventing code words and using euphemisms to deceive the population about the real meaning of German decrees. For example they told Jews they were being "resettled" instead of deported. They also hid and camouflaged the machinery of mass murder as Red Cross ambulances, infirmaries, shower rooms.

German decrees achieved the desired secrecy by strangling the flow of information. Dissemination of news stopped for Jews in occupied territories: Radios were confiscated, all but one or two newspapers were closed, and most of those still functioning became the official voice of the occupier. Communication with other Jewish communities was cut off and forbidden. It was possible—but very risky—for a small minority to listen to Allied radio broadcasts clandestinely and disseminate news of the progress of the war. However, it was virtually impossible to obtain news of the Holocaust, the war against the Jews, except from Jewish sources, like couriers and underground newspapers.

Jews responded to their isolation by defying German restrictions and establishing clandestine means of communication. They sent out couriers, who traveled illegally from one community to another, carrying news, funds, medicine, and eventually arms. These couriers were mostly women, who could hide their Jewish identity more easily than could men. Messengers in national resistance movements and paid smugglers helped Jews communicate externally, informing Jewish representatives in England, Switzerland, Palestine, and the US about Nazi atrocities and mass murders, hoping that the information would be widely disseminated. Jewish leaders believed that if Allied governments knew what was happening, they would act to stop the slaughter.

They needed to inform the world—and one another—that the Germans were not committing **isolated** war atrocities, or pogroms in the traditional sense, but genocide—the systematic murder of an entire people.

In May 1942 the Jewish Labor Bund smuggled a report to Shmuel Zygielbojm, its representative in London, detailing the locations of death camps and the use of poison gas in mass murder, estimating that the number of Jews who had been killed to date was 700,000. In September 1942 Zygielbojm disclosed that the Polish Government-in-Exile was receiving reports from the Bund that 7,000 Jews were being deported daily from Warsaw. When the Free World did not respond to these communications, Zygielbojm committed suicide in an attempt to call attention to the dire situation.

The Jewish tradition of recording history for posterity reaches back more than two thousand years. During the Holocaust countless Jews kept diaries. Many wrote eyewitness accounts and sociological studies, and published newspapers clandestinely. These underground newspapers were disseminated by the full spectrum of Jewish political groups in many European countries, often reflecting a particular group's ideological priorities or interpretation of events as well as a universal and Jewish concern with preserving the historical record for the future.

Underground newspapers had several goals: to inform the Jewish population about the progress of the war, to counter the false information that the Nazis were spreading about the destination of deportation trains, and to encourage Jewish resistance. *Hechalutz Halochem*, the newspaper of the Jewish Fighting Organization of Hechalutz Youth, reported on October 8, 1942: "A year ago the first of our units went into the forest.... For the first time in their lives they were holding weapons.... A year passed...thousands of people were killed. In the forest, too, there were great losses.... But the chain was not broken...the underground fight continues and the bloody battle for a better future...is still raging" (p. 64).

At first Jews expected to use their documentation at the end of the war to write an accurate and comprehensive history of the Jewish experience. Jewish communities were administered by a Jewish Council appointed by the Germans. Some councils, like those in Amsterdam, Lodz, and Lublin, established archives to document ghetto conditions and the organized responses of the ghetto councils. The German Jewish photographer, Abraham Pisarek, created a vivid visual record of vibrant Jewish community life in Germany under Nazi rule (p. 29).

But as the extent of the disaster became evident, Jews realized that German secrecy might result in the destruction of European Jewry and their total eradication from the historical record. They began to write for posterity, and to take steps to assure that their documentation would survive them. Emanuel Ringelblum, the founder of the Oyneg Shabbes archive in the Warsaw Ghetto, (p. 52) is perhaps the best-known archivist to have clandestinely assembled a group of historians and writers, but similar group efforts were made in other large ghettos.

Countless individuals also recorded accounts of what they and their communities were experiencing.

Hermann Kruk in Vilna, Avraham Tory in Kovno, and Mordechai Tenenbaum in Bialystok (p. 80) collected the documents and minutiae of daily life in their ghettos, preserving the story of how Jews coped and responded.

Artists and photographers also used their skills to document Jewish life under Nazi occupation. Some of their work was done secretly; some was permitted. In addition to the work they were compelled to do for the Germans, Jewish photographers and artists clandestinely recorded Jewish life from a Jewish perspective. They preserved a record of that which was positively Jewish, such as the work of social welfare agencies, Zionist youth movements, and cultural life in various ghettos and camps. They also documented the misery and the pathos of Jewish lives in these sub-human conditions. Not all these artists and photographers were professionals, but all used their skills to preserve and document the Holocaust for future generations.

Even in the death camps people with little energy and crude means made an effort to leave a written record of their experiences. Prisoners who worked in the *Sonderkommando* (special squads who were forced to work at the gas chambers) in Auschwitz-Birkenau wrote diaries and buried them in glass jars. *Sonderkommando* prisoners in Chelmno buried farewell notes and listed their names, so they should not be forgotten.

In the Kaufering concentration camp, a subcamp of Dachau, remnants of the Lithuanian Zionist youth movements banded together and wrote, by hand, a ten-page issue of their underground newspaper, *Nitzotz* (*Spark*), voicing utter confidence in Hitler's ultimate defeat and the eternity of the Jewish people (p. 65).

Since all documentation was forbidden by the Germans, it had to be hidden. The Oyneg Shabbes archive, as well as the archives of other ghettos, much personal documentation, and photographic collections, were buried or smuggled out of the ghettos and hidden by sympathetic non-Jews.

Survivors miraculously retrieved much of this hidden documentation and preserved it in Jewish archives in Poland, Israel, and the US, so that the truth could be "screamed at the world."[1] They wanted to insure that the historical record would contain and reflect a Jewish perspective on Jewish life and death during the Holocaust.

Emanuel Ringelblum, born in 1900, was a Polish-Jewish historian and community activist. In the Warsaw Ghetto, he organized a group of writers to document and preserve a record of the Holocaust and alert the world to the tragedy and heroism of the Jewish people. Ringelblum and his colleagues called themselves Oyneg Shabbes, (Oneg Shabbat/Joy of Sabbath), because they met on Saturday. This code name disguised the documentary purpose of their work. They collected diaries, commissioned reports, and conducted interviews with Jews about life under German occupation. They included reports from Polish ghettos and testimony about mass murder in ghettos and death camps. Shortly before the Warsaw Ghetto was destroyed in April 1943, they buried the archive in tin boxes and milk cans in the cellars of ghetto buildings. Although Ringelblum and his family were smuggled out of the ghetto and hidden, they were betrayed and executed in 1944. After the war, part of the archive was dug up; other parts were never found.

# Oyneg Shabbes: A Legacy for the Future

From an essay written by Dr. Emanuel Ringelblum, December 1942

I laid the first brick for the Oyneg Shabbes (O.S.) archive in October 1939. At the time the mood was extremely despondent. The public was terrorized by searches. Everything was burned, including innocent books to which even Hitler would not have objected. People were afraid to write because they anticipated searches. In time, however, people calmed down. So the Jews started to write. Everyone did: journalists, authors, teachers, community workers, young people, even children. Most people kept diaries reflecting daily events through the prism of personal experience.

## Oyneg Shabbes

In the early months of my work on the O.S. material, several associates joined me for this task. When the young historian Rabbi Shimon Huberband was drawn to the job, O.S. gained one of its best co-workers. Unfortunately, however, Rabbi Huberband jotted down his notes as comments in various books so that they might appear to be annotations to the text. It was some time before he could be persuaded that there was no danger in noting down everything and no need to write surreptitiously, as he had done in the beginning.

In May 1940 I thought it expedient to organize this highly important work as a group undertaking. I selected capable people and, as a result, the work was set on the right course and given the proper scope. The O.S. board at the time appointed Hirsh W. [Wasser] as secretary, a position he has held to this day. His daily contacts with hundreds of refugee delegations from all over the country made it possible to produce and amass hundreds of monographs on towns, the most important treasure of the O.S. work.

The establishment of the ghetto [November 1940], the fact that Jews were confined behind walls, provided even greater opportunity for development of the archive. The work expanded but remained clandestine.

Ways were sought to give the work legal status. With this in mind, a competition was proclaimed for dozens of writers, teachers, and intellectuals. We collected so much material that we all thought the time was ripe—if not for a synopsis—then at least for a summary of the various problems and prominent phenomena in Jewish life. Had the plan been realized, it would have been an important contribution to the history of the Jews in Hitler's times.

To our great regret, however, only part of the plan was carried out. We lacked the necessary tranquility for a plan of such scope and volume. Therefore, the writers who outlined various chapters could not conclude them. Several were deported. More than one died from a bullet; some crossed over to the "Aryan" side.

We formulated outlines on topics including the *Ordnungsdienst* (Jewish police), corruption, demoralization in the ghetto, community life, education, Jewish-Polish relations, smuggling, youth, women, as well as polls about Jewish cultural life, creativity, and art during the war, and the situation in various economic areas. Many writers were already at an advanced stage of work when a new disaster descended on Warsaw Jewry—a disaster that cost us 300,000 victims—mass deportations [July 22–September 12, 1942]. The work of O.S. was disrupted. Only a handful of writers continued their work during these disastrous days, writing about what was happening in Warsaw.

The war produced rapid changes in Jewish life in the towns of Poland. The scene changed as rapidly as in a movie. Reduced to the tiniest living space [after the mass deportations], Warsaw Jews now regarded the ghetto period as a veritable paradise and the pre-ghetto period, a veritable idyll…. Pre-deportation and post-deportation existence are as dissimilar as east and west.

The O.S. work was too sacred, too deeply rooted in the hearts of its staff, too important to the community to be put aside. We made an effort to reconstruct the period of deportations and gathered materials on the slaughterhouse of European Jewry—Treblinka. On the basis of accounts from people who returned from various provincial labor camps, we also attempted to present a picture of Jewish experiences in provincial towns during this period. Right now, as I am writing, our work is in full swing and, if we are granted a little more calm time, we will be able to ensure that no important

fact of Jewish life during the war will remain hidden from the world.

## Documenting and Preserving the Evidence

O.S. work was clandestine. Ways had to be found to disguise the collection of material. Few people knew the true purpose of our conversations with eyewitnesses.

There were two types of O.S. workers: permanent workers who devoted themselves entirely to the job, and temporary workers who wrote a single piece on their own experience or on their town or village. Everyone was fully aware of the importance of his part in completing the task. They understood how important it was for future generations to have evidence about the tragedy of Polish Jewry. Some also understood that the collected material would serve present needs as well, informing the world of the horrors perpetrated against the Jews.

Emanuel Ringelblum, 1935.

Our permanent workers, numbering several dozen, were, on the whole, grass-roots intelligentsia. We made a conscious effort to present, simply and faithfully, the course of events in every town, the experience of every Jew—since every Jew living now is a world himself.

Our temporary workers were common people, refugees, who had headed community organizations in their hometowns. Due to the terrible crowding in the ghetto, refugees live in indescribable housing conditions. Sustaining clandestine work in such conditions has been one of our difficulties. Last winter it was cold and most Jewish homes had no electricity. The writing was risky; the hardship indescribable. Add to this the initial fear of being discovered by the Gestapo and the picture is complete. Our co-workers were generally laborers, craftsmen, and so forth, who suffered great hunger in Warsaw, our city of pitiless Jews. The O.S. tried to save these people from starving to death by arranging to distribute food packages to them from communal institutions.

Not only adults, but also young people and, in some instances, even children, worked for O.S. Our aim was to present a photographically true and detailed picture of what Jews experienced, thought, and suffered. We tried to have the same event, the history of a community for instance, described by both an adult and a young person; by a pious Jew who is conscious at all times of the rabbi, the synagogue, the cemetery, and other religious institutions, and by a secular Jew who stresses other equally important moments.

Comprehensiveness was the main principle of our work. Objectivity was the second. We endeavored to convey the whole truth, no matter how bitter, and we presented faithful, unadorned pictures. The horrors perpetrated by the Germans on the Jewish population occupy first place in our work.

This material will supply future historians with information on the thinking of specific groups during the war. It will be of great significance for the tribunal after the war that will hold the guilty responsible—whether Jews, Poles, or Germans.

What type of material has been preserved in the O.S. archive? The most important treasures are the monographs on towns and villages that describe the experiences of a specific community, from the outbreak of the war through its expulsion and liquidation. Because all these efforts were done in conditions of underground secrecy and by people who had never worked in historical research, there is no index of what the O.S. material contains.

Apart from comprehensive monographs, we tried to obtain accounts of singular important events in various towns. We obtained accounts from people who were directly or indirectly involved in a specific event, as participants, witnesses, or in any other manner.

One of the important subjects of the O.S. work were the labor camps, where thousands of Jews perished. Apart from the ghettos, the labor camps were one of the most effective means of destroying the Jewish population by robbing it of its best element—young people and men of working age. The section on experiences in prisons and concentration camps is meager, not because few Jews spent time there, but for the simple reason that from the start, the reigning principle was that no Jews were to come out alive. Thousands of Polish Jews were sent to Oswiecim (Auschwitz), but none

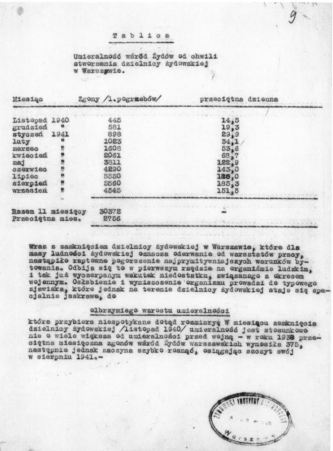

Top: Rabbi Shimon Huberband (1909-1942), a young historian, documented religious life in the Warsaw Ghetto. He and his wife were murdered in Treblinka.
Bottom: A report from the O.S. archive, written in Polish, showing mortality rates for Jews in the Warsaw Ghetto from November 1940 through September 1941. The total number of deaths shown in the left column was 30,372, averaging 2,756 per month. Daily averages are shown in the right column. The report attributes the "gigantic increase in mortality" to the inability of Jews to work in their livelihoods, the terrible living conditions, and the wartime shortages.

ALL IMAGES AND DOCUMENTS ARE FROM THE
OYNEG SHABBES ARCHIVE.

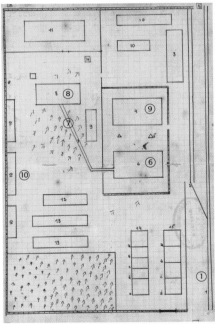

Top: A card listing tenants in a shared apartment in the
Warsaw Ghetto. By mid-November 1940 about 350,000
residents lived in the ghetto, averaging nine people
in each room.
Bottom: Map of Treblinka. Abram Krzepicki was deported
on August 25, 1942; he escaped eighteen days later.
His report on Treblinka was recorded for O.S. by Rachela
Auerbach. The map shows, among other things,
(1) the location of the railroad, (6) the undressing barracks,
(7) the passage to the gas chambers, (8) the building
with showers [gas chambers], (9) the building with the
crematorium, and (10) the ditches [for burning corpses].

returned. The only document on these victims is the
telegram sent to relatives with the typical information
that the inmate died. Those who did return from prisons
felt so terrorized that they were afraid to relate any information. I did, nevertheless, manage to get two former
prisoners to tell about their experiences.

It is impossible to enumerate all the facets of O.S.
work. We can say with confidence, however, that no
important feature of Jewish life during the war was
omitted from O.S. material. A phenomenon such as
smuggling, for instance, which is very significant in all
wars, is represented in O.S. by a work of T-n [Tytelman].
It portrays the overwhelming importance of smuggling
in Warsaw which, so long as the ghetto existed, saved
the community of 400,000 from death by starvation.

Had Warsaw Jewry been forced to live on official
daily rations of 6.3 ounces of bread per individual, every
vestige of Jewish Warsaw would have disappeared. Smuggling took its daily toll of Jewish victims; shortly before
the deportations, smugglers numbered in the dozens.
When Poland is liberated, a monument will have to be
erected to the smuggler who, incidentally, saved the Polish
population in many cities from starvation.

The deportation, which began on July 22, 1942,
marked a new period in the history of Warsaw Jewry. It
also affected the nature of O.S. work, since it interrupted
our activities for several months. At a time when every
second threatened capture and transport to Treblinka,
no one could think about systematic collection. During
the deportations only a handful of people kept diaries
and recorded daily experiences. As soon as things settled down somewhat, people again applied themselves
to the task.

O.S. is not an association of scientists who com-
pete with and oppose one another, but a brotherhood,
where all help each other and strive towards the same
goal. Every O.S. worker knows that his slaving toil and
pain, the risks he takes **twenty-four** hours a day while
engaged in the undercover work of carrying material
from place to place, is for the sake of an exalted ideal
and that in days of freedom to come, society will evaluate
his role properly and reward him with the highest honors
available in liberated Europe. O.S. is a fellowship, a
monastic order of brothers, whose banner is: readiness
to sacrifice, devotion to one another, and service to the
community.

Most artists rely on their imagination to transform reality into images that are moving and often provocative. But the artists who lived in the ghettos and concentration camps realized that the grotesque realities of their existence transcended anything they could imagine. Instead of producing art for art's sake, they used their talent to document the atrocities of living under Nazism and to sustain their sense of purpose and dignity. The Nazis could starve their bodies, but they could not starve their souls. "I believe that my constant urge to draw and thus bear witness was a powerful factor in keeping me alive," recalls Halina Olomucki, who at the age of seventeen began drawing powerful images of inmates in the Warsaw Ghetto and later Auschwitz. "Drawing is my weapon of survival. When I draw I have the impression of being invulnerable... I have to survive."[1] Her works and those of many outstanding Holocaust artists are filled with bleak but moving images of men, women, and children struggling to survive in subhuman conditions. Many of these works were destroyed or lost. Those that were recovered serve as invaluable historical documentation and testimony that the Nazi could not destroy man's creative spirit.

# "Drawing Is My Weapon of Survival"

Text by Barbara Lovenheim

Jewish Councils of the large ghettos—Warsaw, Vilna, Lodz, and Bialystok—often encouraged and assisted Jews with artistic skills. In Lodz artists worked in the ghetto's graphics department, where they had access to art materials, time, and privacy to work. In Warsaw, artists received subsidies. In Vilna and Kovno artists were encouraged to exhibit their work in art shows.

Ironically, the Germans also gave artists a place to work by exploiting their talents to serve the Reich. Halina Olomucki received bread and cheese from the Germans in Auschwitz, who asked her to draw for them. In Terezin, many artists drafted blueprints for construction projects, which gave them access to art supplies. In Bialystok, the SS assigned artists to create counterfeit copies of masterpieces that Germans could sell abroad. In the Sachsenhausen Concentration Camp artists produced counterfeit American and English currency and postage.

These jobs were a godsend to artists who were so determined to continue working that sometimes they traded their bread for paint or paper. As paper became scarce they worked on cardboard boxes, paper bags, the backs of official notices, and even remnants of flour sacks and burlap bags. "Each slip of paper, each pencil butt is a treasure which has to be saved at all cost," recalls Olomucki. "I can withstand hunger, thirst, cold, and fear as long as I can draw."

Olomucki survived both the Warsaw Ghetto and Auschwitz, sustained by the extra food she received for her work and by her artistic passion. Many other exceptional Jewish artists were not so fortunate. The German-born painter, Felix Nussbaum, a recognized artist before the war, became known for his haunting renditions of detainees in Gurs and St. Cyprien transit camps, where he and his wife were interned. They escaped from Gurs and lived in hiding in Brussels for three years. Supported by friends, Nussbaum hid over

100 of his paintings in the cellar of an art dealer. In 1944 he was deported to Auschwitz and killed.

Bedrich Fritta, born in 1906 in Prague, was deported to Terezin and assigned to the Technical Department where numerous artists, including Leo Haas, Otto Ungar, and Ferdinand Bloch also worked. At night they met in the darkened workroom to draw and paint clandestinely, documenting cultural activities in Terezin as well as haunting images of the elderly, the sick, and the dead. They hid their work in walls and in tin boxes to protect it from the Germans.[2]

Leo Strauss, a fellow prisoner and art dealer, used his contacts to smuggle some of their art work outside Terezin. In June 1944 the Nazis came upon some of these clandestine art works. They arrested Haas, Bloch, Ungar, and Fritta and tortured them savagely in the Gestapo prison located in the Small Fortress, trying to find out who had created the "atrocity" art. The artists refused to talk. In the fall all four men and other artists were sent to Auschwitz. Fritta and Bloch died. Ungar was sent on to Buchenwald; Haas to Sachsenhausen, where he survived working for the Germans. After the war Haas returned to Terezin. He recovered his entire collection and many works by Fritta.

Alexander Bogen, a renowned illustrator and painter who now lives in Israel, was born in Vilna in 1916. When war interrupted his art studies, he joined partisans in the Narocz forest. Eventually he joined the all Jewish Nekamah (Revenge) unit. He trained recruits in survival tactics and drew vivid scenes of partisans, using charcoal made from burnt branches and random scraps of paper.

"I would try to record the typical situations that we would encounter," he recalled. "A unit returning from its operation…members sitting around a bonfire, playing cards, drinking vodka. To be creative during the Holocaust was also a protest. This shows that the Germans could not break [the artist's] spirit."[3]

Arnold Daghani (1906-1985), a Romanian artist, was deported to Transnistria in the Ukraine and interned in Mikhailovka, a labor camp, in 1942. In 1943 he and his wife escaped to the Bershad Ghetto. In both places he created art clandestinely, inspired by the harsh life of internment, but he chose to portray the dignity of the inmates rather than their beatings and executions which, he said, "would certainly lower the almost superhuman dignity with which the slaves went to the grave…why cheapen that by atrocities painted or drawn, even if they surpass imagination and 'happen' to be true?"[4]

Left: THE LIQUIDATION OF DR. KORCZAK'S ORPHANAGE by Halina Olomucki, c. 1942. Janusz Korczak (p. 44) was the director of an orphanage in the Warsaw Ghetto, where Olomucki lived. In this sketch Korczak holds a child in his arms as he leads his orphans to the deportation train that took them to their deaths in Treblinka.

Overleaf: ST. CYPRIEN by Felix Nussbaum, 1940. Using watercolor and pencil to create flat, monochromatic hues, Nussbaum conveyed the despair of detainees in the camp where he and his wife were interned. Nussbaum's native city of Osnabrueck, Germany, has honored him by establishing the Nussbaum Museum, designed by architect Daniel Liebskind.

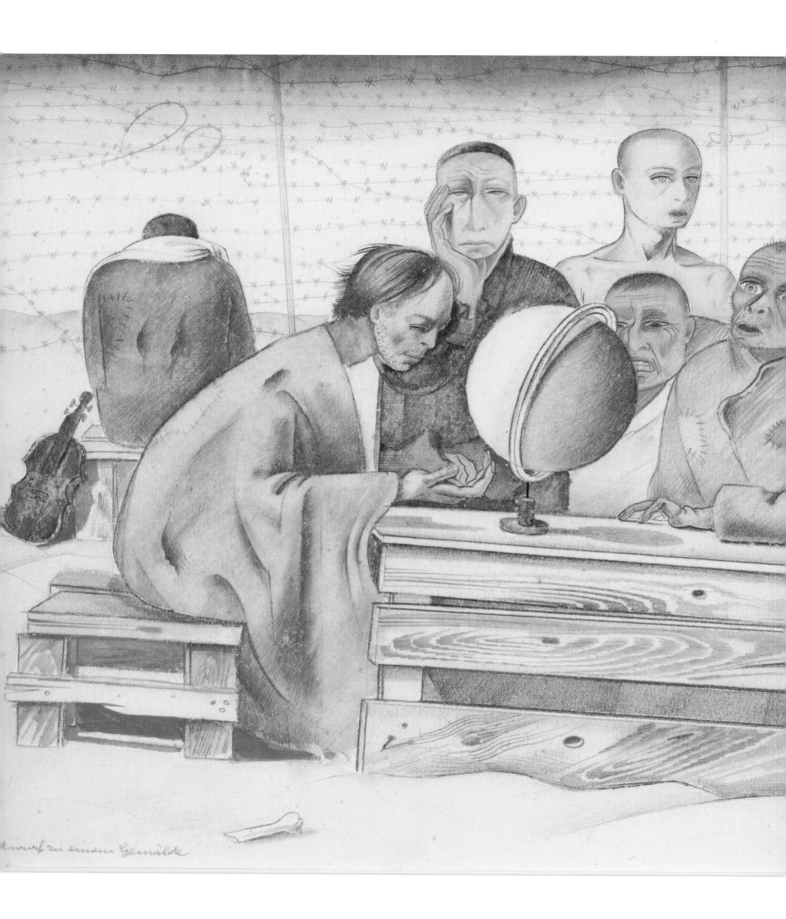

Meiner lieben Familie                    Felix Nussbaum
Weidmann freundlichst gewidmet 1940

Upper left: TYPHUS IN THE CAMP by Arnold Daghani, Transnistria, 1943. Daghani took his watercolors with him to the labor camp in Mikhailovka and became known as the artist of the camp. After escaping to the Bershad Ghetto, he continued painting about the severe conditions in Mikhailovka, where typhoid and other diseases were rampant. Here, the murky dark colors emphasize the bleak environment of Mikhailovka and the fate of its prisoners.

Upper right: FILM AND REALITY by Bedrich Fritta, Terezin, 1940's. This is a satiric ink drawing of Nazis making propaganda films, using Jewish prisoners who, after the filming, will go to their deaths. Notice the symbolism of the camera in the Nazi boot and the corpse behind the curtain. The drawing might have been inspired by the propaganda film, *The Fuehrer Gives the Jews A City,* produced by the Germans in Terezin in June 1944 to promote the camp as a "paradise" for the Jews.

Lower left: PARTISANS EATING by Alexander Bogen, Narocz forest, 1943. "Ultimately, when I asked myself why I was drawing, when I was fighting day and night… [I realized that it was] something similar to biological continuity. Each man, when standing face to face with cruel danger, with death, reacts in his own way. The artist reacts in an artistic way. This is his weapon."

Lower right: UNTITLED by Peter Loewenstein, Terezin, 1944. Loewenstein was deported to Terezin and forced to work in the Technical Department producing "official" art. He also painted and drew clandestinely. This is a powerful ink drawing of men and women hovering together in the cold weather. He was deported to Auschwitz in 1944 and killed.

The Nazis confiscated radios and printing presses in the occupied territories to control news of the war. Only one official Jewish newspaper in occupied Poland, *Gazeta Zydowska,* which was submitted to the German propaganda office for approval, was permitted to exist. In the Lodz Ghetto an additional approved newspaper, *Geto Zeitung*, was published by the Jewish Council. These newspapers printed German edicts, listings of benign ghetto events, and German versions of the war. But for Jews who hungered for real news, these official, censored versions were not adequate. To inform the populace, Jewish political groups published and distributed their own newspapers clandestinely and at great risk. In Poland there were more than 100 clandestine newspapers and journals; most were published in Warsaw.[1] These papers gathered information from outlets like the BBC to report on the real course of the military war and received information about the war against the Jews from couriers and escapees. These publications promoted solidarity with underground movements, encouraged resistance, raised morale, and reduced the isolation enforced by the Nazis.

# Resisting Through the Written Word

Excerpts from underground newspapers

Third Year          *DOS FRAYE VORT (THE FREE WORD)*          No. 1/38
May 23, 1942
Bund Newspaper, Warsaw

## DOS FRAYE VORT

*The Jewish political party known as the Bund (General Union of Jewish Workers) was founded in Vilna in 1897 to organize Jewish workers in the socialist struggle against capitalism in Europe. The Bund considered Yiddish to be the Jewish national language and supported a wide network of services to the Jewish community, including social welfare, youth movements, and education. In September 1939 Bund activists in Warsaw removed two mimeograph machines from their offices, hid them, and used these machines to publish underground*

*newspapers in the ghettos. The newspapers were distributed by Bund couriers to trusted acquaintances, who would pass them on to others. Names of the newspapers were often changed to maintain security, and some were even backdated to prewar times for this reason.* Dos Fraye Vort (The Free Word) *replaced the previous Bund newspaper,* Veker (Alarm) *in 1942. In an article in the above edition the Bund urged workers to hide from German roundups that sought skilled workers. In case they were caught, they advised workers to "work badly and slowly."*

*DOS FRAYE VORT:* In the winter of 1942-1943 Hitler resolved to begin an "offensive" to demonstrate the outstanding bravery of the German army. He thought that German trains and tanks would be ready for the Russian winter and the German soldier would be prepared. The Germans had already secured the sea from a counter-offensive by the Russians and chose a peninsula for their offensive because this was the easiest place. He began the offensive with a concentration of tremendous force, placing 2,000 airplanes in a stretch of fifty miles. He informed his people about the assault five days after it began. And today, on the 19th of May—eleven days after the beginning of the offensive, with many dead, a flow of blood, and a huge waste of military equipment, Hitler has to pay for his local victory that has a very small strategic significance.

Everyone realizes that the German Army of 1942 is no longer the *Blitzkrieg* it was in 1941, when it quickly occupied hundreds of miles. At Kharkov, Marshall Timoshenko's army has begun a great offensive. The first German lines have been penetrated by the Red Army. The German [Field Marshall Fedor von] Bock has thrown all his reserves to counter attack the Russian assault and the Russians are already attacking the second German line. They are also attacking the Leningrad front. The Germans are suffering great losses. The initiative on the Russian front is in the hands of the Russians. They do not allow the Germans to assemble their forces for a greater offensive. The next six weeks will show that Hitler is in no position to "destroy the Bolshevik enemy" and then the final stage of the "Hitler drama" will begin—the German revolution.

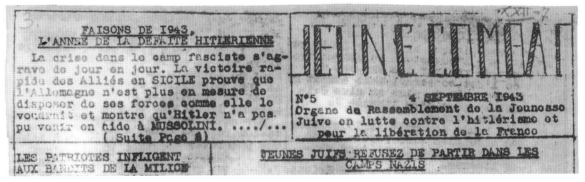

JEUNE COMBAT (YOUTH FIGHTS)
NO 5 / SEPTEMBER 1943
Publication of the Gathering of Jewish Youth Fighting Hitler and for the Liberation of France

### JEUNE COMBAT

*When France surrendered to the Nazis, young Jewish Communists went underground. The Communists provided relief and social welfare services in the poorest Jewish neighborhoods of Paris, assisted the families of interned Jews, and assisted their own operatives who went into hiding. They urged Jews to publicize the plight of internees and their families by writing letters to public officials and the Red Cross. They engaged in armed struggle, and were responsible for two thirds of the anti-Nazi attacks in Paris between July 1942 and 1943. Their clandestine newspaper,* Jeune Combat, *began publication in June 1943 in the south of France, where many of the young resisters had relocated.[2]*

JEWISH YOUTH: RESIST THE NAZI CAMPS!
    Hiding behind registration, new deportations
    and new massacres are being planned.
    Everybody, join the resisters, form groups
    for resistance and combat. This is our cry in
    the face of our families' assassins.

FIGHT BY ANY MEANS, INCLUDING ARMS
After the Jewish refugees, the women, the very elderly, the children, Jewish youth will be the next victims of the Nazis. The successive killing of countless Jewish families is no longer enough for the Hitler beast, who diabolically pursues extermination. The enemy is being beaten on every front. To maintain their power over the occupied countries, the Nazis have increased the terror.

Young Jews, the enemy uses awful tricks. Don't fall into the trap of registration nor into the trap of forced labor. Anything is better than the Nazi concentration camps, which lurk behind the curtain of registration and the *Todt* (forced) labor camp. In the face of these threats, our elders show us the way. All the Jewish parties and organizations have succeeded in uniting at the national level. All over France, the national unity of young Jews must be similarly achieved.

Already, the Jewish youth of l'Isère, Savoie, and Haute Savoie have recently formed a committee of united defense, whose aim is the solidarity of all the young Jews. To organize resistance against the deportations, all French youth should be fraternally united.

Throughout all the towns of France, young Zionists, young Scouts,[3] young people of whatever philosophy have to unite and form their committee of unified defense. Be prepared to defend your life and that of your family. In order to defend yourself against Hitler's rage, it is necessary to increase the defense and combat groups that have been formed by the UGIF (Union of French Jews, the Jewish Council in France.)

Young Jews, save yourselves, join the army of patriots in the maquis that is preparing to liberate France. Join the wonderful FTP [a Communist Jewish fighting group] that includes many Jews and delivers terrible blows to the Nazis.

Let us fight like the hero [Rabbi] Marcel Langer who, in front of the guillotine, proclaimed: "I am dying for France and a better humanity."[4]

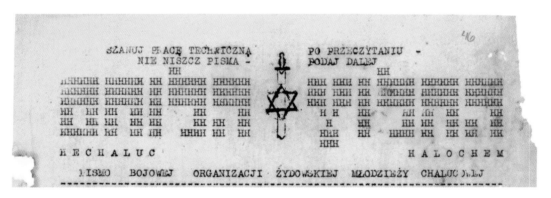

*PUBLICATION OF THE JEWISH FIGHTING ORGANIZATION OF THE HECHALUTZ YOUTH,* KRAKOW
Second Year. No. 36        Friday October 8, 1943 – 8 Tishrei 5704

### HECHALUTZ HALOCHEM

*When the Krakow Ghetto in Poland was established in March 3, 1941, Zionist youth movements went underground. The Jewish Fighting Organization [JFO/ZOB] launched some offensive actions in the "Aryan" side of Krakow, notably an attack on the Cyngaria cafe during which eleven Germans were killed and thirteen wounded. Their underground journal,* Hechalutz Halochem, *was published in Polish in Krakow.*

### ON YOM KIPPUR

A year ago our first unit went into the forest. It was Yom Kippur eve. Crowds glided through the streets of the ghetto toward the last small synagogues. The tones of Kol Nidrei [prayer] reverberated among the houses. Religious fervor swayed the crowd, who were living under the threat of death. Our young people stole away quietly from the ghetto. For the first time in their lives they were holding weapons and for the last time the muffled noise of Jewish alleys said farewell to them. They were never to return to the ghetto, never to unite with their brethren, and only in the far away forest would they fight in the name of freedom against the bloody enemy.

A year went by. The melody from the *beth hamidrash* (Jewish house of study) was silenced. The ghettos were razed to the ground. Thousands of people were killed. In the forest, too, there were great losses. The fighters gave up their young blood for the freedom of the people.

But the chain was not broken. The continuity goes on. The underground fight still goes on and the bloody battle for a better future, which is bound to rise for the oppressed people, is still raging.

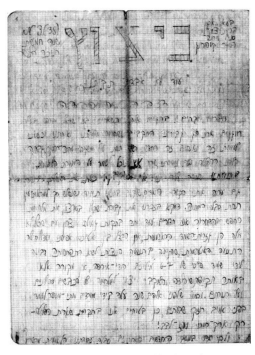

*Nitzotz* masthead and lead article

*Nitzotz* cover page with IBZ logo: The Star of David with Hebrew letters

*NITZOTZ (SPARK)*
Newsletter of United Zionist Organization / No. 3 (38) fifth year
Camp Kaufering Branch / Hanukkah 5705 (1944)

## NITZOTZ

*When Kovno, Lithuania, was occupied by the Soviets, several Zionist youth movements joined forces to form Irgun B'rit Ziyyon (IBZ–United Zionist Organization). Their newspaper* Nitzotz (Spark) *was published clandestinely, first under Soviet occupation, then under Nazi occupation.* Nitzotz *reported on the IBZ activities and goals, reflecting the idealism of the Zionist youth movements. Before the ghetto was liquidated in the summer of 1944, the leaders of IBZ were deported to Stutthof and then to Kaufering, a sub-camp of the Dachau concentration camp. In Kaufering the IBZ leaders organized to insure survival. "We guarded our morale and our lives, and the lives of others," recalls one leader. They hand-wrote an issue of* Nitzotz, *the voice of the surviving Lithuanian Zionists.*

*Nitzotz expressed their hopes for the continuity of their Zionist work, their morale, and their lives. They were optimistic about survival because radio broadcasts related to them surreptitiously led them to think that liberation was imminent. After the Kaufering camps were liberated in April 1945, some of the leaders of IBZ eventually reached Palestine.*

## WE HAVE NOT LOST HOPE

Dear Comrades! At this moment our brothers all over the world are celebrating the holiday of our Maccabee heroes. Meanwhile, we are now in the second month of imprisonment in Kaufering, but we have resolved…to guard our national identity.

These [Nazi persecutions] are not the first edicts of apostasy. Anti-Semitism, which has brought about the physical destruction of six to seven million European Jews, had its origin in that same period that Judas Maccabaeus set out to battle the Hellenistic conquerors and their beliefs. And just as a few rebels, two thousand years ago, stood up to an enemy seven times stronger, so we are confident about the resurgence of the surviving remnant, still strong of spirit and brave of heart!

If in the last months our national work has suffered from various difficulties, we are now resolved to increase our activities and strengthen our ties. In the West and in the East the dawn is breaking and the nations of Europe are coming back to life. We must be ready to seize the historic moment of our nation. We are full of hope that we will succeed in transmitting our newsletter to our comrades in the death camps.

Photographs are rarely neutral images. Often they are social commentary and reveal as much about the photographer as the subject of the photo. During the Holocaust German photographers deliberately photographed Jews in the most unfavorable light possible to promote Nazi propaganda that Jews were inferior, unworthy, and weak. Sadly, these are the images most often used to illustrate the events of the Holocaust. The few exceptions are images taken by Jewish photographers who used their cameras to record the grim realities of Jewish life as a form of resistance. "I don't have a gun," said George Kadish, a photographer in the Kovno Ghetto. "The murderers are gone. My camera will be my revenge."[1] Those who took unauthorized photos of ghetto life operated clandestinely, secretly capturing the brutality of Jewish life as well as the heroic ways in which Jews resisted dehumanization by continuing their religious practices, education, and culture in unimaginable circumstances. Many ghetto photographs were lost when the ghettos were destroyed, but thousands of images miraculously managed to survive, becoming invaluable documentation for future generations.

# Through Jewish Eyes: Documenting with a Camera

Text by Barbara Lovenheim

The Jewish Councils that supervised Eastern European ghettos employed photographers to document official ghetto activities and produce ID photographs for residents. Henryk Ross, a photojournalist, worked in the Lodz Ghetto's Department of Statistics, part of the vast bureaucracy created by Mordechai Chaim Rumkowski, head of the Jewish Council. Ross was required to photograph ghetto officials, social events, and meetings. He also documented the productivity of the ghetto's Jewish work force, hoping that these photographs would encourage German authorities to preserve the ghetto as important for the war effort. On the side, Ross secretly photographed the appalling conditions of ghetto life, often focusing on Jews who had died of hunger and also photographing deportations to death camps.

Mendel Grosman, who worked with Ross in the Lodz Ghetto, was a painter and self-taught photographer before he was hired by the Jewish Council. He often hid his camera inside his coat, where he had cut holes in the inside lining of his pockets, giving him the ability to manipulate his camera with his hands. When he saw a compelling image, he opened his coat slightly and deftly took pictures, unseen by his subjects or the police. Unlike Ross, who organized and photographed groups of people, Grosman captured people in motion, when they weren't aware of his presence. He walked streets and alleyways and rooftops, capturing the poignancy and pathos of human suffering—in homes, soup kitchens, and at the cemetery—with such skill and sensitivity that he managed to turn the most dismal subject matter into moving images documenting a Jewish perspective on the unfolding horrors.

Both men took great risks in operating clandestinely, since they could be caught by German authorities or even Jewish officials. Grosman's work in the Statistics Office allowed him to order extra film without arousing suspicions. As the threat of liquidation neared, Ross hid thousands of his negatives in barrels and buried them. Then he escaped. After liberation he returned to retrieve them. Grosman was less fortunate. He hid 10,000 negatives in crates and buried them. Tragically, he died on a death march to a German work camp, his camera still around his neck. He was thirty-two. When his sister returned to uncover the negatives, she sent them to Palestine. There they were lost during the Israeli War of Independence. Fortuitously, a friend in the ghetto, Nachman Zonabend, had saved hundreds of Grosman's negatives. They are currently the major source of Grosman's photo collections, now housed at the Ghetto Fighters House and Yad Vashem in Israel, and the YIVO Institute in New York City.

George Kadish (Hirsch Kadushin) worked in the Kovno Ghetto in Lithuania. Trained as an engineer, he received orders from Germans to repair x-ray machines in Kovno. He seized the opportunity to barter for film and develop negatives at the German military hospital. Then he smuggled them out, hidden in crutches. In the ghetto, Kadish placed his camera inside his overcoat and snapped pictures through a buttonhole. He took photos of Jews at forced labor and also used his camera to record resistance activities.

Before the ghetto was liquidated in 1944, Kadish escaped across the river and photographed the ghetto going up in flames. He returned to photograph the few Jews who had survived in hiding. Intent on preserving his collection, he enlisted the aid of Yehuda Zupowitz, a Jewish police officer, to help him hide it for posterity. Zupowitz was caught and tortured by the Germans, but he never divulged the location of Kadish's photos. After liberation Kadish retrieved his collection and mounted an exhibition for survivors in DP camps.

Photos documenting the slaughter of Jews before liberation are rare and extremely important. When the Nazis invaded Lenin, Poland, the parents and sisters of Faye Lazebnik (Schulman) were sent to a ghetto; her brothers to a work camp. Faye, who had learned photography from her brother Moishe, was kept alive to develop film. Often she made copies and hid them.

When Faye realized that she would be shot, she escaped and joined the Molotov partisan brigade in the

Top: George Kadish photographed the Yiddish words *"Yid'n Nekamah"* (Jews revenge) that a dying neighbor wrote in his own blood on the ground in Kovno, June 1941.
Bottom: Henryk Ross photographing a group of Lodz Ghetto residents for ID pictures. By grouping them he took several photos in a single frame and saved film for his clandestine work.

forest along the Russian-Polish border. There she nursed wounded partisans, went on missions, and photographed the brigade as they fought and hid in the woods. During a partisan raid on Lenin, she recovered her photography equipment. During the next two years she took over 100 photos, developing them in a darkroom made from blankets. After the war she found her brother, married his partner, and immigrated to Canada.

The jarring photo on p. 73 of prisoners burning corpses on a pyre in Auschwitz-Birkenau is unique and rare as documentation; it records activity that the Nazis took extraordinary measures to keep secret. According to Dr. Piotr Setkiewicz, chief archivist at the State Museum of Auschwitz-Birkenau, the photo was taken by the *Sonderkommando* (Jewish prisoners forced to work at the gas chambers and crematoria) in the summer of 1944. It was smuggled to the outside world with hope that it would incite a response from the Allies, but there is no record of it having an impact.

## The Lodz Ghetto

Above: Henryk Ross took this photo clandestinely of Jewish deportees from the Lodz Ghetto being herded into a transport to Auschwitz at the Radogoszcz Station. At the Eichmann trial in Israel in 1961, Ross testified that he had disguised himself as a cleaner to get into the train station that was open only to German workers. There he hid in a storeroom and took photographs through a hole in the wall (see side of opening on the left side of photo) to document the deportation for future generations. c. 1942.

Left page top: Mendel Grosman photographed a memorial assembly for Chaim Nachman Bialik, the renowned Hebrew poet, and Theodor Herzl, the founder of Zionism, held in the Lodz Ghetto in 1943 by members of the Chazit Dor Bnei Hamidbar youth movement. Members thought of themselves as the vanguard of those who longed to enter the Promised Land. However, like the Biblical generation who perished in the desert, they realized that they might not succeed. Zionist meetings were often held clandestinely.

Bottom: Mendel Grosman photographed a public prayer service on Yom Kippur 1940, held in the courtyard of the synagogue at 21 Zgierska Street in the Lodz Ghetto. In keeping with Orthodox tradition, men and women prayed separately. Unlike other ghettos, Jewish communal prayer was permitted in Lodz in 1940 and some prayer services were specially organized for the High Holidays.

## The Kovno Ghetto

Above: George Kadish photographed violinists performing in the Kovno Ghetto orchestra. Front row, Maya Glad-shtein (later Kapit); third from right, Alexander (Shmaya) Stupel, a well-known German-Jewish violinist; standing behind the violinists, Stupel's brother Boris. The orchestra had thirty-five instrumentalists and five vocalists; it gave eighty concerts in the ghetto's Police House between the summer of 1942 and March 1944. Boris Stupel and Maya Gladshtein survived and immigrated to Israel.

Left page top: During the fall of 1941 residents in the Kovno Ghetto were allowed to organize schools, but on August 25, 1942, formal education was banned. Limited classes for young children continued clandestinely. This photo by David Chaim Ratner shows a class held in a stable at 101 Krisiukaicio Street. Children include Taiba Leibaite (far left), Basia Leibaite (second from left), and David Ackerman Falahi (in background).

Bottom: George Kadish photographed this secret orphanage in the Kovno Ghetto hospital ward, where nurses hid children who had lost their parents. Children (and the people who hid them) were at great risk, since a special Children's *Aktion* took place in the nearby ghetto of Shavli (Siauliai). In Kovno a Children's *Aktion* occurred on March 27-28, 1944; 1,300 children under the age of twelve were shot or sent to Auschwitz.

## Documenting Mass Murder: Poland, May 1942

After the Nazis invaded Faye Lazebnik's hometown, Lenin, Poland, her parents and sisters were imprisoned in the ghetto. Lazebnik, who was trained as a photographer, was kept alive to develop photographs for the Germans. In 1942 the *Einsatzgruppen* (mobile killing squads) massacred the entire Jewish population of Lenin, including Lazebnik's parents and sisters. A few Jews were kept alive to work for the Nazis and were ordered to bury bodies in trenches. The Nazis photographed the burials as evidence of a successful operation. After Lazebnik developed the above photograph for the Germans, she made copies and hid them as documentation of Nazi atrocities. After the war she managed to return to Lenin and recover this photograph, as well as others.

## Photographing Mass Murder: Auschwitz-Birkenau 1944

A rare photograph showing *Sonderkommando* prisoners burning Jewish victims on a pyre in Birkenau in 1944. According to Dr. Piotr Setkiewicz, chief archivist at Auschwitz-Birkenau, a Greek Jewish prisoner named Alex pointed the lens, pushed the shutter release, and hid the camera. Other Jewish inmates involved in taking this photo were Szlojme (Szlama) Dragon, his brother Abram, and Alter Fajnzylberg, all from Poland. Dawid Szmulewski, a Jewish prisoner and member of the Polish underground, who was for many years credited as the photographer, secretly delivered the camera to the *Sonderkommando* and developed the film. He gave the print to his underground group, *Kampfgruppe* (battle group) Auschwitz, which smuggled it to the outside world, hoping that the photograph would incite action by the Allies.

Bronia K. was born in Grodno, Poland, to a family of modest means. A pogrom in Grodno in 1935 aroused her interest in the Zionist movement. She wondered why Jews did not have their own country and why they always lived at the mercy of others. She became active in the Zionist youth movement, Hechalutz Hatza'ir-Dror (Young Pioneers-Freedom), that would prepare her to settle in the Land of Israel. Through her activities in Dror she learned about the Nazi persecution of the Jews even before the Germans occupied Grodno in 1941, but knowing about Nazi actions was not the same as experiencing them herself. Recruited as a courier for the resistance movement, she found sources of courage and strength in herself that enabled her to succeed in risky missions that supported resistance activities.

# To Communicate and Record

From the oral history of Bronia K.

In January 1942, Mordechai Tenenbaum came to Grodno from Vilna, where he had experienced the mass killing of Jews [in Ponar]. He was one of the most important organizers of the Jewish underground and Jewish fighters in the ghettos in Poland. At that time, life in the Grodno Ghetto was very difficult, but there was no killing. Mordechai told us what had happened in Vilna. I think he was one of the first and the very few who understood that the mass killing of Jews from Vilna was not just a caprice of the Germans, but part of a general German policy to kill Jews. And the same thing would certainly happen in other places. At that time, there were not many people who understood this.

After Grodno, he went to Bialystok and from Bialystok to Warsaw (p. 80). When he arrived in Warsaw and told this to the Jewish leaders, they didn't believe him. They didn't believe that such a policy could exist because it was so inhuman. How could a legal government—even the Nazi government—kill millions of people for no reason? Only because we are Jews? Children? Why? It was not believable. They couldn't face it.

But we believed what he said. And he told us what we had to do. Since the Germans did not want the Jews to know what was happening, it was not permitted to communicate between ghettos. The Germans did everything to separate Jews from the non-Jewish population and to isolate Jews in their ghettos so that the Germans could trick them and lie to them. My duty was to communicate with other ghettos. I was sent from Bialystok to other places to tell Jews what was going on. This was my first task.

After Grodno, Mordechai went to Bialystok. He traveled all over Poland, even though Jews were not permitted to travel and he had a very Jewish face. You could be shot 1,000 times if you were caught. But he had false papers as a Tatar and since he had studied Eastern cultures before the war, he knew a little bit of

Turkish. So he made false papers using the name Tamaroff. And he traveled with these false papers. I don't think there was any place in Poland where he did not go to organize youth and instruct them what they had to do.

He told us that the center of our Zionist movement in the northeastern part of Poland would became Bialystok. After a month, another girl from our movement came to me in the ghetto in Grodno and informed me that I had to go to Bialystok to attend a gathering of the members of our organization. All the members of our organization had to go to Bialystok to meet each other and to develop and implement a program of our activities for the future.

My problem was how to leave the Grodno Ghetto and how to come back in, since I had no papers. But I was lucky to have a very not-Jewish face. I went out of the ghetto by some hole in the wall and I went to the train station. Of course it was dangerous because there were many non-Jewish people who knew me. But even Polish people had to have permission to buy a train ticket. Of course I had no permission. And I didn't know exactly how to buy a ticket without permission. Then I saw a German at the station. I went to him and

I smiled nicely and I asked him if he could buy me a ticket to Bialystok.

He said, "All right." So I gave him the money and he bought me the ticket.

Of course when I arrived in Bialystok I didn't know where the ghetto was or when I could get in. My instructions were to go to a place where Jewish girls were working outside the ghetto and to enter the ghetto with them. But when I arrived, it was morning. I knew they would not go back into the ghetto until the evening. I didn't want to wait, so I decided, No. I would try to go in by myself. After all, if I knew how to get to Bialystok, I would surely find a way to go into the ghetto.

Then I looked around and saw a small street about 100 yards from the ghetto gate. When I went to this street, I took my [Jewish] stars out from my pocket and put them on very quickly. I was used to doing this. Then I started running and when I came to the German guard at the gate I told him, "I'm very much in a hurry, please let me in. I went out with my working group, but I forgot that a German gave me some clothes to wash for him and I forgot them and I can't go to work without these clothes. So please let me in and in a while I will be back."

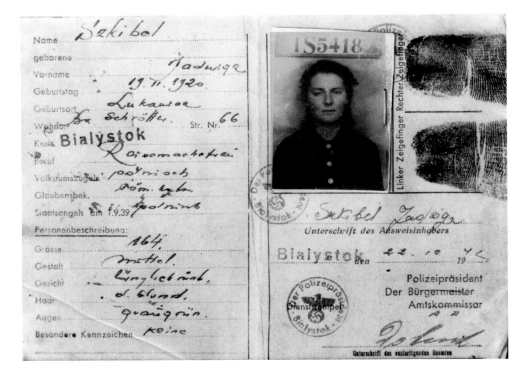

A forged identity card for Bronia made by the underground. This German-language document used the name of Jadwiga Szkibel, her assumed name. The card allowed her to travel from ghetto to ghetto, carrying information.

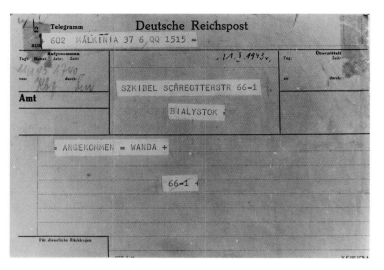

A telegram from Tema Schneiderman, a courier based in the Bialystok Ghetto (p. 86), to Bronia, addressed to her assumed name, Szkibel. The telegram says, "I arrived, Wanda." [Wanda was Schneiderman's code name.]

I was speaking so quickly and I was in such a hurry that he didn't know what to do. He looked at me and said, "Yes, but you must go out from the same gate." I said, "Sure, sure, I will…I just need ten minutes. I will be back." So he let me in. And this was how I got into the Bialystok Ghetto. All of us, from different regions in the Bialystok district, came in our own way. And we all arrived safely.

After the meeting I returned to Grodno. Later I was asked to go to Bialystok and stay there. When I left I didn't know I was leaving my family forever. I didn't tell them where I was going because it was a secret. I remember my mother in the doorway, smiling, looking at me, with such a long, sad look. I didn't even kiss her because I didn't realize that I would never see her or my family again.

This time I went with a boy, a member of our organization. We traveled on foot and sometime by horse cart. On the way from Grodno to Bialystok, we passed different villages where there were ghettos. One was even a labor camp. We visited them to meet members of our organization. But it was more to support our members and tell them what they had to do. They must not be passive. They had to do something. Maybe they had to fight.

We didn't know at that time how we would fight. But we already knew that we must do something. We

had to fight against everything that the Germans would do to us. To mobilize our people, we went to all these places. Then I returned to Bialystok where I worked with young people, persuading them to join our movement and to work in the underground. At the end of 1942, I was sent outside the ghetto [to work as a liaison officer].

*As a liaison officer she moved between the ghetto and "Aryan" areas, facilitating communication among Jewish groups and with non-Jewish resistance groups. In order to travel as a Pole, Bronia obtained a false passport, based on a forged birth certificate made for her by the Zionist underground. Getting this passport involved several visits to police and government offices. At any time, her ruse could have been discovered. Other women working as liaison officers and couriers were already living as non-Jews; one of these women found a room for Bronia.*

My second task was preserving a record of what was happening. Members of the underground movement in Bialystok and, especially Mordechai Tenenbaum, had a rare awareness of history. Mordechai was very concerned that people should know in the future about what was going on now. Since he knew that the Germans were destroying Jewish archives, he was concerned about keeping records and writing reports himself. He also asked people from other places to write accounts.

At the beginning of 1942 some [Jewish communities in] villages had already been liquidated. Some of these people escaped to Bialystok and Mordechai organized people [in the resistance] to interview them. Mordechai kept these reports in underground archives and he looked for a place outside the ghetto to hide them. I was asked to find a hiding place for the archives. I found one outside the house of a Polish man. Three boxes were smuggled outside the ghetto and hidden. These archives are now at Yad Vashem.

*After the liquidation of the Bialystok Ghetto, Bronia fought with partisans in the forest and survived the war. She settled in Israel after liberation and worked at Yad Vashem as a researcher. She is the author of finding aids for several Yad Vashem collections and, with Zvi Szner, she edited and published the papers of Mordechai Tenenbaum. She lives in Jerusalem.*

# SAVING LIVES
# Helping, Hiding, Escaping

*Bonnie Gurewitsch*

Under German occupation, Jews were subjected to relentless and growing persecution that deprived them of their incomes, their assets, and their freedom. Uprooted from their homes, most were forced into overcrowded, primitive, and unsanitary living conditions that guaranteed the spread of epidemics and social conflict. Unprecedented numbers of Jews were suddenly forced to depend upon community resources. Jews responded to these extraordinary circumstances by creating new social welfare services, by organizing escape plans, and by making efforts to hide Jews from deportation and death.

The German Jewish community created the Reichsvertretung, a unified leadership structure that tried to create a sense of cultural and social community for the largely assimilated German Jewish community. Led by Rabbi Leo Baeck, the Reichsvertretung supported academic and vocational programs to teach Jews new skills and cultural activities that employed Jewish artists and intellectuals. The Reichsvertretung also assisted German Jews with the difficult process of emigration. "We wanted the individual Jew, when exposed to persecution, to feel that he could find refuge in the protective mantle of the Jewish community,"[1] said Rabbi Baeck.

Rue Amelot, a social service organization in Paris, supported refugee families, sent packages of food and clothing to Jews interned in camps, and fed thousands of Jews in its soup kitchens. In Eastern Europe, CENTOS (Society for the Care of Orphans) and TOZ (Society for the Preservation of Health) sponsored health clinics, soup kitchens, summer camps, and other services for children. After America entered the war in December 1941, funds from the American Jewish Joint Distribution Committee were no longer available to subsidize these agencies, and they had to depend on local resources. New organizations such as Jewish Self-Help, which was active throughout Poland, and House Committees in Warsaw, helped people in ghettos cope with their crowded living conditions. These organizations and the Jewish Councils that supervised ghetto life worked hard to respond to the desperate social welfare needs of Jews.

In a letter to comrades in Palestine, Mordechai Tenenbaum, a leader of Zionist youth movements, describes how these movements moved into leadership vacuums left in the ghettos, creating schools, soup kitchens, gardens, and organized sports and cultural activities (p. 80). Members of these movements harnessed the idealism and energies of ghetto youth, giving purpose and structure to their lives as they provided much needed social services.

After the outbreak of war in 1939, options for escaping Europe became severely limited. Success in escaping depended on a person's proximity to neutral countries, obtaining documents that would prevent arrest and detention, and the possession of the physical courage and stamina required to practice deception, avoid German patrols, and withstand the rigors of a challenging journey, often on foot over mountainous terrain.

The status of the French Jewish Scouts, Eclaireurs Israélites de France, as a constituent of the French Jewish community, allowed them to move within France with relative freedom. In addition to providing assistance to Jews interned in camps, Scouts created escape routes from France, particularly after the start of mass deportations. As Yitzchak Zakkai describes in his diary, *Crossing the Pyrenees* (p. 94), Scouts forged false documents that enabled Jews to reach border towns and paid smugglers to guide Jews across the border to Spain, where they could get passage to Palestine. Other Jews escaped to Switzerland. Some Scouts chose to join the French fighting underground, either fighting with de Gaulle's troops or in separate Jewish units.

Escape routes from Eastern Europe were much longer and more dangerous. Hungary, unoccupied until March 1944, was a temporary refuge for Jews escaping from Poland or Slovakia. Romania, no longer allied with Germany after August 1944, became a way station for Jews fleeing to Palestine. Several "underground railroad" efforts smuggled Jews eastward from Czechoslovakia and Poland, through Hungary and Romania, to Black Sea ports where fortunate refugees might sail to Palestine on ships flying flags of neutral or foreign countries. Zionist youth movements in Hungary and the Working Group in Slovakia supported escapes from Slovakia and Poland to Hungary.

Zionists called their escapes *tiyyul* (hike) and continued rescue activities even after Hungary was occupied by the Germans, as described by Shulamit Lack (p. 102). An estimated 6,000 to 8,000 Slovak Jews and 1,200 Polish Jews reached Hungary; many crossed into Romania, hoping to go to Palestine.[2] The Working Group in Slovakia pursued several other approaches to protect and rescue Slovak Jewry, including negotiation and bribery, as described in the letters of Rabbi Michael Dov Weissmandel and Gisi Fleischmann (p. 90).

When escape from Nazi held territory was no longer feasible, Jewish communities tried to protect Jews by providing hiding places for them. Young Jewish couriers, usually women, in Eastern and Western Europe used their contacts with non-Jewish resistance groups to locate safe hiding places for Jews, often visiting them in hiding, paying for their upkeep, making sure that they were safe, and moving them when necessary. In Eastern Europe couriers also maintained contact between ghetto and forest resistance groups, preparing the way for resistance fighters to escape from ghettos. For the individual courier there was no respite from the constant need to maintain the charade of a false identity. The betrayal of one link in the chain of clandestine activities could compromise the lives of hundreds of Jews and non-Jews.

Jewish resisters in Belgium cooperated with the national underground, warning Jews of impending deportations and appealing to civilians to assist them. Cooperation between these underground groups resulted in hiding 4,000 Jewish children (p. 124).[3] In Italy, DELASEM (Jewish Committee for Aid to Jewish Emigrants) went underground during the Holocaust and obtained protection for nearly 5,000 Roman Jews within Vatican City and its enclaves, as well as in Roman convents and monasteries.[4]

By the summer of 1942, Jews in Holland who had not responded to registration or deportation orders had to find hiding places. Some, like Anne Frank's family, used personal contacts to arrange hiding places, taking in unrelated Jews as well. In Amsterdam, Walter Suskind, a German Jewish refugee, arranged for Jewish children to be "kidnapped" by Dutch resistance members and taken to hiding places all over Holland. Gerard Sanders, a Jewish Council member in Enschede, worked with pastor Leendert Overduin and Dutch resisters to find hiding places for 1,200 to 1,400 Jews, most Jews of the town. Many were betrayed or discovered and deported; about 500 survived.[5]

Even in Berlin, under the close surveillance of the Nazis, 1,200 to 1,400 Jews survived in hiding. Many, like the members of the Chug Chalutzi resistance group, or the extended Arndt family group (p. 98), were proactive in their own survival; they found hiding places for each other, located sympathetic non-Jews who would help them, shared their limited food rations, and rescued each other from danger.

Jews frustrated Nazi plans to kill them by organizing efforts that helped them stay alive in desperate ghetto conditions; they also organized and carried out rescue operations, and saved lives by providing Jews who could not escape with false documents, food, and hiding places.

Mordechai Tenenbaum was born in Warsaw in 1916. Self-taught and erudite, he became a leader of Zionist youth movements Dror and then Hechalutz. With the outbreak of war in 1939 he fled to Vilna. After the massacres of Vilna Jews in Ponar in the summer of 1941, he joined the Vilna underground. He was involved in drafting the historic manifesto issued on January 1, 1942, in which Abba Kovner first called for armed resistance. He was one of the first to suspect that the Ponar *Aktions* were part of a systematic plan to kill all Jews. In March 1942 Tenenbaum returned to Warsaw to convince skeptical Jewish political leaders to adopt this view. Writing fiery editorials in the underground press, he urged Jews to defend their honor by taking up arms. When massive deportations began in Warsaw in July 1942, Tenenbaum was among the founding members of the unified Jewish Fighting Organization (JFO/ZOB) and trained ghetto fighters in the use of arms. In November 1942 the JFO sent Tenenbaum to Bialystok to lead a resistance movement. In the report below Tenenbaum describes his experiences in Warsaw and the ideological struggle of Warsaw leaders to accept the reality of mass murder. This condensed version is its first English publication.

# We Are Responsible for Our Youth's Future

From a letter by Mordechai Tenenbaum, Bialystok, April 1943

**To the Workers' Committee of the Histadrut (labor union) and the Secretariat of Hakibbutz Hameuchad (United Kibbutz Movement, Palestine).**

In the midst of our destruction and liquidation, I am writing a summary of our movement—Hechalutz—in the last two years. This will not be totally accurate, but it will be close to the truth. Others competent to summarize have fallen. I am the last one and I am in such a mental state that I hope to be forgiven for what is unclear.

*Tenenbaum then describes the acute difficulties of the German occupation of Poland from 1939 to 1941—the confiscation of Jewish assets, the isolation, terrible overcrowding, and extreme starvation of Jews in ghettos, compounded by brutality and random murders. Zionist youth movements saw it as their mission to insure Jewish survival in the ghettos and to raise morale.*

In the early days of German occupation, when it was possible to leave the [Warsaw] Ghetto, the network of our movement expanded. We founded new chapters and intensified educational activities. We held meetings and local and regional seminars. We printed newspapers and material for group leaders. Despite the dangers of bringing people to seminars, this was necessary for our movement.

Later, when I traveled through the Generalgouvernement (occupied Poland) we set up a core of dedicated young activists who could realize our revolutionary ideals. When we held a meeting in our branch in the Warsaw Ghetto, we counted 1,000 members.

It was now the *hachsharot* (training farms) that played the key role in supporting the Zionist movement and Jewish community. We supplied suppers, clothing, shoes, beds, and soap to our members. In the kibbutzim there was singing; now there was singing in the ghetto branches.

There were other areas of work that the movement developed, as we were now the sole force initiating action within the ghettos. Why was this so?

Many older communal leaders had left Poland; others were killed or disappeared; some did nothing, fearing the Gestapo. In contrast, almost all the low level bureaucrats remained at their posts for as long as possible. There was another reason: corruption. Everyone agreed it was necessary to run a [soup] kitchen, but no one was capable of running it honestly because it was impossible—under existing conditions—to do so. The ghetto was a prison—people were isolated and had no knowledge of what was happening outside. Only our members would come and go, crawling under the walls and crossing the barbed wire.

Then we began looking after children and teenagers. Thousands of youngsters had no parents and thousands of families had no food. Children walked around naked and unsupervised. We organized children's corners in large apartment buildings where children played together, studied, and received soup and bread. We organized special kitchens where children ate lunch, learned songs, and listened to story telling.

### They Were the Only Butterflies I Saw

We turned every inch of available land into gardens that produced nutritious vegetables, becoming spots of sunshine and freshness inside the grey prison walls. Children played there, forgetting for a few hours the crowding at home and fights between parents because there were no jobs. They would forget the lack of air to breathe, and the hunger.

On May 5, 1942 [Lag B'Omer, a spring holiday], a children's play was performed on the theme of spring—the renewal of life, the sun rising, the splendor of tomorrow. Children performed as flowers, birds, butterflies. They were the only butterflies I saw that summer in the ghetto.

Since we saw ourselves as responsible for the education and future of Jewish youth, we also set up an underground high school. We hired the best prewar teachers. We also organized informal courses for youngsters. Thousands attended. We had two folk choirs, two children's choirs, and a dramatics club. Every Saturday there was an *Oneg Shabbat*, attended by the leading actors, artists, and Hebrew writers in the ghetto.

Mordechai Tenenbaum c. 1935.

Our weekly newspaper [*Yedies*] carried political and community news for 3,000 readers. We organized workshops for youth, primarily to exempt them from conscription to German forced labor camps and to supply forced laborers with food and clothing.

We accomplished all of the above thanks to the boundless devotion and discipline of our activist core. And we were always the leaders, attracting members of various organizations and movements to our activities. Our members worked in Warsaw and the occupied territories for nearly a full year.

But after June 22, 1941, [when Germany invaded the Soviet Union] Soviet-occupied territory east of the Bug River fell into Hitler's hands. It became necessary for our members who had worked secretly in the Soviet underground to surface. We became publicly political.

We demanded that the Jewish Council write all public notices with traditional Yiddish spelling, that teachers instruct in Yiddish or Hebrew, and that students study Hebrew.

By controlling cultural institutions in the ghettos, there was greater impact to our work than in our political battle before 1939. In all of the ghettos we informally unified all the Zionist movements, from the left

Members of Zionist youth movements at a meeting in Vilna c. 1942. Tenenbaum [middle row, far right] led the uprising in the Bialystok Ghetto on March 16, 1943, and died in battle.

wing Po'alei Zion to the right wing Revisionists. We not only initiated this idea; we bore the burden of the day-to-day Zionist work in all ghettos in eastern Poland. We feared that the Soviets might return and it was necessary to prepare Zionist antitoxin. We saw ourselves as responsible for educating a Hebrew generation, for a national culture, for the Zionist movement.

**A Radical Change**

On June 22, 1941, a radical change occurred in the attitude of German authorities towards the Jews. All Jews were to be eradicated. Germans considered every Jew a spy, a dissident, a Communist. Jews were placed outside the bounds of law; every German, every local policeman, was permitted to kill Jews without answering for it. The only punishment for a Jew was death. It was forbidden to leave the ghetto. If the yellow Star of David was not sewn on properly—death. Purchasing a loaf of bread from a Christian—death. These decrees poured down on us all at once.

The first *Aktion* took place in Vilna. In the course of a few hours, dozens of our members were taken away. From that day on we went from *Aktion* to *Aktion*. But

we still did not know that this was to be the fate of Polish Jewry. We searched for an explanation among the local authorities and in the attitude of non-Jewish Lithuanians. During the quiet times we worked; during the pogroms we "guarded" our people.

We tried to escape to Sweden. But the many *Aktions* did not allow us to succeed. So we transferred our leadership core to Bialystok. There we continued our work. We set up meetings and seminars; we built chapters and *hachsharot*, gardens, cultural institutions, and the like. When after two years we met with our Warsaw members we found to our joy that without any contact our Soviet and German-occupied centers stood on the same principles. Decisions that we had made in Vilna and Lvov were almost identical in their broad formulation to those made by members in Warsaw. Our everyday work under Hitler's whip faced the same problems, difficulties, and the same solutions.

There were some who saw the *Aktion* in Vilna, the subsequent destruction of Jewish communities in Lithuania, and the partial liquidation of communities in Belorussia, as German revenge on Russian Jews for aiding the Soviet regime. Local residents also saw these murders as payback. Occupied Poland was still quiet. But after the first wave of killings and rumors of new restrictions and decrees for Jews, we understood: Vilna was just the beginning. It would be followed by the liquidation of the entire Jewish community. The idea of an uprising germinated.

## An Overcrowded Ghetto; A Narrow Prison

Comrades in Eretz Israel—try to understand our position: From the Soviet underground and the tyranny of the Soviet Secret Police we were thrown into an overcrowded ghetto and confined to a narrow prison. Several families lived in every room.

Every German who wants to—beats us. Every German who wants to—kills us. For every careless act of individuals a policy of collective responsibility is applied to an entire Jewish community. Dozens of Jewish informers serve the Gestapo. There are searches, arrests, individual death sentences, and the murder of thousands organized with military precision. Hunger. Cold. No help from outside the ghetto. Instead: a wall of hatred and derision, of blackmail and robbery.

But we knew that defending the ghetto was not possible. The power that conquered Europe and pulverized entire nations in a matter of days could surely overcome us, a handful of young people. This terrible knowledge filled us with despair but also determination.

We decided to sacrifice our lives for a price—the highest price possible. We began preparations for armed resistance in Vilna. After many more *Aktions* we breathed easier and could meet without fear.

We unleashed the slogan: "Let us not go as sheep to the slaughter!"[1]

## Our Lives Became a Preparation for Death

We became the leaders of our people. We had to take care of radio communication and transportation, armaments and information, espionage and finances, propaganda and defense, partisan activity and political negotiations—dozens of matters with which we were totally unfamiliar. But we were compelled to do this, because there was no one else to do it. We were in a race against Himmler's death squads: Who would succeed first? Would we manage to prepare for our last great act, or would the *Aktion* come first and find us unprepared?

In most cases Himmler won. SS forces and Gestapo offices worked better than we did. But if we forced German armies to destroy the ghetto in a lengthy battle with the help of tanks, aerial bombardment, mines and artillery—we would not be the defeated ones.

In April 1942 we met in Warsaw. We supplied precise details of the destruction of Jewish communities in Lithuania and Belorussia. We determined that the wave of horror was approaching occupied Poland. We insisted that Jews mobilize all resources for defense and actual warfare against the enemy. If it was not possible to fight the enemy in open battle by partisan warfare, diversionary tactics, and sabotage—we would meet him at the gates: defending the ghetto. No other course of action was possible at this time. Everything was lost.

Menachem Kirshenbaum [Zionist delegate] responded: "True—what happened in Lithuania. But in the Warsaw Ghetto there are more than 400,000 Jews. Mass murder of such proportions—inconceivable! Let us not bring about the tragedy with our own hands. Nothing can be done without reaching German ears."

Maurycy Orzech [Bund representative] began: "As Germany weakens, subjugated nations will be called upon to revolt. But now the only response is passive resistance. If a Jewish policeman is told to hang a Jew—he must not. Tell the Jews to go into hiding."

Only Finklestein [Communist representative] and Gitterman [Joint Distribution Committee], our colleagues from the Warsaw underground, were with us.

Meanwhile the first *Aktion* in the Generalgouvernement began in Lublin during the feast of Passover [April 1942]. Optimists could no longer explain former brutalities as revenge on Soviet Jewry. We began to feel the approaching storm.

We searched for ties and assistance outside the ghetto. We met with the PPR (Polish Communist Party) that had reorganized and was willing to work with anybody on the basis of immediate, unconditional battle against the occupier. We needed such a partner.

Why did we contact the Communists? The official circles of the Polish underground movement saw their work primarily as propaganda, education, and civil disobedience, mainly in the economic sphere. They saw every act of active, unconditional battle as a provocation for German repercussions: "The time has not come yet. Wait."

### Every Day We Face Liquidation

But we couldn't wait. Every day we faced the inevitability of liquidation. Every day we were in a race with Himmler. That is why we searched for a different partner and found the PPR. Modeling themselves after escaped Russian prisoners of war, groups of armed partisans filled the forests of Poland. The PPR saw its primary role as immediate, active battle. Every act of diversion and sabotage helped the Red Army—therefore it must be done. Don't wait, take up arms!

We thought about arming the ghetto with their help and sending armed units to the forest. We thought that utilizing our ties with the PPR would enable us to carry out acts of [Jewish] national revenge.

Inside the ghetto—maximum cooperation. Committees on top of committees. Combined expenses. Outside the ghetto, promises on top of promises. Expeditions, searching for ties with heroic partisans, the purchase of guns, which we never received. In general: good will, willingness to help, but the reality—helplessness.

In the midst of these turbulent days of planning and anticipation, the *Aktion* in Warsaw began. [July 22, 1942] It caught us unprepared. Yet, in spite of everything, we are ready to begin our counter-action. We capture guns. It is possible to kill the murderer from an ambush, not necessarily with a rifle or pistol. We equip our people with false papers and begin preparations.

### We Explain, Deportation Means Death

We organize attack units, draw up a detailed plan, prepare materials for arson and diversion, and create posters calling for Jews to defend their lives and their dignity. We explain to deportees that they are not being "resettled in the East to labor units," but to death.

Before the crucial day, when we are forced to take responsibility for the fate of 400,000 Jews, we call for a meeting of "town elders." But they have gone. Institutions and offices are empty. Only we walk the streets.

We meet at night. The leaders are shaking with fear: "Have mercy—don't do anything. This way they'll deport some tens of thousands, but if you start [the uprising], they'll destroy us completely. Do you wish to take upon yourselves the blood of hundreds of thousands of Jews? And why destroy everyone for a nice gesture to history? We know for certain: In three more days the *Aktion* will cease." They decide to wait.

> "We answer: 'We will lead the demonstration.' Everyone is silent. One rabbi says: 'The Torah forbids it.' The rest: 'Wait. Save what is possible to save...' We realize: The responsibility is ours."

Often you cannot control nervous tension. You must go on the transport, go with everybody and share their fate. A second meeting. Most do not show up. It is known with absolute certainty: The murderers have been bribed. They have promised to end it. They will continue until 80,000 people are deported.

Every day designated streets are ordered to report for deportation. Whoever comes 'voluntarily' receives six pounds of bread.

### We Propose a Demonstration.

We will break through the ghetto wall and demonstrate with placards. A mute protest arises from people who don't have weapons, can't defend themselves, and are afraid they will be killed.

We answer: "We will lead the demonstration." Everyone is silent. One rabbi says: "I cannot do this. The Torah forbids it." The rest: "Don't start. Wait. Save what is possible to save…"

We realize: The responsibility is ours.

In the ghetto—the *Aktion* continues. Every day, 5,000 to 7,000 victims. On the other side of the wall—searching for ways to get guns, to contact partisans.

The slogans of the PPR were good for nothing. All attempts to get our people out to the kibbutzim in the Lublin district—the center of partisan activity—ended in imprisonment and death. Other attempts ended in even worse than death.

## A Spy Network of Girls

We organize a spy network of girls who were peddlers and farm workers, and men who worked on trains. All people we trust. In the forest we organize a unit of our people armed with weapons from the PPR and German weapons captured in battle. They carry out a successful attack on a police station and clash with security personnel. In Krakow they capture guns by "cruising" outside the ghetto. In other places they prepare for resistance.

We turn to Sikorski's people.[2] We had been in contact with them earlier and supplied them with information on what transpired in our Valley of Tears. From time to time they printed it in their newspapers and passed it on to London.

We set up the "Polish Jewry Committee." We meet with the underground liaison for Jewish affairs of the Polish government-in-exile.

He asks: "Why don't you turn to the PPR?" We answer: "You represent Free Poland. We are citizens of the Republic. Give us the opportunity to avenge, to fight, and in the worst case—to die an honorable death." He answers: "We must wait for the order."

We argue: "We cannot wait. We are in a unique situation."

A second meeting, a third. Individual assistance—yes. Finding places for a few people outside the ghetto—yes. Arming—no. It is still too soon to arm Poles.

I say outright: "Here too there is good will. The people we meet with are sympathetic. They treat us with understanding. They do what is possible; but the maximum? No, definitely not."

How great is our joy when Tema [Schneiderman] brings the first "eggs" (grenades), the first "colts" (revolvers)!

In Warsaw there are 50,000 Jews left. In Bialystok—40,000 Jews. I leave for Bialystok. Frumka [Plotnicka, a courier]—to Bedzin (p. 87).

On the first of November, 1942, at 9:00 in the evening I reach Bialystok. About eight hours later the *Aktion* begins throughout the entire region. Again, we are too late.

Once again: Meetings. Organizing. Preparations for counter-action. Discussions about partisans.

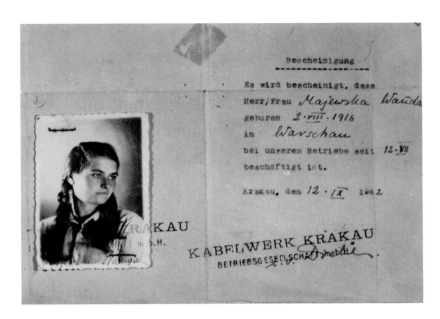

A forged work document for Tema Schneiderman, bearing the name Wanda Majewska. Schneiderman was a courier for the youth movement Dror, and Tenenbaum's girlfriend. She went on some twenty missions between Vilna, Bialystok, and Warsaw, carrying news of mass executions and bringing ammunition for revolt. On January 17, 1943, she went on a mission to the Warsaw Ghetto and was deported to Treblinka in the second great *Aktion*. She was murdered soon after she arrived.

During this time: the final liquidation of the Jews in Poland. Our people fought and resisted.

All fell. Not one member of the pioneering kibbutzim was deported to Treblinka.

They all fell, defending the honor of Israel. To prepare for months for a fine death—was there ever such a thing before?

After such tremendous sacrifice, such great effort and such fine accomplishments—the end of the Hechalutz movement and the Zionist youth groups in the heart of world Jewry—in Poland.

Let history judge if it had to be this way.

M. [MORDECHAI]

*Tenenbaum commanded the Bialystok Ghetto resistance force and gave the signal for the ghetto uprising on August 16, 1943. He died during the fighting. The above report, written in the form of a letter to his Zionist comrades in Palestine, was smuggled out of the Bialystok Ghetto and hidden with additional archival material that he collected for posterity. The archive was retrieved after the war and is preserved at Yad Vashem as the Tenenbaum-Mersik collection.*

Tzippora Birman was a member of Dror, a Zionist Socialist youth movement, and Kibbutz Tel-Hai in the Bialystok Ghetto. Like the courier Tema Schneiderman (see p. 85), she posed as a Christian and carried news from one ghetto to another. Birman began working in Vilna and, when the Germans occupied the city in June 1941, she was arrested and imprisoned. After three days she escaped to the Vilna Ghetto, where she rejoined her Zionist group. She wrote the following letter on March 1, 1943, in the Bialystok Ghetto, to her comrades who had already immigrated to Palestine. The letter was found with the Bialystok Ghetto archives that were assembled by Mordechai Tenenbaum and his colleague Zvi Mersik before the ghetto was liquidated in August 1943. The archives were smuggled out of the ghetto for safekeeping. The original letter is now in the Yad Vashem archives. It was published as an appendix to an article about the Bialystok Ghetto archives written by Bronia Klibanski (p. 74) for *Yad Vashem Studies*, Vol. 2, 1958.

# Couriers: "Bringing Hope, News, and Regards"

From a letter written by Tzippora Birman, March 1, 1943

**To My Dear Comrades Wherever You Are,**

Tema [Schneiderman] did not live in the Vilna Ghetto. Because she looked gentile, she settled in Vilna to help us and bring us news. She told us that members of the Movement were planning a joint course of action that included organizing youth to establish a kitchen that would give some purpose to their lives.

We were the only people who knew definitely that Jews were being put to death. After the second *Aktion* in Vilna [August 1941], Tema went to Warsaw and Bella Chazan [another courier] went to Grodno. Weeks elapsed and we had no news from them. Then Tema returned during an *Aktion*, bringing Lonka Koziebrodzka [a courier]. They looked like two charming *shikses* (non-Jewish girls). Their faces radiated cheerfulness as they brought us new hope, news, and regards from the other parts of the Movement, which had not been in contact with us for some time. They told us a lot about the Warsaw Ghetto, now two years old. They inspired all of us with courage and hope. We began to believe that the Vilna Ghetto, too, would remain.

While we were trying to maintain our group cohesiveness in the ghetto, our gentile-looking girl comrades moved about freely, trying to save the Movement. Many comrades were caught by the Lithuanians. They tried to shoot us, but we managed to get away. It was impossible for the Movement to conduct any kind of activity because of frequent *Aktions*. Many of us received homemade Lithuanian documents. Tema found some members of the Party who were considering transferring the Movement to Bialystok, where life was quiet and comfortable. A German [soldier] named [Anton] Schmidt drove us to Bialystok in his car.[1]

Bialystok felt like a paradise to us. After so many *Aktions* in Vilna and so much slaughter, cold, and hunger, we were received with open arms by our comrades. They learned about the great destruction in Lithuania, where not a single Jew remained in any large town. Only a few thousand remained in the main cities.

As soon as we recuperated a little, we began to establish a new branch. What marvelous youth Bialystok had! We decided to bring the ideology of the Movement to them, to deprive them of their complacency and shock them into disquiet. When the courier Frumka [Plotnicka] arrived from Warsaw, a new light lit up in the Movement. Again news circulated. We were happy with every personal message and shared new impressions. Tema traveled throughout the district, bringing the message of the Movement to Zionists in desolate towns, encouraging them and raising their spirits, and calling them to work for us. At first they refused to believe the "Jewish *shikse.*" They did not trust her, thinking this was probably another Gestapo trap. But after they saw that she really was a comrade, they listened to her raptly, hardly believing that in these horrible days the Movement was carrying on its work, and that the chain had not been disrupted.

Before Passover 1942 the Movement called a convention. Comrades arrived from all over. They risked their lives to attend the meeting. Frumka reported on the work of the illegal Movement in Warsaw. Mordechai [Tenenbaum] spoke about the work in Soviet Russia, and Zvi [Mersik] about the future of our work in the ghetto. The consultations continued for three days. The company dispersed encouraged and abounding in faith.

Passover passed. A beautiful summer. News from Vilna indicated that all was quiet for the time being. Tema and Frumka travelled to Kovel where there was no ghetto yet. They brought us news from Volhynia and from Belorussia and received news from us. How much joy, how many elated moments occurred during these meetings when we heard the news. New life was injected into the group. News and regards, from cities and towns. From Grodno news arrived of a fine branch. Rub'chak [Reuven Rosenberg] had gone to see them.

Then the Golden Days of the Bialystok Ghetto passed. Again, dark days. Our *shikses* were trapped and caught. No news came from Warsaw; it was as if they had vanished. Our nerves were at a breaking point. We needed to hold a seminar; our branch had to be inde-

pendent. We decided to hold a seminar without outside help. Our spirits were at a record low at the time of the opening. We sang *"Techezaknah"* (*"Be Strengthened,"* a Labor Zionist anthem) very quietly and our voices grew weaker and weaker. We were all singing and weeping. The seminar was held for two weeks and we were encouraged and strengthened. Our branch grew. But still no news from Warsaw, as if thousands of rivers were separating us. Meanwhile refugees arrived from Volhynia, telling of terrible slaughter. One didn't know who to think of first—parents, sisters, and brothers killed in the woods? Or comrades killed by the hundreds with other Jews? Terrible days. Refugees from Warsaw appeared. The news about the *Aktion* was confirmed.

We had almost despaired of meeting anybody; then Tema arrived—a ray of light in dark days. She told us about the *Aktions* in Warsaw, more terrible than those in Vilna, and brought a call for us to contact the partisans and fight the enemy with them. We sent two groups out, only to fail immediately. The assistance promised by the PPR (Polish Communist Party) did not come. We could not procure the arms we needed. We thought of what had happened in Warsaw. If it could happen there,

Tzippora Birman

the cup of poison would soon be served in Bialystok. Hitler was keeping his promise. After the war, a Jew would be a museum object. There was no way out. Tema returned to Warsaw.

The work in the Bialystok branch then assumed a different character. These were days of a terrible restlessness. All the roads of life were blocked to us. We felt alone, forgotten. We suffered pain and carried on the work. We did not stop it—God forbid.

We decided to contact the partisans to acquire a few arms. We would not allow the Germans to send us to Treblinka. We decided to falsify documents. We

Three couriers: From left to right, Tema Schneiderman, Lonka Koziebrodzka, Bella Chazan.

made an imitation German rubber stamp and, with the help of party members who had worked in a German printing press, we produced certificates. There was no other way; we had to join the partisans. We also played with the idea of creating our own independent partisan unit. The idea appealed to everyone. With the help of party members and the *Judenrat* we received funds.

After two *Aktions* in the ghetto we sent the first group into the forest. We raised as much money as possible so they could acquire arms on the way. We also sent them to find a path for us. One returned; four fell. Leiser [Rejzner] told us of terrible things he had seen on his way—the dead bodies of hundreds of Jews lying on the ground in the forests of Marcinkonis.

The failure broke our spirits. We were left without a choice. We had no alternative but to die honorably on the spot. We began to prepare a "counter-action," which meant utter liquidation within a few days. We thought that a few thousand might survive. No one was willing to die and, facing death, our will to live grew stronger. We decided: The girls would break out of Bialystok; the boys would carry out a counter-action. Days and nights passed in the shadow of the expected *Aktion*. We prepared for the struggle with death. For eight consecutive days Jews were sent to the terrible slaughter in Treblinka. But it was not easy for the Germans to take people away. Thousands dug themselves in. There were also some cases of resistance, as well as many cases of suicide. We all survived.

Again, there is no news from Warsaw. There has been a counter-action there, organized by our people. It seems they have all been killed. There is no news from Tema, who went there. A terrible feeling. We shall be the last to fall. After us no one will remain alive. There won't even be anyone to take our corpses to a burial site.

But the pain is not that we will be killed. It is painful to know that no trace will remain of the Movement. We continued the chain throughout all these days—openly and clandestinely, when we were strong enough and not strong enough. I am sitting here and writing. Mordechai and the rest are preparing the counter-action. We are producing handmade grenades. We will kill our slaughterers; they will have to fall with us. There is no other way.

Our fate is sealed. We suffer pain and are destined to disappear in silence. Not even to be buried like our forefathers. There is no alternative but to die a death of honor without fear and apprehension. We know the Jewish nation will not die out. We will grow and prosper as a people. We will rise and avenge our innocently spilled blood.

Vengeance! This is our challenge to you who have not suffered in Hitler's hell. This you are duty-bound to fulfill.

Remember, carry out our last will and your duty.

*Tzippora Birman, Reuven Rosenberg, and Leiser Rejzner fell fighting in the Bialystok Ghetto uprising in August 1943. Tema Schneiderman was deported to Treblinka from the Warsaw Ghetto and killed in January 1943. Bella Chazan survived and went to Israel. Lonka Koziebrodzka was caught by the Germans, sent to Auschwitz, and executed. Frumka Plotnicka fell in the Bedzin Ghetto uprising in July 1943 (p. 127). Zvi Mersik died of typhoid in the Bialystok Ghetto.*

Smuggling food into the Warsaw Ghetto. Photo from Oyneg Shabbes archive.

*In his study,* Polish-Jewish Relations During the Second World War, *Emanuel Ringelblum paid tribute to the children who smuggled food and other staples into the Warsaw Ghetto: "The children who were smuggling had the most extraordinary and fantastic courage…These children went through [the ghetto walls] several times a day, laden with goods that often weighed more than they did. Smuggling was the only source of subsistence for these children and their parents, who would otherwise have died of starvation." Henryka Lazowert, a Jewish poet who wrote in Polish, wrote for Oyneg Shabbes. She was deported to Treblinka and murdered in August 1942.*

## THE LITTLE SMUGGLER   by Henryka Lazowert

Past walls, past guards
Through holes, ruins, wires, fences
Impudent, hungry, obstinate
I slip by, I run like a cat
At noon, at night, at dawn
In foul weather, a blizzard,
    the heat of the sun
A hundred times I risk my life
I risk my childish neck.

Under my arm a sack-cloth bag
On my back a torn rag
My young feet are nimble
In my heart constant fear
But all must be endured
All must be borne
So that you, ladies and gentlemen,
May have your fill of bread
    tomorrow.

Through walls, through holes,
    through brick
At night, at dawn, by day
Daring, hungry, cunning
I move silently like a shadow
And if suddenly the hand of fate
Reaches me at this game
T'will be the usual trap life sets.

You, mother
Don't wait for me any longer
I won't come back to you
My voice won't reach that far
Dust of the street will cover
The lost child's fate.
Only one grim question
The still face asks—
Mummy, who will bring you bread
    tomorrow?

Gisi Fleischmann (1897-1944), a leading prewar Zionist activist, and her relative, Rabbi Michael Dov Weissmandel (1903-1956), a major figure in the ultra-Orthodox Agudath Israel movement, were leaders of the Working Group, a Slovak Jewish underground organization intent on rescuing Jews. Most notable was their successful 1942 bribing of Dieter Wisliceny, Adolf Eichmann's deputy in Bratislavia, that stopped deportations from Slovakia for two years.[1] These negotiations evolved into the Europa Plan that aspired to halt all deportations. The Working Group also supported the escape of some 10,000 Jews from Slovakia and Poland into Hungary, aided Jewish deportees in Poland, and was influential in setting up Slovak labor camps where Jews could work and temporarily avoid deportation. The Group maintained clandestine contacts with Jewish organizations outside Slovakia, seeking funds to bribe Nazi officials and inform the world about the fate of the Jews. The letters here reflect their desperate sense of urgency as they try to obtain huge sums of money from Jewish organizations, despite Allied regulations prohibiting the transfer of US dollars to Nazi territories. Eventually, emissaries of the Jewish Agency for Palestine managed to smuggle about $200,000 from Turkey into Slovakia, but this was inadequate to fulfill their overwhelming needs.

# The Working Group in Slovakia

From letters by Rabbi Michael Dov Weissmandel and Gisi Fleischmann

### Letter from Rabbi Weissmandel

*Rabbi Weissmandel wrote his letters in Hebrew, using the words* rasha *(wicked one) and* resho'im *(wicked ones) as codes for Nazis. Wisliceny is referred to as* yo'etz *(advisor). Code words are in color.*

Sabbath eve, *Parshat Bo,* January 15, 1943

Shalom and best wishes.

Thank you for your letter. Please understand that the cancellation of deportation orders for all European Jews is not feasible. For our work here we need two types of funds: (1) secret funds to bribe individual *resho'im* (Nazi leaders); (2) public funds to give to the [Slovak] treasury for support of those in the Slovak labor camps: [Sered, Novacky, and Vyhne.] We can only *hope* to provide funds for canceling deporta-

tions. [Providing] public funds to the government to support those in camps in the land of evil decree (Poland) is not on our agenda at present.

In regard to secret funds, understand that the position of the Jews is very weak and, because of this, it is impossible to negotiate as you thought without causing great harm. God forbid! For three months we have proceeded very gradually. We did not want negotiations to obligate us before the money was in our pockets and we could transfer it. To our great disappointment, negotiations with our opponent went quickly, and negotiations with our allies—namely you, our brothers—proceeded cautiously, regardless of our urgency.

It has now been more than two months since our *yo'etz* (Wisliceny) settled the matter with the chief, the *rasha* who is appointed over all the troubles of Israel, the famous E–(Eichmann) and we are not able to continue negotiations responsibly. Many things were done, and for reasons that I cannot specify here, the negotiations did not reach a dangerous point and we had acceptable reasons to stop them.

But if we now begin negotiations again, we must either ask, "How much do you want?" Or we say, "This is the amount we will give." We cannot ask the first question because they will demand a substantial sum of money, and that response will obligate us. If we do not have the money, they will demand souls in place of money, red blood in place of golden coins, as it happened last Yom Kippur, when there were casualties caused not by disease or hunger but by lack of funds.[2] Therefore, our only option is the second.

As we are dealing with matters of life and death, we must blind them with at least a $100,000 deposit [roughly $1 million in today's market] from our allies. Three paragraphs have already been negotiated with E- and he has agreed to them: (1) Cancellation of deportations to Poland from all occupied countries; (2) Deportations will not be cancelled from Germany, Austria, the Protectorate [German-annexed Czech territory], or Poland; (3) Assistance by legal means, such as sending limited packages, money, and letters to the deported.

These conditions will require three payments: $500,000 for cancellation of deportations; a second payment of $300,000, and a third of $200,000 for aid to deportees. A ten percent deposit ($100,000) will be paid on accepting the agreement. We cannot, under any circumstances, believe the word of a German. But of course this is a matter of negotiation; perhaps we will succeed in conducting business according to your standards, because you have money to waste and tears to shed, and our resources are not equal to yours.

We still hope that we will succeed in obtaining more concessions, perhaps by using your methods of negotiation, such as begging, crying, and pleading. There is no right or wrong way to negotiate. We have strong hopes that we will be able to extend the cancellation of the deportation orders in the Old Reich, Austria, and the Protectorate and also for our brothers, the citizens of Poland. But we would have to offer an additional sum: $500,000 for Germany; $500,000 for Poland. This is our opinion; tell us what you think.

May you be blessed with all the blessings that come to those who concern themselves honestly with community issues, innocents who receive Heaven's pity.

More than anything, we need a large fund [in German money] for supporting people in Poland. The money we are asking for now is just for bribes, which are swallowed up in the pockets of individual *resho'im* (Germans) and don't go into the treasury of the wicked (German) government. This is to appease our Jewish brothers who are afraid to oppose the monetary laws of the land. Of course we aren't able to investigate the nature of the camps in Poland and we don't want to provide money for [the Jews in] those camps. There will be no end to their needs, since they are directly in the power of the *rasha* (Germans).

Here [in Slovakia], where there are no such [concentration] camps, it is a different matter entirely. Camps are under the control of the Slovakian government (that secretly hates the *rasha* in their hearts), and the Germans don't step foot in these camps. The work is only for details [Slovak consumer goods] and not for the war effort.

Please expedite the negotiations between our side and our opponents, which will take time; meanwhile, perhaps the *rasha* will change his decision to destroy everything. It is in God's hands. It is not your fault that it drags out so long. We are not blaming you, people of good hearts and shallow pockets; it is that our adversaries are people of deep pockets and no heart.

Rabbi Michael Dov Weissmandel

May God protect us all from this trouble; may he help and redeem his oppressed people quickly, as we beg him.

P.S. The money matters and cancellation of the order must be done within four or ten weeks; without money on the table the negotiations will be useless.

*Rabbi Weissmandel was deported to Auschwitz in October 1944. He escaped from the train, hid near Bratislava, and reached Switzerland. After the war he arrived in the US, where he reestablished the Nitra Yeshiva in Mt. Kisco, NY, and established a new family.*

## Letter from Gisi Fleischmann

*Gisi Fleischmann wrote her letters in German and used Hebrew words (written in German) as codes. Her Hebrew words are in color and their literal meaning is in parentheses in black. When Hebrew words have a double meaning, the code meaning is in color.*

October 17, 1943

Dear *Chaverim* (comrades),
I confirm your letter of September 25 and will answer only your most important inquiries since the *shaliach* (courier) agreed to take only one letter. Re: *Willy* (Wisliceny). The result of our negotiations was unfortunately negative because Willy received strict instructions from his boss, the minister *le'inyanim pnimim* (for internal matters, Eichmann), not to enter into any agreements with us. The [Nazis] are not willing to fulfill any obligations.

However, *Willy* obtained permission to go to his *birah* (capital/Berlin) to submit suggestions for relief actions for the *megorashim* (deportees). I have presented proposals to him that should serve as a basis for negotiations. Before his departure he received an order to drive immediately to *Fanos* (Greece) and he is now there. As he was leaving he promised to do everything possible on the matter of *acheinu* (our brothers).

Unfortunately I do not believe that he can achieve much because in the end he is only carrying out [Eichmann's] orders. We are in touch with his *kalah* (bride, girlfriend) here through whom possible messages should be transferred, but at this time she has no news from him. In the meantime the *gerush* (deportation) continues and we are helpless. Since we do not have the right *melitz* (intermediary), our work on this matter has begun to flag heavily. Before his departure we put *asarah alafim* (10,000) *Stefan* (Rabbi Stephen S. Wise/US dollars) at his disposal but he said he considers this only a deposit because we do not have contractual relations. I can hardly express how unhappy I am that promising negotiations failed because of the terror of the *tzorer* (enemy) and his *avadim ha'osrim* (accomplices).

Unfortunately I keep thinking that if the demanded *emtza'im* (funds) had been at our disposal, the negotiations would have been favorable. At that time the will was present but we had no funds. Yet, since May 10th, the day of our first negotiation, and during the following weeks, we noticed a slower pace of *gerush* (deportation). Throughout the whole time, however, we offered nothing but suggestions. In the meantime *hamazav hamedini* (the political situation) turned out in such a way that the *tzorer* (enemy) absolutely wants to accomplish his *mifal bitul hayehudim* (destruction of the Jews) and I fear that he could succeed.

Re: *Hatzalat pleitah* (rescue of refugees). This *mifal* (operation) continues. So far thirty-eight *plitim* (refugees) from Rendsburg, [Germany], have come to us; most are with Miklos (Horthy/Hungary). About forty more are on the way and according to the information of *plitim,* about 150 are still *beya'arot bamachteret* (hiding in the forests) and will arrive gradually.

*Plitim* from Bochnia and Krakow are constantly arriving. So far we have rescued *elef plitim* (1,000 refugees) and *tishim yeladim* (90 children). Now there are about *matayim plitim* (200 refugees) here who will be brought to Miklos (Horthy/Hungary). The work becomes more difficult and dangerous. But the biggest *sakanah* (threat) is from the *Ashkenasischen* (German Nazis) because they too have knowledge of it. It is clear that the resolution of these difficulties requires a high *takziv* (budget). The rising demands of the *shlichim* (messengers) [who carry messages from deported Jews to the Working Group] place such obligations upon us that we do not know what funds we can count on. There is still the problem that the *plitim* who reach us from *Ziviah* (Lubetkin/Poland)[3] on their way to *Miklos* are completely penniless and have to be cared for.

We thank you *chaverim* (comrades) for providing greater *emtza'im* (funds) for *hatzalat pleitah* (rescue of refugees). We will, if necessary, take [money] out of the *shloshim elef* ($30,000) intended for *Willy.* Please replace it through the *shaliach* (messenger). We expect your *ezrah* (assistance) so that we can send *shlichim* to where ever they find *yehudim* (Jews) and and bring them here. There are still possibilities, but it is terribly difficult to get to the *megorashim* (deportees) because they are hermetically isolated. Recently a *bilti-rishmi bah* (unofficial letter) came from Poniatow reporting that there are *chamisha assar elef megorashim* (15,000 deportees) from different *aratzot* (countries).

As a trial run, we have sent *te'udot notzriot* (Christian papers) to some *chaverim* to see if *brichah* (escape) is feasible. We also sent *emtza'im* (funds) to some *chaverim* and, if the connection works out, we will start the *ezrah* (assistance). We discovered a group in Sawin, in the Lublin district, and we are trying to contact them. The main *emtza'im* to be considered should be *Stefans* (dollars) although at present *Ella's* (Gisi's code name) *moledet* (homeland, Slovakia) is flooded with this article, because the *plitim* themselves have brought in many *Stefans* and because of the ones that you and Saly [Mayer, from the Joint Distribution Committee (JDC) in Switzerland] have provided. *Stefans* have flooded the little country so the *sha'ar* (rate of exchange) is very low.

Therefore a very high number of *Stefans* would have to be available to fulfill this task. If you could send *zahav* (gold) instead of *Stefan,* this would be preferable. Nathan [Schwalb, Hechalutz representative in Geneva] is trying to procure for us *ketarim* (crowns, Slovakian currency). That would be best since we need *ketarim* for the execution of the *mifal* (operation). For the *hatzalah* (rescue) work we also need *Stefan,* particularly for *Kadmon* (East, deportations) in *Ella's moledet (Slovakia)*.

Re: *Ezrah* (assistance) for *Ziviah* (Poland). We have concluded that provisionally 100 packages with food may be sent to the local Red Cross, based in *Ella's* residence (Bratislava). The JUS [Jewish Self-Help organization] in Krakow, which distributes packages with the Red Cross, has to be informed about sending these packages immediately. According to our information it does not make sense to send heavyweight packages to Birkenau, but receipt of one-pound *Lisbon* (packages distributed by JDC offices in Lisbon) was often confirmed. With the next *shaliach* (messenger) we will send you 100 Birkenau addresses, to which you can send smaller one-pound packages. If you can, send unsolicited gift packages to *Ella's moledet* containing condensed milk and other canned goods. Medicine is also of great interest. We received forty boxes with condensed milk a few weeks ago from Nathan. This mailing arrived smoothly and has been distributed.

Re: *Ella's moledet.* The sky is still full of clouds. For the moment there is no *gerush* (deportation) threat, but now we are again in the midst of a crisis, since *anachnu* (all of us) are to be put into *machanot* (camps). Natu-rally our whole apparatus has been set in motion so that this *sakanah* (danger) is reduced to the minimum. Unfortunately the *Ashkenasischer* (German Nazi) influence is crucial here and what that means I do not have to explain in more detail. There is not a day when we do not feel the lash of the *tzorer* (enemy). Nevertheless our will to live is unshakable and, as long as our strength lasts, we will try to keep ourselves alive and undertake everything to offer *ezrah* (assistance) to those less fortunate than we are.

I thank you in the name of the entire *klal* (Jewish nation) for the *emtza'im* (funds) that were sent and I attach the *ishur* (authorization) that we three have signed. I will sign as "Noemi," Oskar [Neumann] with the name "Yirmiyahu," and Moshe [Dachs] will sign as before. We do what we can and I am certain that you will motivate yourselves to the maximum.

Gisi Fleischmann

My dear *chaverim,* I now close and convey my heartfelt wishes on the occasion of the high holidays. May God pity his people, may we be all blessed with *geulah* (redemption). Your letters are true rays of light. Maybe in normal times we would not have appreciated the strength and the value of your reports as we do in the midst of misfortune. When I think of the possibility of this dream coming true, that I could be with you, our dear brothers in *Eretz* (Land of Israel), then my heart stops beating, and this hope is the meaning of my life. I have to believe in the realization of this dream, because it gives me strength and courage to endure. With warm regards I remain with you.

*Shalom*

Gisi Fleischmann

*Gisi Fleischmann sent her daughters to safety in Palestine; she stayed to help her besieged community. She was murdered in Auschwitz in October 1944.*

By March 1944 many Jews, including Yitzchak Zakkai's parents and leaders of the Jewish Scout movement in France, had been deported. Most did not know the truth about death camps or the fate awaiting Jews. Since the Germans had already dismantled Jewish children's homes, Scouts focused on building an underground network for saving children, hiding them with non-Jewish families or institutions, smuggling them to neutral countries, and providing children in hiding with social services and supportive care. Older youth faced a choice: Crossing the Pyrenees and immigrating to Palestine from Spain with the help of Zionist organizations, or joining the French Jewish military underground. To cross the Pyrenees, Scouts used their ties with the Armée Juive (Jewish Army). To deceive German authorities, they maintained that AJ stood for *Auberges De La Jeunesse (*Youth Hostels). Small groups of teenagers who decided to cross the Pyrenees gathered in Toulouse, equipped with bare necessities. There they were met by hired guides or local smugglers who led them across the mountains.

# Escape from France: Crossing the Pyrenees

From the diary of Yitzchak Zakkai, written aboard a ship to Palestine, October 1944

In June 1940 [after Germany invaded France] I registered in the foreign workers' battalions and was sent to a farm in Soudale [France], where I loaded hay for about two weeks. There I began to learn Hebrew with the help of a small book of Hebrew grammar, and made my first halting steps towards Judaism. My next step was a decision not to write on the Sabbath and to observe the Sabbath when I left the farm. Once a day I tried to learn the meaning of prayers. After the farm work ended, I was sent to break wood into charcoal, working with many Spaniards. I managed to learn some Spanish from them, which proved to be of value later on.

*Zakkai escaped from the work battalion on the morning of Easter Sunday, gambling that the guards would be drunk and hoping that his absence would not be discovered until the evening roll call. He succeeded, and found his way to a* hachsharah, *a Zionist training farm, in Taluyers.*

Early in 1944 members of the *hachsharah* began to crystallize ideas about escaping from France to go to the Land of Israel. Shortly before Passover, Chameau [Shimon Hamel] asked me to make *aliyah* and go to Palestine with his group of sixty-four people (a mixture of young and old Jews, and some Spanish refugees). It was an agonizing decision—to go or to remain in France and wait for you, dear parents, to return. Finally, I too decided to join the *aliyah* group.

After Passover our group went to La Pusok to get organized. We stayed at a farm managed by Chameau's brother, hiding in two cabins in the forest. During the day we worked on the farm, mainly in the vineyard. Finally, Chameau arrived to give us final instructions. Wary of the Gestapo, we made our way in small groups to St. Girons, near the Spanish border. We hid in the forest to await the arrival of all sixty-four members of the group and the smugglers who were to be our guides. Walking was difficult for the elderly, and there was danger from German army patrols.

After waiting for a day, we set out on our main journey. The delay has severe consequences. We have received food for three days from the maquis (French underground)—each person has nine eggs, a package of cheese, two pounds of sugar cubes, four and a half pounds of bread, and a large tin of sardines. After heated arguments with the "elders," we collect all the food and redistribute it according to a rationing plan. But some take advantage and, while the food is collected, they swallow "a few pieces of meat" for breakfast. The delay costs us a full day's food rations.

And so the journey begins at nightfall. We get off to a good start, and cover more ground than expected. Soon we catch up with the group that set out before us and had camped about a half a mile ahead of us [for security reasons]. The wiser for yesterday's experience, we decide to empty over half the contents of our backpacks, hoping to do better on the grueling journey ahead. We leave the cabin piled high with suits, shirts, underwear, kerchiefs, socks, books, work tools, and all sorts of useful and useless belongings, realizing that we had loaded ourselves down with impossible bulk and weight for such a trek. To commemorate our decision, we name the place "Fresh Start."

It is necessary for us to cross extremely dangerous places [visible to the German patrols in the area]. Sometimes we take paths close to villages; at times we run quickly, crouching, across exposed terrain. Often it is forbidden to utter a sound and we move on virtually without stopping, double-time. The two smugglers are armed with sub-machine guns; six of our people have pistols. We finally stop at 4 am near an empty barn and are able to sleep for an hour.

At dawn we can make out high above us, in the distance, the Montgary mountain ridge. "That's where you'll eat Spanish soup tonight," we are told by the smuggler Adrian. Meanwhile, the second smuggler has been replaced. A rest stop. Soon we are moving on. "Close ranks, close ranks!" Now we are walking continually uphill and encounter our first snow. Excited, we sink our walking sticks into it. We have no idea what this snow holds in store for us!

A small stream. We wash up. Onward again. A ridge above us. Now only those with guns proceed, almost crawling, towards the exposed ridge. Nothing

arouses their suspicion. Adrian approaches a small cabin some distance away and with his sub-machine gun ready, kicks open the door. The cabin is empty. This is the same place where his friend had been ambushed and killed by a German patrol. Adrian gathers us around him and we take an oath of revenge with the cry: "Louis, we will avenge your blood." And now, our first real rest stop. For lunch, a few sardines, noth-

Members of the *hachsharah* working in the vegetable garden in Taluyers, France, c. 1942.

ing more. The sugar cubes are our main sustenance.

Onward. We climb upward for hours. Another cabin. But onward! Now we are sinking into deep snow as we walk. We see another cabin, which later we call "The First Shelter." It is Friday, at dusk. After a short rest, we move on again, slowly, because of the deep snow. After a few hundred yards the smugglers lose their way in the thick fog. We return to the shelter. Later the smugglers try to find the correct route but the visibility is so bad you can't see 100 yards ahead. We have to make do in the shelter. The women get the upper berth; the men crowd together on the floor.

At 4 am we set out again by moonlight. Visibility has improved. But people are weaker, just as the slope becomes steeper and the climb more difficult. Some want to rest. Finally we reach the ridge. Beyond it, a steep and long downhill stretch. But our relief is premature. Again we are climbing upward. Finally, another cabin that we name "The Second Shelter." We are on

Mount Vallier. One smuggler explains the rest of the route to us. We burn our false papers. We don't waste any more time and the people from Limoges set out right after us. (Individuals and small groups had arrived at the shelter at intervals of time after us.) After a few paces, we come to a fork in the trail. "Right or left?" we call out to those behind us. "To the right," comes a reply. But the correct path was to the left.

We turn back and reach the "Second Shelter," trying again to find the right direction. We must climb to the top of the mountain before nightfall. We haven't eaten for twenty-four hours and had little food the day before. One woman collapses. Later she manages to follow us slowly, with the assistance of others. With great difficulty we manage to reach the shelter by Saturday night. We are crowded in the cabin, squashed together like sardines. Nobody has enough strength to think. Someone lights a small fire and prepares a drink from melted snow and saccharine for the weak and the sick. Our food situation has become life-threatening and we decide now to eat our tins of non-kosher meat.

Robert Gamzon, leader of the French Jewish Scouts.

The next morning we set out again. Staying in the cabin could lead to death. But Freydo, Charlotte, Emily, and Sami are too weak to go on and they stay there, assisted by Jacques and Claude. We promise that when we reach our goal, we will send a rescue party. We leave most of our meager belongings and most of our food. But when we reach the ravine we hear shouts in the distance. Germans? Theo moves ahead to identify them. A long time passes and we are soaked to the skin. We can't sit down and rest because the snow is melting and everything is wet. Theo finally comes back. It is the other group in the distance, he says, and they are coming towards us. He wants to return to the Second Shelter. True madness, but all our pleas do not change his decision.

*Guessing the correct route by means of ambiguous landmarks, they climb a treacherous cliff covered with melting snow. Three people are nearly killed when they slide down the slope, one while trying to save another.*

In the distance, an avalanche of snow thunders down to the valley. A shriek—someone is not sliding downward like the others; he's rolling head over heels! Horrified and helpless, we watch the "human snowball" falling, his backpack flapping around him with every turn. It is Felix, our brave comrade, who has not yet complained about his smashed kneecap, broken elbow, and skull fractures. (Later he was to say the *Hagomel* prayer for surviving danger.) His fall is broken by the snow. We climb cautiously.

Suddenly a rock disintegrates under my leg and I begin to fall. Snow swirls around me and I can't see anything. "Feet first, feet first," flashes in my mind. It works. Out of nowhere, someone extends a stick, which I try to grasp. But my hand slips because it is covered with snow, and I slide rapidly downward. I manage to slow down by braking with my feet. Finally I stop. I have fallen about 150 yards. Not far above me, most of the convoy has already stopped. They begin to go around the base of the cliff to reach the slope beyond. I climb in their direction. "Wait for us, wait for us," wails Fanny, but it's impossible. Everyone has to save his or her own life. We can't hang on to each other; it's too dangerous.

Finally everyone reaches the convoy. We are faced with a steep, rocky slope, covered with running water. We climb in zigzag fashion to the ridge above. Manfred is in the lead, making a path in the deep snow, step after step. When we finally reach the narrow ridge, we seem to hear the babble of a stream in the ravine before us, but we can't manage to spot it. Fog blankets everything. But we begin our descent, or rather, our downward slide in the soft snow.

Finally we get to our destination (the saddle of the ridge.) When everyone has arrived, we continue to climb. I take the lead with a compass. After a while, we see our scout below, gesturing to us. He has found a shelter cabin. Some go to the cabin. The rest continue to climb—until we discover that the iron content of the mountain has been causing the compass to point all along to the mountain top! With no sign of the sun, it is impossible to determine true compass points. After climbing for a few hours, we find a downward slope.

With heavy hearts, we return to the cabin. And

discover it is very small. Fifty-seven people have to stay here! The sick and injured lay on a wooden shelf on one wall. The rest of us pass the night standing crushed together, soaked to the skin and burning with fever. We are no longer hungry. We doze on our feet. But sleep doesn't rest our bodies or renew our strength.

I can no longer relate how we got through the next day and night. We sat crowded together or lit a small campfire, or pushed our way to get hot water [melted snow]. "The Germans are coming, the Germans are here," our guide called out every so often, "Everyone outside!" Was I sleeping? Was I dreaming? Was I walking? When I opened my eyes, I found myself in the cabin. But the moment I closed them again, we were walking. Suddenly Fanny woke up. "Why are we walking?" Everyone was hallucinating....

Jewish Scouts marching in Taluyers, c. 1942.

*They set out again three days later, leaving the sick and the exhausted in the shelter. That same day, a second group manages to follow them. They all return to the mountain peak and the sun burns off the fog, allowing them to regain their direction. The sight of a distant mountain peak covered by a forest convinces them that ahead there is a settlement—and Spain. With renewed strength and optimism, they make their way through the snow in that direction.*

Our confidence increases. We descend and see an empty cabin. Occasionally we come across a patch of ground without snow. And now, even cattle dung! Never in my life was I so happy to see cattle droppings! Then we pass what seems like a border marker, convincing me we are in Spain. There are cut branches—a sign of people! We go deeper into the forest.

Some of us see a house. Are we really in Spain, or is this a German border post? Since I'm the only one who knows Spanish, I proceed with caution, accompanied by Alfred. The others follow us from a distance. A light rain soaks our skin. Gradually the thick underbrush gives way to a clearing in the forest. If we are in Spain, we are twelve or fifteen miles from Montgary. But we can't get there today. We find an empty shed for sheep and see a shepherd with his flock. He hasn't discovered us yet. We walk towards the man....

"Good morning," I call out in my best Spanish. "¡Hola!" he answers. He is a Spaniard, but does he live in Spain—or in France? "I live in Spain!" he says!

We are saved! We are saved!

I send a silent prayer heavenward. Then we make yodeling sounds for the others to come. We return to the shepherd and ask him for food. He can't give us any, because he isn't in charge of the flock. But further on, he says, "there is a village...it's Montgary!" We shout wildly to the group. Everyone surrounds the shepherd and we decide: Onward. An hour later we reach our first Spanish village! By now it is Tuesday evening. We have been traveling for a week....

*They split into smaller groups, finding food and lodging at farmers' homes. The remaining groups straggle in, bearing harrowing tales of those who didn't survive. All the hikers, even the non-believers, decide to observe a half-day fast in gratitude to God for their miraculous deliverance. The refugees turn themselves in to the Spanish police, who do not send them to a prison camp. Slowly regaining their strength and health, they travel on foot and by bus toward Barcelona. The Joint Distribution Committee assumes responsibility for the needs of those headed for Palestine. They receive legal aliyah certificates from the British Consulate and study Hebrew while waiting for a Portuguese ship that will take them to their final destination.*

By early winter 1942 there were some 33,000 Jews still alive in Berlin; many were working as forced laborers in munitions factories. It was around this time that Erich Arndt, a 19-year-old Jewish worker at Siemens, heard rumors of an upcoming raid through the factory's underground *Mundfunk* (rumor mill). The raid would purge factories of all Jewish workers and their families. Erich persuaded his father, Dr. Arthur Arndt, to take the family into hiding, as well as Erich's girlfriend, Ellen Lewinsky, and her mother Charlotte. Dr. Arndt, his wife Lina, their children Erich and his older sister Ruth, went into hiding on January 9, 1943; Dr. Arndt took medicine and instruments with him. A year later, Erich's friend, Bruno Gumpel, joined the group, bringing their number to seven. During their ordeal in the shadowy underworld of Berlin, they lived without identity cards, food ration stamps, or secure shelter, aided by more than fifty non-Jewish Germans and sustained by their fierce will to survive, their strict codes of behavior, and their commitment to take care of each other. Of the roughly 1,200 to 1,400 Jews who survived in hiding in Germany, the extended Arndt group is one of the largest that survived intact.[1]

# Berlin: Survival in Hiding

From the oral history of Ellen Lewinsky Arndt and the memoir of Ruth Arndt Gumpel

In 1941 I was sent to the firm Schubert in Reinckendorf. I was only seventeen. The firm manufactured parts for weapons. We did small sabotages: Putting a little sugar in the transmission, or breaking a tool on the machine, making the machine stand idle until the foreman fixed it. We did these with great care and not too often.

I made friends in the plant with Heinz Birnbaum. Unbeknownst to me, Heinz was a member of the Baum Group [a Communist underground group comprised mainly of young Jews].[2] At night, Heinz fabricated items since he had finished an apprenticeship as a toolmaker. I took the parts out of the plant in my clothing.

One day Heinz said, "I made a detonator. I need you to take it out. Put it in your bra." We had to pass a control leaving the plant, but he checked our purses, and we never carried stuff that made us look suspicious. I did not know what these parts were for. But a long electric cable was needed for it. A fellow named Geisenberg was recruited to smuggle out the cable. He was taken into the side room, where he undressed, and the cable was wound around his body.

The Baum group hoped to flee to France, and Heinz asked me to come along. I had a passport picture made. But the plan made no progress. Something was holding up the fabrication of the false passports. Then Heinz did not show up for work. After one morning's shopping, Heinz came to my house and hid in the stairwell. He said, "They are after me. In my room in Wilmersdorfer Strasse, you will find handbills and brochures in the bookshelf. Do me a favor and get these papers and bring them to the following address."

I got the papers and delivered them in west Berlin. The idea that the Gestapo was probably watching Heinz's house and could have followed me came to me a day or so later and I was terribly scared. But since I had no formal connection with the group, my name was not on the Gestapo's list and nothing happened.

## Preparing for a Life in Hiding

Meanwhile people started disappearing. We knew where they were going, but we didn't know what was happening to them, not in the beginning. Soon we knew it was really bad, that they separated the young from the old. We knew that they killed people. It all got out in bits and pieces. In November 1942 my boyfriend Erich Arndt, a slave laborer at Siemens, heard a rumor that by April all the factories would be empty of Jews. Erich, his sister, Ruth, a slave laborer at Erich & Graetz, and I knew we couldn't wait for that and we decided to go underground. We sat down with Erich's parents to plan for survival. Erich's father, Dr. Arndt, had been a very good German, an officer in World War I, and he had gotten an Iron Cross.

When Erich told him we weren't going to the camps, Dr. Arndt said, "It's the law." Erich said his parents had a choice either to go with us into hiding or we would go alone. Erich also insisted that he had to take me and my mother Charlotte. But we needed Dr. Arndt. He had done a lot for his patients and he was the only one who knew enough people to help us. Finally he said, "Okay. I will speak to some people I trust."

First he talked to his former patients Anni and Max Gehre. They agreed to hide Dr. Arndt and he stayed with them until the end of the war. Anni also insisted on helping us find hiding places and jobs. She talked to another patient, Max Koehler, who owned a small machine shop. Max despised Hitler and he agreed to hire Erich as a journeyman and give him an "Aryan" name. Anni found a hiding place for Erich, Ruth, and their mother Lina with Purzel, also a former patient.

Erich and his family went into hiding on January 9 [1943]. *Mutti* and I went into hiding a month later, after I found a hiding place for her with Frau Harm, the wife of a German soldier, for a small sum of money. When *Mutti* was settled I went to Purzel's.

Soon it became dangerous for Erich to ride his bike to Max's factory. Young men not in uniform were suspicious and often stopped by police. Max invited him to move into the factory. *Mutti* Arndt (Lina) went to live with the children's first nanny. Later, when I ran out of hiding places for myself, Erich asked Max if I could move into the factory. Max said, "If the Nazis are going to kill me for hiding one Jew, they might as well kill me for hiding two."

One of my jobs was with the Bachman sisters, former patients of Dr. Arndt's who ran a tailoring shop. I got an excellent meal and a few marks. Across the street was a "madam." I sewed for her and often saw another woman there with a little girl. It was obvious to me they were also Jews in hiding.

When I told the madam that my mother had lost her hiding place with Frau Harm she sent me to contact one of her girls at a bar on Kurfurstenstrasse. I offered to pay the girl if she would hide my mother. She said "okay" and rearranged her schedule to see clients during the daytime, so my mother could sleep there at night. But neighbors became suspicious. Why was an older woman there? Charlotte had to move.

*During the next year Ruth and Charlotte went from one hiding place to another. Since Ellen and Ruth were young, they got jobs as maids and cooks for a wide spectrum of Berliners, many of whom knew they were Jewish. In the spring of 1944 Bruno Gumpel, Erich's school friend,*

Ellen Lewinsky (Arndt) wearing a hat she made from scraps of mink given to her by her aunt before her aunt was deported to Riga. Ellen wore the hat during her time in hiding; it helped her image as a Berlin citizen. c. 1942.

*joined the group. Bruno had been on the run since his parents had been deported to Auschwitz. When he lost his hiding place, he tracked down Erich. Max hired Bruno and gave him shelter. In the fall Ruth moved into the factory; three months later Lina moved in.*

## Life in the Factory: Winter 1944

There were now six of us in the factory. We got mattresses that came in three parts, so you could shift them. We put packing paper on the floor for the mattresses and had two folding beds. Every morning we got up at 5 am and had to put everything away in cupboards. We took turns at the sink to wash. Then Ruth and I left for our jobs.

Erich and Bruno worked alongside the other six or seven workers, most of them elderly men. But there was a young apprentice, Hörst, a fervent Nazi. Once he

A photo of Erich Arndt (far left) in Max Koehler's factory; Erich had an "Aryan" name, Walter Driese. The elderly man on the right was known as "Uncle Willy." None of the factory workers knew that Erich was Jewish. c. 1943.

threatened Erich by saying there was "something not right going on." Erich took him into the back storage room and beat him and told him never to insult a "good and great" German again. The next day Hörst brought in a few ration stamps to appease Erich. Naturally, after that he got "reminded" of his lowly status and his misdeeds quite often.

On weekends, when the other workers were not there, we bathed. We put an old oil drum on a Bunsen burner and filled it with water and bits of soap that Anni Gehre had given us. We allowed each person two basins of warm water, and hung an old blanket over a beam to provide some privacy. We also boiled all the wash. Then Ruth and I washed and rinsed the clothes. Erich and Bruno had to wring them several times so they would dry overnight. We rigged lines over the machines and hung up everything.

Every seven days we went through the same procedure. I mended all the clothes and cut uppers off socks to make new soles for other socks. Ruth ironed, cut everyone's hair, and gave manicures. We also cut fresh brown packing paper to make a new table cover with cut-out designs and fringes for Shabbat.

We were determined not to become dehumanized and tried to normalize our lives. We played gin rummy and listened to news on the BBC. Erich and Bruno played chess with pieces cut from a pipe. Erich rigged up a wireless to intercept German military reports, so we always knew when bombing raids were coming.

Food was our worst problem. Ruth and I brought home food from our jobs, often saving half of our lunch for the others. Bruno got ration cards posing as a bombed-out Berliner. Sometimes I joined him. Since we were both blonde no one questioned our identity.

As the war went on, we got very tired and irritable and worse, we got very hungry. I was in charge of food that I kept in a black leather tote. I was very strict. I carefully divided bread into slices; two slices for Erich and Bruno; one slice for each girl. Otherwise the boys would eat their rations at night and would be hungry during the day and tempted to eat the rest of the bread.

Near the end of the war we all broke out in lumps and bumps from malnutrition. Then Dr. Arndt would come late at night and give us vitamin B shots from the medicine he took into hiding. That didn't totally eliminate the lumps but made it better.

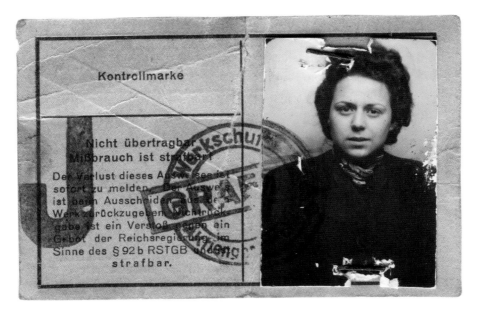

The work permit of Ruth Arndt from Erich & Graetz, where she worked as a slave laborer from 1940 to 1941. Before she went into hiding, her mother sewed the work permit into the seams of her winter coat, so she could use it for identification after the war.

## Surviving the Last Days

*From the unpublished memoir of Ruth Arndt Gumpel*

By now [February 1945] all our previous daytime hide-outs were gone. I had to stay in the storage room with my mother and Charlotte [where Erich and Bruno had set up wooden bunkers]. It had no windows and we could not use lights, because they would have shone through the cracks between the wooden wallboards and be seen by the German employees. I suffered from a recurring urinary tract infection. Not being able to use a bathroom was sheer torture. We had to use a pail and that presented an additional danger—the tinkling noise. Only when the machines in the shop were going full blast or when Erich came in and made noise could we take turns emptying our bladders. The few old Germans still working there never knew of our presence. [The Nazi worker Hörst had joined the navy.]

It became more difficult to meet with my father at night since air raids had increased tremendously. He could never go to the air raid shelter because somebody could recognize him. All around us houses were destroyed and there was an ever-present stench of burned flesh. For the next two months we had less and less to eat. Only a few pounds of grits, full of worms, and burned rolls, hard as a rock, made into soup by Ellen, kept us going. Damage to the factory from air raids was relatively minimal. Some windows were blown out and splinters lodged in our clean, hanging laundry. We had a hard time removing glass from our raw, home-made noodles, drying on the workbench.

By April we were under constant artillery fire and we four women went into the air raid shelter with the other tenants from the building; we no longer cared if we were seen. It was scary and some people cried. One woman placed a feather pillow over her head.

It was my turn to get fresh water from the only available source, a pump, located a block away. When I came to the corner, wearing a steel army helmet, I thought for a moment I was dreaming. There, right in front of me, stood two or three Russian soldiers eating pickles from a large barrel. I did not know what to do first and I almost forgot to take off my helmet; with it they might think I was a German soldier. I offered them water to drink. Then I ran back into our shelter.

When I told them about the soldiers, the German women became even more frightened, with good reason, of course. It never occurred to Ellen, our mothers or me that we too might be in danger. My mother opened the seams of our coats and took out our Jewish ID cards. The Germans around us just could not believe that they had four Jewish women sitting right among them! We had been in hiding for more than two years.

It was April 26, 1945.

*Ellen and Erich married on June 16, 1945; Ruth and Bruno married on September 19, 1945. On October 7, the two couples had a double Jewish wedding in the synagogue where Erich had his bar mitzvah. The entire group of seven immigrated to the US in 1946. Erich lives in Rochester, NY. Ruth lives in Petaluma, CA. Ellen died in 2006; Bruno died in 1996.*

Shulamit Gara, an only child, was born in Budapest in 1924 to assimilated, upper-middle-class parents. Her father, an attorney, was a decorated veteran of World War I; her mother was well-educated. In 1939, at the age of fifteen, Shulamit joined Hechalutz, a Zionist youth movement. She changed her name from Maria to Shulamit and began observing kashrut (Jewish dietary laws). Although Hungary had passed anti-Jewish laws in 1938 forbidding Zionist meetings, members met secretly in private homes. In 1939 Shulamit and other young Zionists began helping Polish Jews who had fled to Hungary—still an unoccupied country—immigrate to Palestine. By networking with Zionist branches in several countries, Hechalutz obtained funds from Jewish sources to purchase and prepare false identities for refugees. They paid smugglers to assist Jews to cross the Hungarian border to Romania. In Romania they guided them to ports on the Black Sea where they hoped to escape to Palestine. After Germany occupied Hungary in March 1944, Hechalutz sent emissaries to provincial cities to warn Jews and persuade them to go into hiding. Between May and August 1944 young Zionists helped a few thousand people cross the border into Romania. Although Polish Jews brought reports of mass murder, most Hungarian Jews felt that they were safe and did not believe these reports.

# Hungary: "I Saved as Many People as I Could"

From the oral history of Shulamit Gara Lack

On March 19, 1944 [when the Germans occupied Hungary], about ten or fifteen Zionist leaders went to the mountains near Budapest to decide strategy. When we returned to Budapest, we saw German soldiers and tanks. We started to get false papers to help Jews escape, because there were no forests and nowhere to run. I told my mother to hide while I got her papers. But she was too scared. "Look, I will not run," she said. "You go, you do whatever you have to do, I can't." So I bought veronal, a poison, and I gave it to her, warning, "Take it before you get to the gas chamber. There's nothing I can do where you're going." She was deported before I could help her and she died in Auschwitz.

To get false papers, we walked into government offices asking for the birth certificates of non-existent Hungarians. While the clerk went to look for them, we looked in the book on the counter and found real names. Of course he couldn't find these fake names, so we left. We returned the next day to another office and asked for birth certificates of real people. The only risk was that sometimes the person had died or might be in the office. So you always went in with your stomach in your mouth.

When we had the birth certificates we could go to a church and get a Christian baptismal certificate. But there we could have the same problems. We also forged a lot of documents ourselves because we couldn't get as many as we needed.[1] We sold them to Jews who had money so we could rescue the young people and send them, illegally, to Palestine. If we could save someone, we had to save young people, since older people would have a hard time adapting to Palestine. Also, you couldn't send more than ten or twelve people in one transport through the border.

At that time Jews were supposed to wear yellow stars. I put on the yellow star when I went into my house. When I left, I took it off and put it into my pocket. When I wanted to bring people out from the ghettos I had to go as a Christian. I had Christian papers in my pocket, which I wrote myself. I went into the ghettos to take young people to my apartment in Budapest and hide them there until I could send them over the border to Romania. A lot of parents did not want to let their teenagers leave and the children wouldn't leave without their parents' okay. Other parents said it was fine.

From the time they took my mother away until August 1944, I had ten to twenty youngsters in my apartment every day and I had to feed them. I let the superintendent think I was a bad girl because there were so many young men coming and going to my home. It was much better for him to think that I was a bad girl than for him to know what was really going on. And I succeeded. From every group I sent, one or two were caught but the rest got across safely.

We tried not to use our real names so that if anyone was caught by the Germans and beaten they couldn't give out our names. Nobody in a transport knew anything except the leader. I was the head of Hano'ar Hatzioni, which was one particular branch of the Hechalutz youth movement. We tried not to stay in contact with the other branches. We didn't want to know their names because we didn't want to jeopardize their safety. I even worked with the Communists and we bribed as many Christians as we could.

I rented a bunker from a Hungarian officer who let us use his name on an apartment in exchange for my father's furniture and money. During air raids everybody was supposed to go down to the bunker, but you couldn't take anyone who didn't live in the building, which meant I was the only person who could go. In the meantime people came and searched apartments to see if anybody was there—you had to leave the doors open because of the fire hazard. Can you imagine what kind of work I had to do to hide ten or fifteen people in my apartment? They were sleeping on the floor. It was an unbelievable risk but I had nothing to lose except my own life and that was worth the risk. We had no other apartment.

Levi Yehudah, who worked with me, made a connection with the farmer or person who took groups from Hungary to Romania. Levi went with every single group. He is alive today, thank God, in Israel. He did a fantastic job. He was the one who talked to people and got the money to give to the man who took the people across the border.

I couldn't meet more than three people in one place without being asked by the police what I was doing. So I set certain times—2 pm, 4 pm, and midnight when people who were going to be part of the escape group would meet in front of the theater or at the train station, where people are usually standing around and waiting. One day the superintendent of my building came up to tell me that the police were looking for me. That was around 11 am. I said, "What do you mean they're looking for me?"

"Yes, they have a paper that says they have to take you into the police." I gave him money to tell the police I wasn't there. They were stupid enough to leave a note

Shulamit Gara and her mother, 1930's.

# "Perhaps my purpose was to live in times that were historic and terrible, but gave me the opportunity to save lives."

saying they would arrest me later that day. I waited until 3 pm because I didn't want the people I was hiding to be picked up instead of me. After 3 pm I walked out and lived two weeks in the mountains of Budapest with two guys. It was a terrible two weeks but I had to stay because I had to gather my escapees.

Then we went down to Budapest and I picked up my boyfriend, Dov, and Ruth Kurtzweil. Her parents would only allow her to leave if she went with me personally on a transport. So the last transport to Romania could have been Dov, Ruth, and myself. Somehow we lost Dov. We had to go back for him, because if he was standing alone on a street the police would certainly catch him. He was there and we also picked up six Polish Jews from another group, whom I couldn't just leave there. Then I traveled with them towards Cluj [a city in Hungary].

From there we were supposed to take the train to Nagyvárad [Hungary]. In the train I started to give everyone money and tell them what they were supposed to do. They started to talk in Yiddish and a civil detective on the train saw us and I realized that he knew what was going on. I knew I would be arrested. I told everyone not to follow me when the train stopped in the station but to leave me and go with Dov. I wanted them to be able to cross the border. I also told Ruth to go with Dov, but Ruth refused to go with Dov, and she and I landed in jail in Nagyvárad. There they called the police in Budapest to find out if lived at the address on my false paper. When they found out I didn't live

there, they knew I was Jewish. Furthermore, I had sewn a lot of money into my clothing to use when we crossed the border. They found the money and since it said on my papers that I was a seamstress, they knew no seamstress had that kind of money. So they beat me. But I kept quiet until midnight. Then I told them I was Jewish. By that time I knew that the rest of the group was safely over the border.

We were kept in Nagyvárad a couple of days. Then Ruth and I escaped. We were caught and sent to Budapest to a holding place. From there they sent us to an internment camp in Szarvas, Hungary, where you could receive letters and packages and even visitors. The next morning, Germans sent us to Auschwitz. I wasn't shocked when we got there since I knew what was waiting for me. What I didn't expect was the terrible screaming of children when they were taken away from their parents. I had nobody to be split from because Ruth and I were the same age; so there was no reason to separate us.

My only purpose was to stay a human being and not to become an animal. And because in Auschwitz it was impossible to do this, I wanted to die there. I felt I had fulfilled my purpose; I had saved as many people as I could. I was sure that that the State of Israel would be born and the people whom I had sent there would live as free citizens. If I couldn't be with them, all right. Moses couldn't go into the Promised Land. One person doesn't count; the purpose is what counts.

*After a week in Auschwitz, Shulamit and Ruth were transported to Stutthof, a concentration camp in Germany, and then to Thorn, a forced labor camp. Because she spoke German, Shulamit was selected to be the Blockälteste [barrack supervisor]. She tried to use her position to protect her women charges, but on a five-day death march where no one was fed, she lost Ruth because Ruth could not walk. Shulamit and nine other women survived and made it back to Hungary. In Budapest Shulamit worked for Aliyah Bet, helping Jews immigrate to Palestine illegally. After reuniting with Dov, her Zionist comrade and boyfriend, they moved to Palestine and fought in Israel's War of Independence. Eventually they divorced. Shulamit remarried and moved to the United States with her second husband. She lives in New York City.*

ATTACK, drawing by partisan
Alexander Bogen, 1943.

# ARMED RESISTANCE
# "To Get Killed or To Kill"

*Bonnie Gurewitsch*

n a poem titled, *To the Teachers*, Hela Blumengraber, who had been a student at the Jewish high school in Krakow, blamed her teachers for teaching students "to strive for a life of ideals… to search relentlessly for the truth…." Instead, she argues, her teachers should have taught them:

> How to kill to avoid getting killed
> And get used to the glitter of blood.[1]

The transformation from humanist to fighter was a difficult one. The first step was psychological. Jews had to believe the unimaginable: the historically unprecedented reality that Germany, a civilized country, had discarded earlier anti-Jewish policies and was murdering them *all*. Jews also had to internalize the fact that no defensive measures would protect them. Tuvia Bielski, in his oral history, said that after witnessing the massacre of 5,000 Jews in Lida, Belorussia, he understood: "I saw there is only one way: to get killed or to kill." He then left to fight as a partisan in the forest.

But for the great majority of Jews this realization came late in the process of annihilation. Because of the Nazi policy of deception and deceit, most Jews did not know that the Nazis were killing all the Jews. Most hoped that if they could only hold out long enough, an Allied victory would rescue many of them. Reports brought to them by couriers about mass murder seemed unbelievable. Many leaders of the ghetto youth movements, however, *did* believe these reports. But when they tried to organize armed response, both the Jewish Councils that governed ghettos and the general ghetto population opposed efforts to obtain arms or contact partisan groups operating in the forests, fearing severe reprisals from the Germans.

There were notable exceptions. In Pruzana, Poland, the Jewish Council's vice-chairman helped people escape and was in charge of ammunition collected by the ghetto fighters. In the Minsk Ghetto the Jewish Council was in close touch with Belorussian partisans, providing them with warm clothing, shoes, information, hiding places, and forged documents.[2]

More than ninety ghettos had armed undergrounds. But in most ghettos, it was only after their families were deported and their communities decimated that youth movements felt they could actually mount armed resistance. Resistance fighters faced another choice: Stay and fight in the ghetto at the moment of liquidation? Escape before liquidation and fight in the forest? Inspired by the Warsaw Ghetto uprising of April 1943 that lasted more than a month, young Jews in more than half a dozen ghettos took up arms at the moment of liquidation. Facing German tanks and artillery with a few weapons and homemade grenades, none of the fighters expected to win anything except a moral victory, choosing the moment and the manner of their deaths.

Some young fighters who left the ghetto were tormented by the choice they made to leave their family behind. Abba Kovner, a partisan commander, wondered later in life: Would he be remembered as a hero, or as a son who abandoned his mother? But as partisan

Frank Blaichman explained in his oral history: "The Germans were the enemy; they murdered my family. So if you could lay your hand on one, why not?"

Even when Jews decided to fight, they lacked the resources for armed resistance. Few had any military experience or expertise with weapons. They had scant contacts for purchasing weapons. Their physical isolation made communication with national resistance movements difficult. In countries like Yugoslavia, Greece, and Italy, Jews could join partisan groups and share the fight with compatriots. In Eastern Europe, however, a tradition of anti-Semitism discouraged Jews from joining local partisan groups. Some units would not accept Jews at all. Those Jews who were accepted were often betrayed or killed by their "comrades."

Could Jews fight on their own, as Jewish groups? In Eastern Europe, Jewish partisans had no support from local civilians; they had to force civilians to provide them with food and necessities, often punishing them for betrayal. Since the Soviet Union did not tolerate independent Jewish units, Jewish groups often had to surrender control to Soviet commanders. Tuvia Bielski, who commanded a large fighting brigade, managed to achieve a modus vivendi with Soviet partisan commanders by demonstrating the usefulness and loyalty of his fighting unit. Nekamah [Revenge], a Jewish unit led by Abba Kovner, struggled to exist and had to accept Soviet command.

Most fighting groups were all male; they rarely accepted women (p. 120). Jewish partisan Family Camps were unique because they offered refuge to women, children, the elderly, and men who could not fight. These camps provided support for the fighters by supplying meals, doing laundry, making clothing and boots, caring for the sick and wounded, and repairing weapons and equipment. The Bielski brothers commanded the largest Family Camp, caring for 1,200 Jews (p. 114). Shalom Zorin commanded 800 Jewish partisans and a Family Camp near Minsk. Yehiel Grynszpan's group had 400 Jewish fighters and a Family Camp of several hundred Jews near Parczew, Poland. Dr. Yeheskel Atlas commanded a unit of 120 partisans plus a Family Camp.

Fighting and living in the forest was difficult: It meant facing the dangers of a primitive, hostile physical environment and battling an enemy that was infinitely better trained and equipped. It often meant fighting the anti-Semitism of local civilians and partisans, in addition to the Nazis. It is estimated that eighty percent of those who went to the forests perished.

Geography also played a large role in the feasibility of armed resistance. Partisans needed cover, like the dense forests and swamps of Eastern Europe, or isolated villages high in the mountains of Italy or Greece, where the mechanized German Army couldn't easily maneuver. In flat, densely populated countries like Belgium or Holland, where fighting groups had no place to hide, partisans concentrated on sabotage, defensive work, and clandestine work. In Belgium, Jewish partisans stopped a deportation train. In France, Jews fought with the maquis (a national resistance army) or in the Armée Juive (Jewish Army).

Desperate choices to fight back were made in three of the six death camps. In August and October 1943, Jewish prisoners in Treblinka and Sobibor organized revolts, killing key Nazi personnel, setting fires, and creating chaos that facilitated escapes. Several hundred prisoners escaped; only a few dozen survived.

Knowing that they would inevitably be murdered, prisoners who worked at the gas chambers and crematoria in Auschwitz–Birkenau organized a revolt. Jewish *Sonderkommando* prisoners planned a general prisoner uprising in conjunction with the Polish underground in the camp. When on October 7, 1944, the Polish resistance did not participate, Jews revolted on their own, damaging two crematoria, putting one out of commission, and killing several SS guards.[3] Although most rebels died, their heroism inspired hope and pride in other prisoners.

Jewish resisters knew that they had no chance of defeating the Nazis. But the Jewish definition of success was different: It meant simply mounting armed resistance and demonstrating to themselves, to the Nazis, and to the world, that Jews could fight back.

Shalom Yoran's mother told him to leave his parents, take revenge, and tell the world what had happened.[4] He and others fulfilled this charge by fighting evil, risking their lives to damage the Nazi regime, and leaving a legacy of physical and moral courage.

Abba Kovner grew up in Vilna, where he became a leader of the Hashomer Hatza'ir Zionist youth movement. When the Germans occupied Vilna in June 1941, Kovner and others hid in a Dominican convent. In December, they returned to the ghetto to learn that the Germans had killed 20,000 Jews in a series of massacres in Ponar, a nearby forest. Kovner intuitively realized that these executions were part of a "well thought-out system"[1] and that escape was not feasible for millions of Jews. He concluded that armed resistance was the only alternative. His famous rallying cry, "We will not be led like sheep to the slaughter," was taken to other ghettos by couriers, inspiring young Zionists to take up arms. In January 1942 Kovner met with Josef Glazman (member of Betar), and Itzik Wittenberg (leader of the Communist cell) to form the United Partisans' Organization (UPO). But the UPO lacked the popular support it needed in the ghetto to stage a rebellion. When liquidation of the ghetto began on September 1, 1943, Glazman led a group to the Rudnicki forest to fight as Jewish partisans. In the ghetto's final days Kovner and 100 other Jews joined them. In March 1944 Kovner wrote a letter explaining why the UPO had been unable to fight and defining future goals for Hashomer Hatza'ir.

# "The Vanguard of Armed Resistance"

From a letter to Hashomer Hatza'ir partisans by Abba Kovner, March 17, 1944

*The edited excerpts below are from an original copy of the letter, written in Yiddish, that the Jewish partisan Zelda Traeger copied into a notebook. It was hidden from the Soviets, brought to Palestine after the war, and later deposited in the Moreshet Archives for safekeeping. Kovner translated the letter into Hebrew. In 2002 it was translated into English. This is the letter's first publication in the United States.*

Our life today is too cruel for us to remain united only by the ties of the past instead of being united by a clear political goal for the future. This letter will not only recall memories but will reconsider and strengthen the ideal of the *shomer* (a member of Hashomer Hatza'ir).

The major aim of the UPO was to serve as the vanguard of the armed resistance movement and to organize a unified fighting force in the ghetto to defend the Jewish masses who faced destruction. But the UPO did not achieve its goal. The Vilna Ghetto was liquidated and the battle to defend the ghetto did not materialize. We were forced to retreat to the forest. Why did we fail?

Individual Jews had various options for escape—hiding out in bunkers, disguising themselves as "Aryans," and becoming partisans. In contrast to these strategies that served only to rescue individuals, the UPO presented a communal strategy—combat.

For us, members of the UPO who were organized and armed, there was nothing simpler than escape to the forest. But that choice meant abandoning the Jewish masses without a fight and betraying our national responsibility. That choice appeared to us immoral.

In light of our new experience as partisans and our reevaluation of the UPO, I can state emphatically that if we had we carried out a major battle in the ghetto, and if tens of thousands of Jews had dispersed and fled to the forest, their fate would have been bitter.

Although a small number of young Jewish men can still join the partisans, the immense forest is too small to protect masses of Jews.

But what is the UPO accused of? That instead of organizing combat in the ghetto, we should have organized a mass flight to the forest. Instead of an answer, let us point out the bloody blot in the history of the general partisan movement—the liquidation of Jewish fighting groups in the forest and the confiscation of their weapons in Narocz and elsewhere (p. 123). Many of our dearest comrades fell in a tragic struggle defending their right to fight.

To arm masses of Jews in the ghettos or [labor] camps would have been no simple task. The fear of collective punishment was so great that UPO Commander Itzik Wittenberg halted the operation of purchasing weapons and smuggling them into the ghetto.

The tactics of the UPO grew to fruition logically, as we determined that our people should not go helplessly as sheep to the slaughter. The only answer we could give to the Jewish masses in the ghetto was struggle. If we fall—the enemy should pay dearly. If we die—then with honor. Even if we had achieved battle it would not have been an empty demonstration, just as the Warsaw Ghetto revolt [in April 1943] was not a futile demonstration.

*As the UPO continued to advocate rebellion, Jacob Gens, the head of the Vilna Ghetto, opposed it, believing that armed revolt would bring harsh reprisals from the Germans. At a meeting with UPO leaders, Lithuanian policemen, possibly alerted by Gens, arrested Itzik Wittenberg, UPO military commander. As police led him outside, UPO members attacked and freed Wittenberg, who went into hiding. The next morning Gens announced that if Wittenberg did not surrender, the Germans would liquidate the entire ghetto—consisting of approximately 20,000 people. Ghetto residents began attacking UPO members with stones and Wittenberg, knowing that he was doomed, turned himself in. Before leaving he appointed Kovner his successor as commander of the UPO. To avoid death by the Nazis, Wittenberg took his own life with a cyanide pill on July 16, 1943.*

[In September] the Gestapo in Vilna carried out the liquidation in a new manner, using great wile and sophistication. On July 10th, when we had resorted to arms to get Wittenberg out of the hands of the Gestapo, and after the [subsequent] provocation in the city, the UPO was exposed to the Gestapo. After their experience in the Warsaw Ghetto, the Gestapo had misgivings about liquidating the Vilna Ghetto directly. They devised a better method of deception: separate deportations to work camps in Estonia, promising life and not death, at least for a few months. [Due to these false German promises] the Jewish authorities, fearing the UPO as much as the Gestapo, instilled a deadly fear in ghetto residents that armed struggle in the ghetto [would lead to death]. The result was that the Jewish masses went willingly to the deportation.

The strategic plan of the UPO was to revolt in the eventuality of a Gestapo attack on the ghetto, to allow as many of the masses as possible to disperse and escape. The unexpected, [gradual] deportations (the opposite

Left to right: Rózka Korczak, Abba Kovner, and Vitka Kempner, Kovner's wife. Vilna, 1944.

Jewish partisans in liberated Vilna, 1944. Kovner is standing in the center, rear.

of what had occurred in Warsaw), and the attitude of the populace towards us, paralyzed our action, which was significant only as a response to a mass operation.

If the staff of the UPO had had at least some limited experience in partisan warfare, we would have behaved differently with regard to the Jewish authorities. But as we felt the burden of collective responsibility deeply, we made at least two major mistakes: We shouldn't have handed over Wittenberg or permitted Glazman and his group to escape to the forest.

The strategic mistake was that on the morning of September 1, 1943, the first day of the Vilna liquidation, when the German army encircled the ghetto and the first column entered the gate—we should have opened fire. We would have confronted the masses with an existing fact and swept each and every Jew into the battle. That, however, did not occur, because of the sudden appearance of the German army, our meager supply of weapons and the lack of a prompt decision by the underground command. During the first moments it would have been possible to attack; half an

hour later the situation changed radically. The Jewish authorities, aware of the possibility of a clash with us, took a treacherous initiative. The German Army retreated from the ghetto and the Jewish Police began to carry out the *Aktion*.

### The Dualism of the UPO

The UPO was initially organized to oppose our people going feebly like "sheep to the slaughter." (Our Shomer proclamation of January 1, 1942, was the basis for the establishment of the UPO. We proclaimed a revolt by youth against the despondency of their existence.) The UPO bore the first message of encouragement—the first creed: Battle! But in early 1942, after the initial series of mass killings [at Ponar], our social organization was still weak. Only a few political organizations succeeded in gathering members. For example, not a single Communist cell existed and those movements that succeeded—such as the Bund and Revisionists— were busy grabbing "jobs" in the "ghetto kingdom." The great mass of youth were in despair, robbed of all beliefs and hopes. Our vanguard role—to serve as a fighting force for the bleeding Jewish masses in defense of their lives and their honor—was the first awakening call, the Promethean flame in the darkness of our lives! It was a torch meant to arouse other Jewish communities in Poland and shed light for future generations.

Only after a great delay did we grow close to the idea of partisan activity as an alternative for young people in the ghetto. Members in the ghetto began receiving messages from relatives who were with partisans in the forests. People began to mobilize. Young people began to run off to the forests. All this reverberated in the spiritual world of the UPO.

The UPO demanded of each fighter an ultimate willingness to sacrifice, to look forward to battle, no matter what the outcome. For the vanguard of the UPO the meaning of such battle meant—Death! And then a new reality appeared on our horizon—Rescue!

An ideological dilemma was thus created for many: The choices were, battle and rescue, or battle and death? Some lacked a rooted national consciousness and did not share the sense of responsibility and moral strength of the *shomrim* that prepared us to give our lives, to stare death in the eye! A large segment of the youth favored rescue. The Communist organization sought out a synthesis between these two directions.

When the expulsion took place on September 1, 1943, the danger of liquidation took us by surprise and we decided not to abandon the ghetto on the eve of its destruction. This was correct for all of us, but in the hearts of many this dualism between battle and rescue grew into a spiritual conflict (especially among the Communist youth). The choice to take up arms [in the ghetto] was not taken, not only as a military decision, but because from the beginning there was an alternative to sacrificing our lives in battle in the ghetto.

In the last dramatic and historic deliberation of the UPO in those fatal moments, the question was raised: to commence combat, even with limited forces (part of the armed members were not in the ghetto)? Or to retreat? One Communist representative voted in favor of immediate evacuation. The Bund representative gave a shameful speech, directed at me: "Who do you want to defend, 13,000 Jews? 150 fighters are worth more than those 13,000—they have to be rescued for the continuation of the struggle!" The Revisionist represen-

tative and myself were the only ones who voted in favor of fighting, and it was clear to me that there was no longer enough support for battle.

Thus ended the epic of the UPO [in the Vilna Ghetto]. A great potential of heroism, saturated and illuminated by the ideals of the UPO, melted in the flames of cruel fate.

### Our Path as Partisans

*During the final liquidation of the Vilna ghetto on September 23-24, 1943, Abba Kovner led a group of about 100 members of the UPO out of the ghetto. Sonia Majdesker, who was sent out earlier, led them to the Rudnicki forest, where they began their partisan operations. As more Jews escaped from Vilna, Kovno, and other Jewish communities, the number of Jewish partisans grew to 600, divided into four groups. They were under the command of "Jurgis," the Soviet partisan commander in the Vilna area.[2]*

We did not come to the forest as individuals. After losing the opportunity to fight in the ghetto we viewed the partisan movement as our only alternative. Despite our small numbers, our decisions have been and will continue to be communal and not for the benefit of the individual.

No less dramatic than the history of the UPO is its epilogue: the path of the partisans. How did it happen that the UPO fell apart in the forest? Who bears the guilt for that tragedy?

An unpredictable, tragic onslaught of anti-Semitic persecutions by Soviet partisans, who disarmed us and stole the weapons that were obtained with our blood—this was the reception for our people who arrived in the forest, prepared to sacrifice their lives on the altar of revenge and struggle. In Shomer tradition I bow my head in hallowed and honored esteem to those martyrs who died in the battle for our right to fight.

Our first task was to establish a Jewish fighting unit. Immediately, we became aware not only of the great difficulties, but also the plight of having few weapons and the anti-Semitic atmosphere. It was almost impossible to transform hundreds of Jews into a Jewish fighting unit. In our first meeting with Jurgis he stated that there was no justification for the existence of a Jewish-national unit and cited the example

# "At least one Jewish unit must continue to exist ....we will struggle to maintain it, and we will justify its existence.... As long as the war continues our lives belong to the battle.... A *shomer* goes on until the very end!"

of Narozc [Jewish units in the Narocz forest].[3]

A Jewish unit would constantly suffer from persecution, false accusations, and would never obtain a sufficient supply of arms. Nevertheless, Jews streamed to us, and even though we warned them that they would ease our burden if they transferred some people to other [non-Jewish] units—nothing useful came out of our warnings. We expanded and grew into four units! And the thought came to me that this was all a joke of fate. I was to be the commander of a Jewish camp instead of the commander of a fighting unit. More than once I vacillated between the desire to be a simple combatant among other fighters, or the commander of a Jewish unit. The commitment to my people and my communal obligation won.

Today, March 1944, when our units have obtained many more weapons and the other units have grown, the issue again rose about the dissolution of the Jewish unit. The [Soviet] partisan command decided to disperse the Jews among non-Jewish units.... Our position is that at least one Jewish unit must continue to exist. We will insist on the existence of one Jewish unit, we will struggle to maintain it, and we will justify its existence.

## The Arrival of the Red Army

The victorious Red Army is drawing near and will liberate our area from the yoke of the German conquerors. For most, that day will be a day of liberation. But for us, the *shomrim*, that will be a day of great triumph and joy but not liberation. The entry of the Red Army into Vilna is not our political goal nor is it our ideal. We will have two choices: to go west and continue the partisan struggle or to join the Red Army and go to the front. Which of the two we shall choose depends on a situation which we cannot , as yet, talk about. But one thing

is certain. Whether a *shomer* goes to the forest or to the fronts, he will fight, avenge and help to achieve victory. A *shomer* lives within the struggle! As long as the war continues, our lives belong to the battle! We will not permit any personal concerns to turn us away from this path. A *shomer* goes on until the very end!

## The War and our Vision of the Future

Even the unprecedented present catastrophe did not encompass the entire Jewish Diaspora. The Nazi beast killed five to six million Jews and nine to ten million people![4] The brain [intellectual centers] of Judaism may have been destroyed but its heart and many of its vital organs live on! The pessimistic view of America, the main Jewish surviving community, is unjustified. Serious inquiry will prove that American Jewry has a separate sociological direction of its own and this Jewry has within it great national potential for Zionism and pioneering Zionism. [After the Spanish Inquisition, 15th century] only three million Jews survived a wave of persecution and destruction. Five hundred years later there were eighteen million Jews. Zionism, the renaissance movement of the Jewish people, has suffered a hard and tragic blow, but it has not lost its genuine roots: the Jewish people, in all its tragedy, lives on!

Zionism cannot emanate from negative motivations—only from positive ones. What the Jewish people and the Zionist movement experienced during the war does not negate the Zionist ideal. On the contrary. The idea of the need for a Jewish homeland is reinforced by the tragic truth and plight of our people. Although a Soviet victory will mean life and freedom for hundreds of thousands of Jews who live in Soviet lands, it will not mean independence for the Jewish people [as a nation].

The postwar period will see the rebuilding of the peoples within the Soviet Union, the Ukrainians, Belorussians, Lithuanians, and the Latvians. But regarding the Jews, they will only write books and gather documents about the shocking acts of murder by the Germans. As opposed to other national groups, the Jews will attempt to assimilate into the mainstream, but they will encounter strong anti-Semitism.

The task of Socialist Zionism now is to concentrate maximum national resources to create a Jewish homeland in the Land of Israel. We must work towards achieving a maximum number of Jews in the Land of Israel to aid in the struggle for a Socialist world and a Jewish-Arab republic in the Near East. As difficult as it may be for us to leave the Soviet Union after the war, our desire must be to struggle for a Socialist Land of Israel! Our political and moral right is to go on *aliyah* [immigration to Israel] to our country! If we are unable to achieve *aliyah* through a peaceful agreement with the British, then the revolutionary Zionist ideal gives us the right to make *aliyah* in any way possible!

### *Yizkor*—In Memoriam

Let us, the last ones, remember our dead who fell in battle and sanctified their names and the honor of their nation.

Let the movement remember its loyal members, heroes of the destruction, who in the hour of catastrophe and death raised the banner of battle and revenge, and with their last strength carried it to the very end!

Let our homeland remember the memory of its fully committed members—the last who fell on foreign soil—soaked in the blood of millions of our brethren, with the cry of revenge on their lips.

\* \* \* \*

These lines were written in order to remember, to awaken, to strengthen.

Far, far off lies Vilna, bleeding, gray [ghetto] wall, empty gates, silent streets, empty.

[I believe] the day will come when by the campfires of Merchavia [Israeli kibbutz] someone will tell

Of the holy flames,
Of faith, of eternity!
To battle and revenge!

Abba Kovner and Shmerke Kaczerginski, a Jewish writer, poet, and partisan, July 1944.

*Chazak Ve'ematz* [Be strong and have courage, the Movement's greeting]
Abba
March 17, 1944
The Nekamah [Revenge] Brigade

*Abba Kovner and a few surviving Jewish partisans were among the liberators of Vilna. Kovner became active in clandestine Zionist work in Europe and was a founder of Bricha, an underground organization that smuggled Jews out of Europe to Palestine. Near the end of 1945, Kovner was arrested by the British and jailed in Palestine for these activities. After his release he joined Kibbutz Ein Hahoresh, with his wife, Vitka Kempner, a fellow partisan. Kovner served in Israel's War of Independence and wrote several volumes of poetry, winning the 1970 Israeli Prize in Literature. He continued to be actively involved in Holocaust commemoration throughout his lifetime; he was a major force behind the establishment of the Diaspora Museum in Tel Aviv. He died in 1987.*

The Bielski brothers, Tuvia, Asael, Zusya, and Aron were born in a small village in eastern Poland (today, Belarus). In the spring of 1942, after the Germans massacred the Jews of the area, the Bielskis set up a camp in the dense forests, near Novogrudok. Tuvia (the oldest brother) was the commander. Beginning with a core group of relatives and ghetto runaways, the Bielski fighters killed enemy soldiers and informers, sabotaged enemy operations, and constantly moved to elude the Germans. They sought out and encouraged Jews of all ages to leave nearby ghettos and join their camp. Tuvia's priority was to rescue Jews, regardless of age or military ability. The Bielski group was divided into two units: the fighting group, composed mainly of young men and women who, under Soviet military authority, went on joint missions with Soviet partisans, and a family camp containing kitchens, an infirmary, and workshops that evolved into a small town. By 1944 there were 1,200 people in the Bielski Family Camp, making it the largest Jewish partisan group in the forest. They survived many German raids, lost only fifty members, and killed many German soldiers.

# Forest Jews

From Tuvia Bielski's memoir, published in Israel in 1954

When the summer crop in eastern Poland was harvested in 1942, we made plans to sabotage the Germans' grain supplies. They had taken over large estates and most farm collectives, planting the fields for themselves. The granaries were full. Why should we leave them food? As for the small farmer, if he had food we had food. But the enemy had all the estates. The verdict—burn them!

We divided the estates between us and the partisans under Viktor Panchenkov [a Soviet partisan leader who cooperated with Bielski] and set the date for arson.

One autumn night fires broke out simultaneously on all the estates worked by the Germans. We opened fire on anyone who came to put out the fires. The sky blazed red above the forests and fields. The peasants understood who did it and why. Our stock went up: We had challenged the Germans. But fires alone didn't do

the trick. Soviet airplanes returning from bombing missions realized the significance of the fires and dropped some of their bombs.

Fear gripped the enemy: They understood that we had ties to Soviet headquarters and were coordinating our actions. We set fires; the Russians sent airplanes to complete the job. We were ready for battle.

Now the peasants looked upon us with great respect: The Germans no longer dared to fight us casually; instead they made preparations. We received intelligence surreptitiously from [sympathetic] peasants about the German plans. The arson operation put our group on the resistance map. Our reputation grew.

When my brothers and I consulted with Viktor about strategy, we decided to kill the local mayors, who were all allied with the Germans, and the heads of villages, who were collaborators. We would go out at night in groups of four and attack village heads who were working with the Germans. The attack groups always included me or one of my brothers. Young Aron was helpful, serving as a guide and sometimes getting us all out of a tight spot. We killed five or six village leaders.

After burning the Germans' grain, we decided to disrupt their food requisitioning in the villages. We had to do this to deny them supplies and to mollify the peasants, who otherwise would argue: "You take, the Germans take; what's left for us to take?"

We decided to ambush German vehicles carrying food they had collected in the villages. We joined forces with Viktor's group and planned to send out twenty-five armed men, led by Asael and myself, with the same number from Viktor's group.

We would station ourselves along the Novogrudok-

Fight and avenge! Avenge even at the price of death!"

We left for the site of the ambush and waited in the forest for word from our contacts in a nearby village. A military convoy passed, but it was too strong for us to handle. We aimed to ambush a small supply convoy under the command of Germans and local police.

The honk of a car horn. Aim well, men! It was a small, speedy car. Four officers sat in it. We shot and missed. Viktor's group shot and missed. Less than three minutes later the truck we were expecting came along. This target was bigger and slower.

Raaaat-tat-tat! The truck stopped. We hit the tires and the driver. We rained down a hail of bullets. Eight Germans and Belorussian policemen jumped out of

Tuvia Bielski: Commander of the Bielski Partisans

Asael Bielski: Second in Command and Head of the Fighters

Zusya Bielski: Head of Intelligence Operations

Aron Bielski: A Scout

Novoyelnya road, at the curve where vehicles slowed down. Our men would attack first; Viktor's men would be held in reserve. If the Germans regrouped to attack us, Viktor's men would hit them from behind; their ambush would come from the other side of the road, a few dozen yards from us. We returned to our camps. The next morning it would start.

Mothers and fathers of our fighters were kept fully informed. Some didn't want their sons to be sent; wives pleaded for their husbands. I threatened to expel dissenters or shoot them: "There is to be no interference in combat matters. We didn't come out to the forest just to eat. Have you forgotten the slaughter? We ourselves go out to fight, with no thought for our own safety.

the truck, took cover and fired with a machine gun.

Viktor's men stormed the Germans shouting "Hurrah!" from behind the bend in the road. The enemy panicked and fled. Later we found out that most of them were already wounded. We rose up to pursue them, but they vanished among the trees. We swooped down upon the machine gun and the rifles, the boots and the chickens, and the crates of bullets. We trampled the eggs and butter but we took bags of sugar. Shooting into the containers of gasoline, we set them on fire. Everything exploded. All this—in a few short minutes. We came away with two machine guns, four rifles, and thousands of bullets. Excited, we went deep into the forest, far away from the site. Our first victory

Bielski Partisan Family Camp in the Naliboki forest, Poland, 1943.

over an armed enemy force!

Later, the German army collected their dead and pursued the attackers. But our great joy was in overcoming fear. We had clashed with the Germans face to face! It was possible to confront them. It was possible to wound them. We would meet them once more, and we would accomplish more. But caution dictated that we move beyond the forest. We walked until nightfall. We ate well and went to sleep, waiting until the next day to discuss the victory. In that discussion we encouraged each other and committed ourselves to more action. Viktor and I each got one machine gun and two rifles.

## A Great Disaster

In March 1943 we sent out Avraham Polonski with ten of our members to bring back food. Polonski's brother and my brother-in-law Alter Tiktin were also in the group. They acquired their quota of supplies and started back. About three miles from Novogrudok, they went to the large farm of Bilous, an acquaintance of Polonski's, and asked to stay there for a day since the German garrison was close by and it was better to hide during the day. Bilous welcomed them with food and

drink and even prepared a place for them to sleep. They posted sentries, but at midnight the farm was surrounded by police.

Later we learned from Bilous's godmother that Bilous had sent one of his sons with this information to the Novogrudok police. When our comrades awoke in a panic, it was already too late to fight. They were all shot to death, except for Avraham, who hid under the stove in the chicken coop.

When the police and their officers left, and the family was joyously celebrating their victory, he came out of hiding and called out to Bilous: "The partisans will take revenge on you." At that, an axe wielded by one of Bilous's son came down on his head. The Bilous family thought that the matter was finished—with the death of the witness the terrible crime had been wiped out.

We waited a day or two for the return of the contingent. No sign of life. We went to search in the villages. We checked and investigated until we heard every detail from neighbors who had been told by the family and their godmother.

We couldn't pass over this in silence. If we didn't take revenge on these informers, how would we end up? Every farmer would turn us in. We sent out a patrol to investigate and they found a group of Jews hiding in a remote farmer's cabin. One had heard about the terrible incident and knew that Bilous's godmother was present when it happened. The patrol went and interrogated her. At first she denied knowing anything, but after she was hit a few times, she told everything. The patrol returned and reported to us.

Asael took our top twenty-five men and set out on wagons to wreak retribution on the Bilous family. My orders to Asael: Do not take even a thread from the Bilous house. Everything must be burned and go up in smoke. I reminded him of how [the Biblical] Joshua gave orders against looting, and of the incident with Achan. I said to him: "Act like our forefathers." He promised.[1]

Asael and his men surrounded the house at midnight, and banged on the door. They spoke openly right from the start, saying they had come to avenge the blood of our ten comrades. Bilous understood what was in store for him and resisted. When four partisans pointed their rifles at him, he grabbed the guns and fought. After he was stabbed several times, he still fought. Asael shot him in the head and gave orders for action. They finished the job in a few minutes and set fire to the house, the stable, and the barn. One partisan took a coat with Asael's permission. In a coat pocket was a letter from Traub, the German commander of Novogrudok, thanking Bilous for turning over the ten Jewish "bandits" and expressing his hope that all of Bilous's neighbors would follow his lead.

*In the summer of 1943, Bielski settled his group in the Naliboki forest near other Soviet partisan groups. Now a group of 750 people, they built a bakery, a weapons workshop, a blacksmith shop, and an infirmary, often offering these services to Soviet partisans in exchange for food. Surrounded by swamps and jungle-like growths, the camp seemed less accessible to the Germans. Then rumors began circulating about an imminent major German assault designed to wipe out all partisans in the area.*

### The Big Manhunt: August 1, 1943

We sent out a hundred of our fighting forces, along with two hundred partisans from Soviet brigades, to set up an ambush near Naliboki, ten miles away. We blocked the roads with logs and planted mines in them. When Army vehicles became visible, a Soviet

## "Our great joy was in overcoming fear. We had clashed with the Germans face to face! It was possible to confront them. It was possible to wound them."

partisan betrayed us and [prematurely] shot at the lead vehicle. Soldiers jumped out and began firing in every direction. Not interested in an open battle, the partisans withdrew. The ambush was unsuccessful. The mines remained in the dirt roads. Our people reported to me in detail about the ambush. Everyone could have been killed because of one traitor, they argued.

The mood in the camp became tense. We had survived one manhunt; now we faced a bigger one. The forest was gigantic, the swamps deep, and there was no place to flee. The only thing to do was to try to hide. But there were plenty of traitors—local farmers and Soviet partisans. Many thought we were done for. But some in our group sized things up according to our mood. As long as the leaders were calm, they felt secure.

Milashevski [a Polish partisan leader near Bielski's camp] and two assistants arrived. Soon two partisans arrived on horseback, breathless, and reported that the Germans were less than two miles away. Milashevski wasn't concerned for himself. His group consisted entirely of fighters, but our group had women, children, and elderly people. "Be strong," he said leaving. "We are surrounded on every side."

Asael and I rushed on horseback to [the Soviet commander] Kovalev, who told me that the Polish partisans had fought the Germans and were badly beaten. They would surely reach us by the next morning.

We couldn't hold our own in open battle. We had to get out, fast. I tried to keep our community calm, but I was confused and couldn't come up with a solution. I decided not to follow the Soviet partisans who were going along the Shobin River to escape.

"We quickly advanced several hundred
yards towards our group, when a storm of
rifle fire erupted nearby. I thought:
'We're done for; they've spotted us, and
are blanketing us with fire.'"

Two resourceful members of our group came up with good advice—Mechlis, a teacher who had worked in the forest as a lumber surveyor, and Akiva, a merchant who had traded with local peasants. They proposed that we take the least likely route—through a big swamp. After walking through it for about eight miles, we would come to a dry island, Krasnaya Gorka, where we could hide.

Mechlis promised to guide us to our destination. I felt we couldn't waste a minute and ordered every man to carry whatever food he could in his pockets. The head quartermaster supervised the work. We finished quickly and everyone awaited the order. Then we freed the cattle and horses because we couldn't take them with us. We carried the children on our shoulders, along with guns, food, and equipment. Those carrying children went first, because the swamp became deeper and stickier from people walking in it. The strongest men and those carrying guns went last. We walked single file, so as not to leave many footprints.

At times we sank up to our navels. Later, the water became shallower. But in three hours we walked less than three miles. Then we saw drier ground ahead, where we stopped to rest. People fell asleep, despite the wetness and mud. The air was choking. We forbade speaking out loud. At dawn we decided to remain there, since we heard no more shooting. I decided to return to our camp with Mechlis, Asael, and two other volunteers to see what was doing there. Guards were posted in shifts. Akiva was given orders to lead the group out if it became necessary.

Instead of going through the swamp, we walked slowly and cautiously along a path that Mechlis found, approaching the road where the Germans were supposed to appear. Mechlis checked for tire tracks to figure

out when the road had been used. Since he found none, we set out again, our spirits rising. Had the danger passed? Then we heard the whistle of a shell exploding and noted the direction of the firing.

We hit the ground and crawled between bushes. Then—another shell, and another. A large gun was firing continuously—undoubtedly from a tank directed at our camp and at the Pervomayskaya [Soviet] brigade. The shells exploded close to us, near our bushes.

We lay there for about twenty minutes, until the guns fell silent. I was sure the Germans were beginning to advance after the barrage, since they were only a mile away. We quickly advanced several hundred yards towards our group, when a storm of rifle fire erupted nearby. I thought: "We're done for; they've spotted us, and are blanketing us with fire."

We flattened ourselves on the ground. We could make out voices in Belorussian: "Hurrah, get the Jews! Get the animal. Get it, get it." They were storming our abandoned camp. We were so close we could hear the crack of dry twigs under the feet of the Germans and the police, but we couldn't see a thing—the forest was that thick. I realized that they were shouting in order to scare us, in case we were lying in ambush. The local police went in first; the Germans, as usual, went in last.

We ran back to our group. They were in a panic, lying on the ground, crowded together and quivering in fright. It was a terrible sight. We decided not to reveal the full gravity of the situation. We had to give them courage, because things were really bad. We roused them to move out, silently, going further away from the danger. Once more we walked into the swamp, sinking in the high grass, where only the tallest among us were visible. This was good, making it possible for us to move during the day.

Then the swamp became even deeper. We had no more strength to continue. We hadn't eaten enough; Everyone chewed on pieces of bread, dried peas, grains of barley or rye. The children didn't ask for food. They were hungry, but they didn't yell and didn't cry.

We didn't reach another dense part of the forest until evening. There we rested. I undid the strap of my submachine gun and attached it to my pants belt. Sitting down next to a tree, I tied myself to it and dozed off. Others did the same, tying themselves to tree trunks. Some climbed up into the trees. That's how we spent the night.

It was pleasant in the morning and we walked north. We got into some very deep water and it was nearly impossible to survey the end of our column. We feared that people would be lost. Several yards later we climbed onto dry land, a delightful hill called Krasnaya Gorka.

When we did a head count, there were six people missing, including two children. Three men set out to find them and were gone for a day. Towards evening they returned with the six; they had fallen behind from exhaustion. One man carried the two children himself.

Later we learned that our safety was tenuous. A few miles away Germans lived in empty forest ranger houses. But at the time we felt far from the enemy. They would not cross the swamps, and as for coming from other directions—the distance was too great. To the north there was a very deep body of water, impassable without a bridge.

We began to tend to our clothing and underwear. The rain had passed and the sun was warm. We sprawled on the grass. Despite our gnawing hunger, the joy of being safe strengthened us. But the German manhunt in the forest was still in full force and it was impossible for us to move. We set up guard duty around the perimeter since we would have to camp there for many days. The noise of German artillery in the forest continued from morning to night. We ate mushrooms, blackberries, and grain seeds that we had put in our pockets. A few people had peas; some had handfuls of flour from the camp, which our doctors distributed to the elderly and the children.

As hunger increased, people weakened. Gunfire thundered close by; shells exploded. At night we could hear individual voices of the enemy in the distance. One night I sent Akiva and two others to Kleszczyce to find food. When they approached the village, it was lit up from the headlights of German army vehicles. Akiva returned empty-handed, but the information about the German troops was important.

Later we learned that there were thousands of Germans in the village that night. They rounded up all the farmers, shot the animals they couldn't take with them and burned the village. The farmers were transported to Germany. Only a few dozen escaped.

The Germans burned seventeen villages during this raid, hundreds of large farmhouses. and the Polish town of Naliboki. Their intention was to destroy the villages bordering the forests in order to make it impossible for partisans to find food and shelter in these villages and farmhouses.

*Soon after the raid the Germans retreated and Bielski's group left the island. The family camp grew steadily as the few surviving Jews from the area found refuge there. But there was a constant tug of war between the Soviet desire for control of all anti-Nazi forces, and Bielski's need for independence, so the Jewish fighters could protect their families in the family camp. Tuvia charmed the Russians and made his unit useful to them. He accepted Soviet command, cooperated with Panchenkov in joint military operations, and continued to accept additional Jews into his unit and protect them.*

*In 1944 the Soviets liberated the area. Asael was drafted into the Red Army and died in battle. At the end of the war Tuvia brought his unit to Novogrudok, where the Soviets supplied them with identification documents. In 1945 Tuvia and Zusya immigrated to Palestine and fought in Israel's War of Independence.*

*Soon after settling in Israel, Tuvia's memoir was published in Hebrew.*

*In 1955 they settled in Brooklyn, New York, and maintained close relationships with the survivors of the Family Camp who lived in the US. Tuvia was in the trucking business; Zusya had a fleet of taxis. Aron lives in Florida. Asael's widow, Chaya, lives in Israel. In 1986 Touro College established a scholarship in Tuvia's name. He died in 1987. In 1988 his remains were brought to Jerusalem and reburied with full military honors. He left an extended family of children, grandchildren, and descendants of the 1,200 Jews whose lives were saved by the Bielski brothers.*

Chaya Porus, one of six children, grew up in Swieciany, a small town fifty miles from Vilna. Her father, an educated man who owned a printing and bookbinding company, was a talented violinist and active Zionist. When the Germans occupied Lithuania in June 1941, all Jews were put into ghettos. Instead of studying medicine in France, Chaya joined a resistance youth group. When the Swieciany Ghetto was liquidated in April 1943, she fled to Vilna and joined a resistance unit led by Josef Glazman, a leader of the Betar Zionist youth movement. After learning of the murder of her entire family and most of the Swieciany Jews, Chaya escaped with the Glazman group to the nearby Narocz forest and joined the Jewish unit Nekamah [revenge] in a partisan brigade led by Fedor Markov. Nekamah derailed trains, sabotaged German weapons and food supplies, and spread information about mass extermination and active resistance to nearby ghettos and villages. It was eventually dismantled by the Soviets because they didn't tolerate independent Jewish fighting units. Chaya fought in the Markov brigade until liberation.

# "Since I Had a Gun I Was Accepted as a Partisan"

From the oral history of Chaya Porus Palevsky

I was a teenager when the Germans occupied our town and ordered all Jews to live in a ghetto. After the Germans killed 100 men in a nearby woods, we decided to do something. In our house, which had three bedrooms, two apartments, and two kitchens, we housed about fifty people, including runaways from Lodz and Warsaw. We shared our food with them and smuggled more [food] through the barbed wires strung around the ghetto.

Another house with a large library had a hidden hospital behind bookshelves that concealed a secret door leading to a room with beds and a special bath for sick people. My sister Rochel, a registered nurse, worked there day and night and was called the "angel of the ghetto." My parents also helped and I brought food to patients. If the Nazis knew about the hospital they would have liquidated the ghetto, because they were afraid of a typhoid epidemic.

One of the men in our house, Shika Gertman, a tall blonde educated man in his early twenties, organized a group to fight back. We were the first resistance group in our ghetto and eventually had about thirty members, mostly men in their late teens and early twenties and three or four women. But the *Judenrat* (Jewish Council) that ran the ghetto was against our youth group. When we asked for money to buy ammunition so we could fight in the ghetto or as partisans in the woods, they refused, fearing that the Germans would find out about us and kill everyone in the ghetto.

Soon our house became a meeting place for people who wanted to know about the war. We had a hidden radio in a small storage room in our cellar. There Gertman listened to the radio secretly. We shared war news with everyone, even the *Judenrat*. We knew when the Russians were losing and that made us really afraid that we would all be killed.

Outside the ghetto a group of Poles was working with the Germans, fixing ammunition and airplane parts. Our resistance members volunteered to work with the Poles to smuggle out ammunition and bullets. We collected a large arsenal that we hid in two pails in a nearby ruined house. This was September 1941.

*At the end of 1941 the Germans collected about 8,000 Jews from Swieciany and the vicinity and moved them to Poligon, which they said was a new camp. Chaya's family was sent back to Swieciany to work in a factory. Gertman and other resisters had remained in the ghetto and it soon filled up with Jews who had been hiding in nearby villages. Later they found out that the Germans had massacred all the Jews in Poligon, ordering them to dig their own graves before they were shot.*

After returning to the ghetto, Gertman and other resisters started working on their connections with the partisans in the Narocz forest, mainly Fedor Markov, a respected teacher from Swieciany who had taught Gertman. In March 1943 Gertman and twelve others left to join Markov. Gertman returned in April with two other partisans to bring the rest of us to Markov. They were there when [Jacob] Gens (the head of the Vilna *Judenrat*) arrived with ten Jewish policemen and announced that the Swieciany ghetto had to be liquidated, since the *Judenrat* didn't want Jews to be associated with

Soviet partisans in the area. We would be sent to Kovno or Vilna. We didn't think about being killed.

My family was assigned to Kovno. Since I was extremely sick at the time, I refused to leave. But my mother said if I didn't go she would stay with me and we would both be killed. Then Gertman and a friend carried me seven miles to the train station. Just as we were boarding the train to Kovno, Gertman said, "I have a bad feeling, Chaya. Jump! Please jump!" When he jumped I fell down, out of the train, and Gertman picked me up and we moved away from the railroad.

### Arrival in Vilna

When we arrived on April 5th I found out that everyone on the Kovno train—including my whole family—was killed [in Ponar] by the Nazis. I couldn't move or cry. Later I went to a concert and heard a violinist who played the same song that my father had played. I closed my eyes, saw my father and cried hysterically. I couldn't stop and cried through the night.

In Vilna we met with Abba Kovner (p. 108) to learn about Vilna's underground group. Gertman, who had been with Markov, wanted to return to the forest with others as a Jewish group, but Kovner wanted to stay and fight in the Vilna Ghetto. By the end of May 1943, we decided to organize our own group.

Left: Prewar photo of the Porus family. Chaya is second from left. Above: Chaya's sister Rochel, a nurse, called the "angel of the ghetto," was murdered in Ponar. Chaya was given her belongings and took her blouse with her to the forest.

A *zemlyanka,* a primitive, camouflaged, dugout partisan dwelling in the forest, that provided some protection from the elements and could not be detected from afar.

Vilna underground, UPO] had just committed suicide (p. 109). Because there now seemed to be no way of staging a rebellion in the ghetto, Kovner [who took over Wittenberg's role] and the other resisters were planning to escape to the forest.

A week later, on July 24, Glazman led out our group of about twenty-five people. All of us carried guns and bullets. One fellow, Itzke Potskevits, wore bullets around him on two big bandoleers under an overcoat; the bandoleers were so heavy that he could barely walk. On the way to Narocz a few newcomers joined us. We told them to destroy their [identification] documents and memorize the route so that if we were ambushed they could go to the woods on their own without their identities being detected.

A group then went to Ponar to collect belongings from the Jews who had been slaughtered there. One woman brought me a package from my sister Rochel containing the the blouse that I had embroidered with her initials and given to her for her last birthday. There was also a towel, a coat, and a family album. I left the album with friends and took the blouse. I would not part with it. I would take it to the woods with me.

*In May, Chaya left Vilna with a group of about forty young Jews. It took them about nine days to reach the Jewish partisan group led by Markov in the dense Narocz forest, about ninety miles east of Vilna.*

Markov welcomed the men, but he didn't want women in the group. Since I had a very small Belgian gun with seven bullets that fit into a purse, and I knew how to use it, I was accepted. Another woman, Rochele, returned to the Vilna Ghetto to get a gun.

When we told Markov that in the Vilna Ghetto there was a large group of armed youth who wanted to join him, he gave us a letter for Gens that I hid in my boots or my bra. Then he sent three of us to Vilna to get the group. When we arrived, everyone was in mourning, because Itzik Wittenberg [commander of the

### Night Turns to Day

It was a beautiful quiet night and we started walking. But when we crossed the Viliya River at Vileika we were fired on from all sides. Night turned to day. We told the group behind us to run back to the woods. My hat was shot off and I got down on all fours and crawled into the woods. A few of us found each other and we stayed put for several days until we found more members of our group. Later we learned that some newcomers were captured by the Germans, taken to Vilna, and shot. The Nazis also killed the neighbors and families of those who had forgotten to destroy their ID papers. Our trip back to Markov's base took around ten days. Soon other Jewish groups joined us and we proposed to lead a Jewish unit with the name Nekamah (revenge).

"You should be proud," said Markov. "You are young and very brave people."

We started to build our underground bunkers, called *zemlyankas.* Everyone helped. Our *zemlyanka* was about 200 square feet, supported by small trees chopped from the woods. We made beds from straw and in the middle of a room put a stove that we took from a village. It kept us warm during the winter. We camouflaged the top of the bunker with leaves and branches and made a hole to enter. Twenty people lived in the large bunker. There were smaller bunkers for ten people and one for sick people. There were also bunkers for families who had escaped.

We had a good relationship with Markov, but there was a high ranking commissar from Moscow who said there could not be a Jewish fighting unit. The Jews could only remain together as a support unit and work behind the lines for the Soviets.

The Soviets took our ammunition and gave it to Polish and Lithuanian partisans. The Soviets also took our jewelry, good clothing, leather coats, and boots.

To keep our morale high, we decided to keep our group of ninety people together and fight any way we could. Gertman and I and eight others were sent to Linkmenys near Swieciany to burn an electric station. We stayed in a peasant's house about 500 yards from the station. That night I dreamt that our group was surrounded and I heard shots. When I woke up I learned that three people had been killed; Gertman had been wounded and shot himself to avoid being captured by the Nazis. We promised ourselves that when we were liberated, we would bury the corpses in Swieciany.

When we returned to Markov's brigade, Nekamah was dissolved. I remained as a nurse on the base. I bandaged wounded partisans and took them to a field hospital where a doctor examined them and gave them medicine that was dropped by parachute from Russian planes. We used a small airport that the Germans couldn't use because it was surrounded by partisans.

## Women Had a Hard Time

Once two of our women were sent on a special mission with a Soviet parachute group. When they returned, they had syphilis and said they had been raped. We paid a peasant to keep them in his house and give them penicillin so the syphilis wouldn't spread, They recovered and led normal lives after the war.

Women were assigned to cook and serve food, do laundry, and keep the bunkers clean. We tried to eliminate lice, that were all over, and to keep morale high. On some evenings we sang around the fire and read poems to keep our hopes alive. Even in the woods, you fall in love with each other. My husband, Simon, and I are an example. He lost his family; I lost my family and we were looking for more closeness.

We all told stories from our past and talked about our future wishes. We hoped that we would find our families. We hoped there would be no more wars, especially for the Jews, and we hoped to spread the words of unity and peace, to be able to fight against bigotry for ourselves and our own people.

Then the Soviet commander left without taking any Jews. There were about eighty-five of us and we didn't have enough ammunition [to survive]. We did not know where to go until a young boy told us how to go through marshes to reach a small island. Germans wouldn't go there because they were afraid of getting stuck in the mud.

When we got to the island, we were starving and didn't have any food. One of the babies died. Then a cow suddenly appeared! A live cow! Two butchers in our unit killed the cow, cut it in pieces, and grilled it on the fire. We lived on the meat until we received a summons to return to Markov's base. When we arrived everything had been burned by the Nazis and we had to rebuild all the bunkers.

I wasn't physically wounded but I was wounded mentally. I was a fighter but I was not only fighting the Germans but sometimes my Russian male comrades, who assumed that they could do whatever they wanted with women. One night our [Russian] commander asked me to sleep near him. Looking straight in his face, I spit on him. He was so surprised that that he expelled me and I went to another bunker. Simon also left. I was soon recalled to my unit and the commander was dismissed. But not all women could refuse the commanders. In contrast our Jewish boys respected us and never touched us unless we wanted them to. They protected us.

*In 1944 Chaya and Simon were liberated by the Soviets. In 1946 they immigrated to New York City where Simon's cousins took them in. Simon and Chaya opened a jewelry business. They had two sons and were active in finding jobs for Holocaust survivors and in various Yiddish cultural organizations. Simon died in 2003. Chaya lives in New York City.*

The Germans occupied Belgium on May 10, 1940. Six months later they confiscated Jewish assets, registered the Jewish population, and began to isolate them. The Jewish Community Council was replaced with a Nazi-appointed Jewish Council. In late 1941 left-wing Jewish political leaders teamed up with the national Belgian resistance movement. In Brussels the Committee for the Defense of Jews (CDJ) was formed and local Jewish defense committees were set up in Liége, Antwerp, and Charleroi. The CDJ produced false identification papers, obtained funding, published clandestine newspapers and propaganda, administered communal aid, and provided help for Jewish partisans who worked in the city. These partisans were involved in armed activities against German targets. They also identified and eliminated Jewish informers, destroyed records of the Jewish Council containing deportation lists, and fought manufacturers who were working for the Germans. To sabotage the German war machine, they set fire to German-run factories, attacked German army garages, executed Nazis and their collaborators whom the CDF found guilty, and stopped a deportation train, freeing hundreds of deportees. Jacob Gutfreund, a Polish-Jewish refugee, organized and commanded one of three groups of Jewish partisans in Brussels.

# Armed Struggle in Belgium

Adapted from a memoir by Jacob Gutfreund

One of CDJ's most important and difficult endeavors was hiding Jewish children in safe havens, a complicated task that involved establishing contact with Belgian institutions, children's homes, churches, Catholic clergy, and hundreds of Belgian families. Secrecy was mandatory: Mothers were not even allowed to know the names and addresses of the institutions or families hiding their children.

Fortuitously, these rescue efforts began at the end of 1941—six months before deportations from Belgium started up in August 1942—allowing the CDJ to rescue 3,000 children from certain death.[1]

In some instances, partisans took individual initiative. When Paul Halter learned that the Gestapo was planning to raid a church where nineteen Jewish children were hidden, he had no time to contact his partisan commander. Instead, he immediately mobilized his partisan group, entered the church, and evacuated the children. Partisans then found temporary refuge for the children with trusted Belgian families. Later that day the Gestapo arrived at the church to seize the children. They left with an empty truck. The CDJ subsequently found permanent homes for the children.

## Sabotage

In July 1942, the deportation decree became law, creating confusion and panic in the Jewish community. For Jews the burning question became whether to appear or not to appear at the collection point where they were ordered to assemble for deportation.

In response to these agonizing issues, Jewish underground organizations conducted a campaign *against* appearing for deportation, imploring people not to believe Jewish Council officials who told them that they were being sent to work. Instead, resistance members urged Jews to go into hiding. Even so, many hoped that by appearing voluntarily, they would save other members of their families from deportation, since the Germans threatened to punish an entire family if one member failed to obey a deportation order.

It was then that I met with partisan leaders Weichman and Rakower in a café in central Brussels. We discussed how to resist deportation and strike back at the Jewish Council for its traitorous role in providing Germans with the identities and whereabouts of Belgian Jews. We decided to raid Council headquarters and destroy the list of names and addresses that Jewish officials were planning to hand into the Gestapo. The next day two of our partisans, posing as German security agents, entered the Council building and, with drawn revolvers, gathered all officials into one room, ordering them to be quiet and not make a move. At the same time two other partisans equipped with bottles of gasoline slipped into the head office, poured gasoline on official documents and lists of names, and set them on fire.

## Convoy 20

*Deportations to concentration camps began on August 4, 1942. Most transports carried about 1,000 Jews. Jews who were not citizens of Belgium were deported first; by September 1943 Belgian Jews were deported as well. Most were murdered in Auschwitz.*

In the first five weeks 10,000 Jews were deported. Despite the secrecy surrounding these departures, Jewish partisans succeeded in learning that on April 19, 1943—the very first day of the Warsaw Ghetto uprising—a transport carrying 1,500 Jews was scheduled to leave for Auschwitz. Since partisans obtained this information at the very last hour, there was no time for the elaborate preparation needed to stop the transport. The CDJ and the partisans had to act quickly.

They enlisted the aid of Jewish partisans Georges Livshitz and his brother Alexander, both experienced in sabotage activities as members of the national Belgian partisan movement. The brothers went to the Tirlemont region with a group of partisans and, in the evening, took up positions on the railway line. As the train approached, Georges signaled the engineer with a red lantern. The train slowed down and came to a stop. Partisans rushed to the cars and pulled the doors open; 600 to 700 Jewish men and women jumped from the cars and ran in the direction of the nearby forest.

Germans shone their searchlights and opened fire on them, managing to kill more than twenty escapees. At the same time Germans pursued the fleeing group, capturing about 300. The other half—roughly 350 Jews—escaped safely. Eight wounded Jews were taken by the Germans to the Tirlemont hospital.

The CDJ was determined to save these eight Jews from being deported. On May 2, 1943, three automobiles left Brussels for Tirlemont. One was a Red Cross car that had been stolen for this operation. When they arrived at the Tirlemont hospital, two groups of partisans forced their way in, overpowered the guards, tied them up, helped dress the wounded, and exited quickly from the hospital, speeding away in the cars.

Georges Livshitz and other Jewish partisans stopped a deportation train.

The first car carried partisans armed with machine guns, to clear the way for the other two cars. As the cars approached the center of Tirlemont, their path was blocked by German police. Partisans in the first car opened fire, cutting the roadblock, and making it possible for the other two cars to escape through side streets.

The partisans sped off, leaving behind some German dead, abandoned their cars, and escaped to a nearby forest. The next morning they made their way safely back to Brussels. Unfortunately, however, one of the drivers was an informer. Some of the wounded were subsequently rounded up by the Nazis and deported.

*The attack on Convoy 20 is the only documented episode of partisans stopping a deportation train and freeing its prisoners. Georges and Alexander Livshitz were eventually executed in the Belgian camp Breendonk. In the course of his underground activities, Jacob Gutfreund was arrested by the Germans and deported to Auschwitz, where he managed to survive two years. In 1957, he immigrated to Israel and became a leader of the Organization of Partisans, Underground Fighters, and Ghetto Rebels in Israel.*

Prior to 1942 the Jewish Councils in most large ghettos discouraged armed rebellion against the Nazis because they believed it would lead to immediate annihilation. But as deportations increased and news of the death camps spread, young activists were motivated to determine their own fate through armed resistance. A week after the planned liquidation of the Warsaw Ghetto began on July 22, 1942, Zionist and socialist youth groups united to form the Jewish Fighting Organization (JFO/ZOB). By early October, 265,000 deportees from Warsaw had died in the gas chambers of Treblinka, reducing the original ghetto population to 60,000. As the decimation continued, the Bund and several Communist groups joined the JFO. When German troops entered the ghetto on January 18, 1943, armed Jewish fighters opened fire on them. The Nazis withdrew and discontinued the *Aktion*. As news of the successful rebellion spread to other ghettos, it inspired Jewish underground groups in more than ninety ghettos in Poland and Lithuania who had organized armed resistance units. Few Jews survived the ghetto revolts, but those who died did so for the honor and pride of future Jewish generations.

# Rebellion in the Ghettos

Accounts from the Warsaw, Bedzin, and Czestochowa Ghettos

### Warsaw: "A Jewish Defense in the Ghetto"

**W**hen the Nazis entered the Warsaw Ghetto on April 19, 1943, they were attacked by Jews armed with homemade Molotov cocktails, pistols, and grenades. The combat lasted for nearly a month, until Jewish fighters were burned out of their bunkers and hiding places by flamethrowers. Mordechai Anielewicz, the 23-year-old commander of the uprising, was killed in the command bunker at Mila Street 18 on May 8, 1943, when the Nazis attacked it with poison gas. By that time some of the underground leadership, including Yitzhak Zuckerman, had escaped through sewers to the "Aryan" side of Warsaw. This letter was written from Anielewicz to Zuckerman on April 23, 1943, and delivered clandestinely to Zuckerman in Warsaw. Zuckerman was a founder of the Ghetto Fighters Kibbutz (Lohamei Hagetaot) in Israel and died there in 1981.

Dear Yitzhak,

I have only one expression to describe my feelings and those of my comrades: Things have surpassed our boldest dreams. The Germans ran from the ghetto twice. One of our units held out for forty minutes; the other for more than six hours. The mine planted in the brushmakers' area exploded. We had only one casualty: Yehiel, who fell as a hero at the machine gun.

Yesterday, when we got information that the PPR (Polish Communist Party) attacked the Germans and that the [clandestine] radio station *Swit* broadcast a wonderful bulletin about our self-defense, I had a feeling of fulfillment. There is still a lot of work ahead of us but whatever has been done so far has been done perfectly.

We are now switching to guerrilla warfare: At night, three or four units go outside the ghetto on an armed reconnaissance patrol and to acquire weapons. We know the pistol has no value and we rarely use it. We need grenades, rifles, machine guns, and explosives.

Only a few individuals will hold out. All the rest will be killed sooner or later. The die is cast. In all of the bunkers where our comrades are hiding, you can't light a candle for lack of oxygen…. Of all units in the ghetto, only one man is missing: Yehiel. That too is a victory. I don't know what else to write. I imagine you have many questions. For now, be content with this.

The general situation: All the workshops in the ghetto and outside it have been closed, except for *Werterfassung* (SS enterprise for collecting Jewish property), Transavia, and Daring. I don't have any information about the situation in Schultz and Toebbens. Contact is cut off. The brushmaker's workshop has been in flames for three days. I have no contact with the units. Yesterday the hospital burned down. Blocks of buildings are in flames. The [ghetto] police force was dismantled, except for the *Werterfassung*.

Mieczyslaw Szmerling [commander of the Jewish police at the deportation point who survived an assassination attempt] has resurfaced. [Marek] Lichtenbaum [head of the *Judenrat* after Adam Czerniakow's suicide] has been released from the *Umschlag* (deportation point). Not many people have been taken out of the ghetto. But it is different in the shops. I don't have details. During the day, we sit in hiding places. Be well, my friend. Perhaps we shall meet again. The main thing is the dream of my life has come true. I've lived to see a Jewish defense in the ghetto in all its greatness and glory.

### The Underground in Bedzin

*After the Germans entered Bedzin in 1939, Zionist youth movements created an active Jewish underground that was ultimately in contact with the JFO in Warsaw. In May 1943 Bedzin Jews were moved to a ghetto in the Kamionka suburb and resistance members began planning for armed revolt. When the final liquidation of the ghetto took place on August 3, 1943, resistance fighters held out for two weeks. Frumka Plotnicka, a courier sent by the JFO in Warsaw, fell in battle. Bedzin deportees played a major role in the Auschwitz underground and uprising. Below is an excerpt from a memoir by Aaron Brandes, a Bedzin fighter.*

Immediately after the first *Aktions* in 1942 we had thought constantly of resistance, but we were isolated by the indifference of the Polish population and even the indifference and refusal of our fellow Jews. Since it was impossible to get arms in Zaglembie, we sent Edzia Pesachson to Warsaw. She returned with a courier, Astrid. They brought pistols and grenades, but were arrested at the Czestochowa train station. Astrid escaped

# "I've lived to see a Jewish defense in the ghetto in all its greatness and glory."

Left: Prewar photo of Mordechai Anielewicz, the leader of the Warsaw Ghetto uprising.
Above: Zionist youth, Bedzin, Poland.

but Edzia, who had three pistols and grenades, was imprisoned, tortured severely, and shot for not revealing her contacts.

Astrid continued to bring us arms from Warsaw, always evading checkpoints. Using the grenades and Molotov cocktails that she brought us as models, we began making our own. At night we began building bunkers [to hide weapons, supplies, and food]. Comrades were stumbling with weariness, but we continued to build. We were getting ready.

Then Rivka Glantz, from Kibbutz Dror in Czestochowa, brought us a letter from a Dror member who was working in Treblinka, sorting clothes from Jewish prisoners. "Every day I see them bringing thousands of Jews here, and the next day they are no longer alive," he warned us. "I see my people being destroyed. Do whatever you can, but don't let them send you here—to kill you with poison gas!"

After the deportation of 7,500 people in July 1943, the attitude of the Jews changed; even the attitude of the Judenrat changed. The atmosphere was similar to that in Warsaw in January 1943 [after the first act of armed resistance]. Our comrades in Warsaw wrote to us: "If you want to do something, you have to organize an action that will surpass that of Warsaw. The *Judenrat* knew it was the last in Zaglembie. If members were destined to die with the remnant of Zaglembie Jewry, they were obligated to help us.

In the Kamionka Ghetto, located near the new railroad station, one could hear screams splitting the stillness of night: *Shema Yisrael* (Hear, O, Israel), Help us! These were the screams of the condemned. Over 100 people were crowded into one cattle car. Many died on the way. But it was not permitted to remove the corpses; they remained among the living until trains arrived at the death camps. [By then] Jews were so broken and demoralized that they were incapable of any action, let alone escape. Our comrade Herschel Springer said that when the Germans sent a convoy of 2,000 Jews from Bedzin to Auschwitz, he tried to convince them to escape. If they all started running, the Gestapo would probably kill 200 to 300 people, but many could get away. No one listened to him. They were so despondent that death seemed like a salvation.

After the liquidation of the Warsaw Ghetto [in May 1943], arms shipments stopped. So our female couriers went to Warsaw and bought arms by themselves. Zvi [a male liaison] knew a Jew named Tarlow, who lived as an "Aryan" on the "Aryan" side of the city. For a fee he helped make some arms. Ina Gelbard, and sometimes Renia Kokalka, also brought arms from Warsaw.

In the last week before the [August 1, 1943] deportation, Ina traveled to Warsaw to bring pistols and grenades, to send comrades to partisan units near Krakow that were led by a Polish captain. At the border station, she was caught. She escaped to Kamionka and was caught again. She escaped one more time. With no place to go, no money or documents, hungry and exhausted, she arrived in Zawierce, where Jews still lived, and went to a comrade She had just managed to wash her face and was lying down to rest when the police arrived, arrested her, and turned her over to the Gestapo. They executed her.

## Czestochowa: With Arms in Hand

*In Czestochowa the first acts of armed resistance occurred during the* Aktion *on January 4, 1943. Jews were ordered to gather in the marketplace and when resistance members arrived late, they were arrested. One member, Fishelevitz, shot a German lieutenant with his pistol; Feiner attacked another with his knife. Twenty-five Jews were shot in retaliation. The remaining 300 Jews, including the resistance fighters, were transferred to Radomsk to wait for deportation. Some tried to escape before the deportation began, but only one woman succeeded. Below is an excerpt from an account by Leiber Brenner, a teacher and Bund activist, who survived.*

**February 1943.** The first grenades are ready. The fighters' eyes glitter. But doubt begins to eat at their hearts—the grenades are untested! "We have to test the grenades!" Members sneak out to Meirov behind Czestochowa. They test the explosive power of the grenades, and bring good news the next day, encouraging everyone. Until now they felt themselves suspended over a terrible, bottomless pit. Now they have a source of support. "From now we will no longer go to the trains like obedient sheep to the slaughter! We'll sabotage bridges, we'll remove bolts from railroad tracks, we'll explode army and ammunition trains, we'll kill the German criminals, and we'll get caught with arms in our hands!" These are now the dreams of our

Zionist youth from Czestochowa, Poland.

Jewish fighters. They work with increased energy, training a Jewish fighting unit for specific tasks. They steal aluminum, lead, carbide, mercury, dynamite, and other chemicals needed to make the grenades, from ammunition factories and other work places. They smuggle it all into the ghetto in vats from the ghetto kitchen.

Other fighters dig underground tunnels. The opening of the most important tunnel is outside the ghetto in the old marketplace. The opening of the second stretches into an empty field. There are openings from the tunnels to various houses. Entrances and exits are well camouflaged and there is no danger of detection. People work in two shifts, 100 people per shift, including teenagers.

**June 25, dawn.** All are mobilized in the tunnels. The largest group is in tunnel number one, where the ammunition supply is stored: tens of pistols, tens of grenades, two rifles, Molotov cocktails, carbide lamps, and even German army uniforms. They distribute arms to all the groups and take roll calls. In tunnel number one Marek Folman from the JFO in Warsaw is in command. All faces are serious. Everyone clearly recognizes the gravity of the situation. They know what is imminent and they are ready for the events that will occur.

Messengers from groups that are already in the forests participate in the roll call. A representative of the fighting groups in Upper Silesia is also present. People recall resisters who have died. Marek tells of the brave fighters in the Warsaw Ghetto. He gives instructions and calls for fighting until the last bullet. People are moved by his descriptions and filled with admiration for the brave Warsaw heroes.

Every fifteen minutes the reconnaissance scouts bring news from the ghetto. At the moment the ghetto is quiet. At 3 pm all scouts report that workers are returning from work as usual. Nothing suspicious. The mobilization is cancelled. One by one the fighters leave the tunnels. Only the command remains in tunnel number one: commander [Moitek Silberberg], who is ill, and Lutek Glickstein, who is guarding the ammunition supply. Silence in the ghetto. The fighters do not realize that it is the calm before the storm.

An hour later, fierce machine gun fire is heard in the ghetto, announcing the entry of the Gestapo and Security Police. On Nadrzeczna Street, 86, 88, and 90, the crucial points for the Jewish Fighting Organization, are surrounded and bullets rain on them. Blood is spilled in the streets. Members of the JFO, who only an hour ago had left the tunnels, rush to return. They quickly grab their arms to pay in blood, death for death! But they are shot before they get to the tunnels.

The Germans throw grenades into the tunnels; they murder the small group of fighters, who stand in desperate opposition. Other Jews, who live at the above addresses, also fall. Thirty grenades, eighteen pistols, and two rifles fall into German hands. Only Lutek, who guarded the arms, manages to escape. Moitek kills himself at the last minute rather than fall into their hands alive. The Germans take revenge on his corpse and shove him head-down into the tunnel. The only fighters who remain alive are those in the tunnel whose entrance is at 40 Nadrzeczna Street. This entire group holes up in house number 17 in the old market. Here they wait, with their few arms, for the enemy.

**June 27, morning.** The entire group leaves and take their arms to fight with comrades in the forests. Only six remain under the command of Rivka Glantz. They are attacked by the security police and Gestapo. They fight a bitter battle of self-defense, using only two pistols and one grenade. They wound one Gestapo agent and one policeman. After using up their ammunition, the six fighters continue the battle, throwing stones at the Germans, until they are all killed.

On December 8, 1941, poison gas was used to kill Jews in Chelmno in western Poland. Three more death camps were soon set up: Belzec, Sobibor, and Treblinka. Majdanek, a labor camp, and Auschwitz-Birkenau also became major killing centers. Most Jewish deportees were sent immediately to the gas chambers, often camouflaged as "showers." A small number were forced to work as *Sonderkommando* at gas chambers and crematoria. They were murdered regularly and replaced with new arrivals. A few prisoners worked in technical or maintenance jobs needed to run the camp. All inmates could be killed for the slightest infraction of the rules. Anticipating their own deaths, prisoners in three death camps organized revolts, miraculously rising up and killing some guards. In Auschwitz-Birkenau Jewish prisoners were in contact with the Polish underground, but did not get the assistance they hoped for. Yet they blew up one crematorium and damaged two others. In Treblinka and Sobibor almost all prisoners were Jewish; they were on their own. Most Jews who participated in these three rebellions were killed; a few dozen escaped from Sobibor and Treblinka.

# Death Camp Uprisings

## Accounts from Sobibor, Treblinka, and Auschwitz-Birkenau

### Sobibor: Rebellion and Escape

*From the testimony of Alexander Pechersky*

n late June, 1943, a transport of 600 prisoners arrived in Sobibor. They were the last Sonderkommando of the Belzec death camp, sent to Sobibor to be gassed. A note found in their clothing warned prisoners: "Know that death awaits you, too."[1] The prisoners realized that Sobibor would cease operations and they, too, would be gassed. Leon (Baruch) Feldhendler, a rabbi's son and resistance leader, had tried to plan an uprising, but he was unsuccessful. On September 23, 1943, eighty Soviet Jewish POW's arrived from Minsk. The arrival of a cohesive group with military experience raised the morale of the Sobibor prisoners. Feldhendler approached Lt. Alexander Pechersky, an officer in the Soviet Army. Impressed by his bearing and his experience, Feldhendler asked Pechersky to organize and command an uprising and escape.

One week after I arrived at Sobibor, I knew everything about its hell. Camp No. 4 was on a hill; each section was surrounded with barbed wire and was mined. I was informed of the exact place occupied by the personnel, the guards, and the arsenal. Our group of eighty men was led to camp No. 4. I was working near Shlomo [Leitman]; another prisoner [whom he knew from a labor camp in Minsk]. He approached me and whispered, "We have decided to escape; there are only five SS officers, and we can wipe them out. The forest is near."

I replied, "Easier said than done; the five officers are not together. When you finish with one, the second shoots at us; and how shall we cross the minefields? Wait, the time is near."

At night, Baruch [Feldhendler] told me, "It is not the first time that we have planned to finish with Sobibor, but very few of us know how to use arms. Lead us, and we shall follow you." I asked him to assemble a group of the most reliable prisoners.

**October 7:** I gave Baruch instructions on digging a tunnel [through the barracks to the outside]. It would take fifteen to twenty days. But the plan had weak spots: Between 11 pm and 5 am 600 people had to file through the thirty-five yards of the tunnel and run a significant distance from the camp to avoid the SS posse. I said, "I also have other ideas; meanwhile, let us prepare our first arms: seventy well-whetted knives or razor blades." Baruch said that the *kapos* [prisoner trusties] were interested in our plans and could be very helpful, since they could move freely in the camp. I also thought their help was vital.

**October 14:** At 3:20 pm Geniek came to [Boris] Cybulski's barrack with Shlomo [Stanislaw Szmajzner] and two others. Two officers were killed by [Arkady] Weisspapier in the shoemakers' barrack while Jacob [Boskovich] was giving them boots. At 4 pm I met Luka, the Dutch girl, [Pechersky's girlfriend] and told her: "The officers will soon be dead; be ready to escape." As she trembled, I added, "What we are doing is the only way to survive; we have no right to give up living, we must avenge ourselves."

At 4:15 pm I heard that Cybulski, Michael, and Baruch had accomplished their mission at camp No. 2. At 4:30 Brzecki, a sympathetic Kapo, returned from camp No. 4 with the commando and the SS lieutenant. Soon Gaulatisch arrived. Shlomo told him, "We have done the repairs in the barracks; now workers don't know what to do." Gaulatisch went in; Shlomo's hatchet awaited him.

Later we learned that the SS officer Ryba had been killed in the garage. Now it was vital to leave; Brzecki whistled and prisoners were directed to camp No. 1 in a disorderly way. This infuriated the guard; he was killed with an axe.

A new group from camp No. 2 entered camp No. 1, where prisoners were just learning what was happening. A Ukrainian guard began to shoot; a mighty "Hurrah" was heard. "Forward! Forward!" shouted the prisoners. They were running towards the gate, shooting with rifles, cutting barbed wire with pliers. We crossed a minefield and many lost their lives. My group marched towards the SS barracks and several of us were killed. Between the camp and the forest there was an immense clearing; here, too, many fell.

Fifty-seven escapees finally reached the forest and walked two miles, where they found other prisoners. They built a bridge with tree trunks to cross a canal; they reached a railway and posted sentries as lookouts, hiding under trees during the day. After another three miles they reached the forest and split into small groups of five or six people.

We set off eastwards at night, guided by the stars. We hid during the day. Our goal was to cross the Bug River. We approached villages to beg for food and ask our way. We were often told, "Prisoners escaped from Sobibor, where people are being burned; they are looking for fugitives."

We reached Stawki, a mile from the river. At sunset three of us entered a hut. A 30-year-old peasant was gathering tobacco leaves; an old man was near a stove. In a corner, a young woman was rocking a baby's cradle, hung from the ceiling.

We said we were escaped war prisoners and wished to return home. At last the young man responded, "I will show you the direction, but I won't go with you. The river is guarded

Alexander Pechersky

everywhere, since prisoners escaped from a camp where soap is made with human fat. The fugitives are being chased, even underground. I wish you luck."

"Take some bread for the way," said the young woman. We thanked them and the old man blessed us with the sign of the cross.

That night, October 19th, we crossed the Bug. On the 22nd, we met a unit of partisans of the Voroshilov detachment. A new chapter began.

*In the revolt, most of the SS staff of Sobibor were killed by the rebels. About 300 of the 600 prisoners broke out and reached the forests. The Nazis shot about 100 escapees; others were killed by local Poles. Pechersky and some Soviet POWs managed to survive with partisan groups. After the war Pechersky returned to Rostov, his hometown, where he lived until he died in 1990.*

### Treblinka: Uprising of the Doomed
*From the oral history of Richard Glazar*

*Twenty-two-year-old Richard Glazar escaped from Prague to a remote Czech village, where he hid. Discovered there in 1942, he was sent to Terezin, and then to the Treblinka death camp. He was selected to work and assigned to the camouflage unit, cutting branches in the forests around the camp that were used to disguise the perimeter fence so the camp would not be detectable.*

Richard Glazar's forged identity card that he used to work as a "volunteer" Czech laborer after escaping from Treblinka.

Treblinka was very small. Since I worked in several *Kommandos* [labor units], I knew Treblinka well. Prisoners often tried to escape on their own or in groups. Most of them were caught and killed in a horrible way. They hung them naked between two trees in public. After one attempted escape, SS Lieutenant Kurt Franz executed an entire *Kommando* and told us that for every person who tried escaping in the future, ten people would be executed. After this, individual escapes stopped and we thought instead about a common action or a revolt. The first common action occurred in November 1942, when we sent two men outside, hidden in a load of clothing from prisoners.

They were to join the Polish underground and let the world know what was going on in Treblinka. We had different ideas but we always had to postpone them. It took us from December 1942 until August 1943 to succeed. This involved a young boy from Warsaw named Edek. He was allowed to go into the SS barracks because he played the accordion. He was given the job of putting a small metal chip into the lock of the door of the munitions storage units. When the door wouldn't open, the SS called prisoners from the work unit, including a *schlosser* (locksmith). The workers said they would have to take the door to the shop.

The uprising had to take place on a Monday because on Monday prisoners had to clean up the SS barracks; under the litter they were able to hide guns and grenades from the munitions store. On Monday, August 2nd, we succeeded. But the revolt was not a heroic one, in my view. It was an act of desperation. We set fire to the SS barracks; we didn't capture the towers, guarded by Ukrainians, who defended them strongly.

Some 450 people were involved in the revolt: about 250 from the first section of the camp, and 200

from the second section, where the gas chambers were located. The gas chambers were the only buildings made of masonry; all other barracks were made of wood and they were all burning.

I did not have a gun. I just had an axe. We attacked the Ukrainian barracks. Fifteen minutes later we got the order to escape. We passed through the barbed wire fences while guards shot at us. But my friend Charles Unger and I knew the outskirts and jumped into a pond. We hid in the water, under branches of trees, for about eight hours.

When we got out, Treblinka was still burning. While we were hidden Germans were canvassing the entire area with a plane and dogs. It was lucky that we had been in the water [where dogs could not trace their scent].

We fled to the Moravian border where we knew there were partisans. We traveled mainly at night and hid in the woods during the day. Then 250 miles west of Treblinka, we were captured by Poles and turned over to the police. We said we were Czechs who had been sent to work in Poland and, on the way, were held up by partisans, tortured, and captured. We were sent to Germany to work in a factory.

*Glazar and Charles Unger, using false Czech names, managed to survive for more than a year, working in a German factory in Manheim, as Czech "volunteer" labor. They maintained their false identities and survived Allied bombings. In March 1945, while searching for food and supplies in bombed out buildings, they were captured by American soldiers. Glazar convinced them that he was Jewish by reciting some blessings in Hebrew. They were free.*

## Rebellion in Auschwitz
*From the oral history of Noach Zabludovits*

*Roza Robota and Noach Zabludovits belonged to the Hashomer Hatza'ir youth movement in Ciechanow, Poland. In 1942, they were deported to Auschwitz. Roza was assigned to the Birkenau death camp, sorting clothing adjacent to Crematorium IV, where the bodies of gas chamber victims were burned. Noach volunteered to do heavy labor in the main camp, where conditions were better. He became active in the Auschwitz underground composed initially of Polish prisoners. They began planning an uprising in early 1944. Noach contacted Roza.*

We knew for certain there was an anti-Nazi underground, but there were no Jews in it. We didn't know how to begin, to organize [in cooperation with the Polish underground]. [In March] I went to my friend Roza Robota and said, "Comrade Roza, I would like you to contact the women who work in the *Pulverpavilion* (gunpowder room) in the Union (munitions factory), and ask them to smuggle gunpowder into the camp." Roza agreed and organized a group of women to carry tiny amounts of gunpowder [in their clothing] and in matchboxes between their breasts. When they brought it into the camp, Roza placed it under the corpses on wagons that went to the crematorium. There the *Sonderkommando* took it.

And then, one day—this hurts terribly—the Germans murdered the *Sonderkommando* and changed the guard. The new *Sonderkommando* told me, "Noach, tomorrow we are rising up." I said it was impossible, because the command to revolt was supposed to come from the Armja Krajowa (Polish Home Army), who were supposed to join the prisoners after the first shot. Sons of dogs! Not one came. The Jews were all killed.

*In the revolt on October 7, 1944, crematorium II was exploded, crematorium III was burned, and a fire damaged the ceiling and roof of crematorium I. Four SS men were killed in hand-to-hand combat; others were wounded. The Germans put down the uprising with overwhelming force.²*

Investigators from Berlin planted a man in Birkenau as a "new prisoner" from Germany and gave him a Jewish [prisoner] insignia to find out how gunpowder got into the camp. He was told that a certain woman knew. The Germans took her and tortured her until she talked. Four women were arrested. [Despite repeated beatings, none revealed the names of Roza or her smugglers.]

In January, Moshe Kulka [a member of the underground] came to me and said, "Roza Robota is in the punishment bunker." Moshe took me inside where an SS officer was sitting and introduced me as his cousin. Then he took a bottle of liquor from the cupboard, filled three glasses, and signaled me not to drink. I offered liquor to the officer, who filled his cup again and again. Soon he was lying down, dead to the world. Yakov [the Jewish guard] took me to the cell.

From every door, from every corner, we heard cries in every language. "Yakov, help me! Yakov!" But Yakov, focused on his task, took me to Roza's cell and left me there until 2 am. It was the night before her death. She and the other prisoners were naked, without any blanket or cover. Condemned to die. I saw her body, cut from top to bottom.

"Noach," she said, hearing my voice. "How did you get here?"

"Don't ask. I'm here. Don't cry. At the last minute we'll get you out."

"Noach, you know what I did." She told me, as she lay on the floor, "Noach, bring my greetings to everyone."

Roza Robota

They hung her the next day. She sang *Hatikvah* before she died.

*Roza's last message was a note scratched on a piece of paper smuggled from her cell:* Chazak Ve'ematz (be strong and have courage). *She was twenty-three when she and Alla Gaertner, Estusia Wajcblum, and Regina Saperstein were hung on January 6, 1945, before Birkenau inmates. Noach died in Israel a few years ago.*

# On Blaming the Victim

*Eva Fogelman*

How could a highly civilized group of people so integral to Western culture be the victims of mass murder? Many of us look for answers not only by examining the perpetrators' behavior, but also by probing the behavior of the victims. Some people even blame the European Jews for cooperating in their own destruction. Yet innocent sufferers should claim our support and validation.

This is not a new bias. Beginning in Biblical times, victims of oppression have often been reproached. "Who ever perished, being innocent?" asked Job's friends. In current society, when a woman is raped, the act of questioning the woman's innocence dilutes moral outrage. She may be accused of making seductive overtures or of being in unsavory places with sleazy men, inevitably exposing herself to unnecessary risk. In cases of domestic violence, one spouse may be accused of inciting uncontrollable rage in the other spouse. And when physical violence leaves no visible scars, the victim is often not believed.

Similarly, Holocaust survivors often encounter not empathy, but emotional numbness and judgmental queries. According to Susan Sontag, many people are introduced to Nazi savagery through "a photographic inventory of ultimate horror." Yet, she says, "living with the photographed images of suffering...does not necessarily strengthen conscience and the ability to be compassionate.... Images transfix. Images anesthetize."[1]

The vivid testimony of death camp photographs compounded by the survivors' graphic details of the starvation and horrible living conditions they experienced in the camps, their near-death personal experiences, and the murder of loved ones, sometimes elicit inappropriate questions instead of empathy: "Why didn't you leave Germany after Hitler became chancellor, or after your business was boycotted, or after your property was confiscated?" Hungarian Jews who lost loved ones during the last year of the war are similarly challenged: "How could you not know, in 1944, what fate awaited you with the Germans on your soil?"

Many visual representations of Jewish life in the ghettos, concentration camps, hiding places, and escape routes depict Jews as passive victims. The famous image, taken by a German army photographer during the final liquidation of the Warsaw Ghetto in May 1943, shows a neatly-dressed boy holding his arms up, frightened and bewildered. He is amidst other Jews holding their worldly possessions, surrounded by armed soldiers. This indelible image reinforces the perception of Jews going "like sheep to the slaughter."

Since Germans took most existing photographs documenting the destruction of European Jews, it is not surprising that Jews are portrayed as victims. But why does this same passive image persist in many films about the Holocaust, where men, women, and children often appear as helpless victims and Germans appear as powerful persecutors?

With the exception of a few films that dramatize armed resistance, such as *Ashes and Diamonds*, *Samson*, *Last Stop*, and *Partisans of Vilna*, Jews are shown in deportation lines, or as naked and covering their genitals, waiting to be killed, as emaciated bodies in concentration camps, or as individuals dependent on non-Jewish rescuers.

Psychologist Bruno Bettelheim actually reprimanded Anne Frank's family for not having a gun with which to kill the police who arrested them.[2] How odd for Bettelheim, a German Jew, who was incarcerated in Buchenwald and Dachau for a year, to blame the victims! Upon his release, Bettelheim was ostracized by his family when they mistakenly assumed that he had been incarcerated for "outrageous crimes."

Strangely, Bettelheim rationalizes Nazi policies and violence, writing that Germans found it incongruous to live in a world without "law and order."[3] The bourgeois German population could not imagine that any government would act without law and order. The Nazis reinforced this view by insuring that all acts in Germany between 1933 and 1939 were "legal."

Bettelheim witnessed inmates who vacillated between identifying with the Gestapo and demonstrating the courage to resist. Although he admits that in the concentration camp system it was impossible to physically resist and remain alive, years later he concluded that inmates could have resisted by forming "democratic groups of resistance of independent, mature, and self-reliant persons, in which every member backs up, in all other members, the ability to resist."[4]

According to film historian Judith Doneson, Jewish victims of mass murder were criticized more acutely after Israeli warriors triumphed in 1948-49, 1956, and 1967. The challenge for Holocaust filmmakers, she argues, is to balance history and the unimaginable, history and psychological grief amidst terror.[5]

In Roman Polanski's 2002 film, *The Pianist*, a prominent Polish-Jewish pianist avoids deportation from Warsaw. Most other ghetto Jews are depicted as immoral, helpless, or in denial about the prospect of impending murder. The viewer is never shown the life-affirming resistance that existed in the Warsaw Ghetto, including the creation and maintenance of schools, soup kitchens, theaters, and political organizations.

Yet, sometimes, survival under conditions of extreme terror can most effectively be conveyed through films. Consider the scene in Steven Spielberg's *Schindler's List* (1993) where Jews in the Plaszow labor camp are assembled while the German commandant watches from a balcony, ready to shoot anyone whom he deems unfit for life. The viewer constantly feels the intensity of the thin line between life and death.

Ironically, victims sometimes blame other victims. Jews who managed to escape Germany before the outbreak of World War II often criticize Jews who did not escape for being short-sighted.

Although Jews who survived the war deserve awe as part of a "saved remnant," many were not even accorded respect in the communities where they sought refuge. Young Zionist leaders who left for Palestine in the 1930s were criticized by some ultra-Orthodox Jews for only saving their own kind.[6] Some Zionists, in turn, asked those who did not emigrate: "Why didn't you flee Europe?" Young men and women who escaped from ghettos to the woods and took up arms, like Abba Kovner, asked themselves: "Am I a hero in Israel? Or have I betrayed my mother?"

Shock at hearing about the Nazi atrocities might arouse sympathy. But sympathy is a kind of pity. It is not empathy. Survivors feel blame—not empathy—when asked, "How did you manage to stay alive?"[7]

What accounts for these attitudes that range from blame to sympathy to shock? By focusing on the victim, contemporary Jews, many of whom have been brought up to feel that they can do anything, often defend themselves against feelings of passivity and helplessness, feelings that are disparaged in our society. They avoid imagining themselves in an overwhelmingly dangerous situation and avoid confronting the question: What would I have done? And would I have survived? Instead, they focus on: What did "these people" do in order to survive such hell?

Many fantasies have emerged about Holocaust survivors. In Orna Ben-Dor's film, *New Land* (1994), a pregnant survivor has a medical check-up. As the woman exits she overhears the doctor saying to the nurse in Hebrew, "Her child is an offspring of an SS officer she slept with. That's how all the pretty women survived the concentration camps." The woman takes a hot iron and burns the number off her arm.

By now, it is commonly known that in the *Yishuv* (pre-state Israel), Holocaust survivors encountered an ambivalent reception. On the one hand, they were sought out to fight in Israel's War of Independence. But they also experienced suspicion, disdain, and isolation.

Many women were considered whores who had slept with Germans to survive; men were considered immoral because the "survival of the fittest" often depended on focusing on their own needs.

In America of the late 1940s and 1950s, anti-Semitism was still a significant force and McCarthyism was rampant. Many Jewish leaders feared that any attention drawn to the Jew as victim would result in increased contempt for all Jews. Thus, when *The Diary of Anne Frank* was performed on stage, the play was universalized by removing specific Jewish references. For example, the phrase, "Why do Jews suffer?" was changed to "Why do people suffer?" The Franks' Jewishness was also downplayed.

Another response was to portray Jews as heroes rather than victims, which complemented the new image of the Israeli soldier who had proven to be a triumphant warrior. Arnold Forster of the Anti-Defamation League exaggerated armed Jewish resistance during the Holocaust, noting that a million Jews were killed in armed struggle against the Germans.[8]

During the 1961 Eichmann Trial in Israel, some individuals in power blamed the survivor witnesses. Prime Minister David Ben-Gurion had conceived of this as a "historic trial," the purpose of which was to unite Israeli society by signifying that Israel was the only heir of the six million murdered Jews. The prosecutors, Jews who had settled in Palestine before 1939, created a climate of opinion that was described by the underground leader and partisan Abba Kovner: "Here in the air in this courtroom there hovers the question why they [the Jews] did not rise in revolt."[9]

Kovner testified that on January 1, 1942, he had called upon Jewish youth in the Vilna Ghetto to revolt in the well-known manifesto: "Let us not go like sheep to the slaughter....True, we are weak and defenseless, but resistance is the only reply to the enemy! Brothers! It is better to die as free fighters than to live by the grace of the murderers. Resist! To the last breath."

After Kovner's unforgettable testimony, the chief prosecutor Gideon Hausner asked: "Forty thousand Jews were taken away to Ponar [site of mass shootings outside Vilna]; why did they not rise [in revolt]?"

Kovner explained that one needed independent authority to organize. The underground group was only an internal movement "in a glass cell" surround-ed by Germans. "I saw desperate people committing suicide," he asserted. "I did not see desperate people who were also good fighters....I influenced people to die one hour earlier to sacrifice themselves for something that had meaning....[But] out of this despair an underground fighting organization existed."

Hausner's view—that Jews should have fought against all odds—was apparent after Moshe Bejski, who had been rescued by Oskar Schindler and who was to become an Israeli Supreme Court justice, testified about the hangings [of Jewish prisoners] in the Plaszow camp. In a harsh voice, Hausner challenged: "[You are saying that] 15,000 people [Jews] stood there, facing a few dozen or even hundreds of [Nazi] police. Why didn't you lash out, why didn't you rebel?"[10]

In response to Hausner's challenge, journalists and poets implored people to respond to survivors with humility, arguing that we should beg forgiveness from those who were judged. Survivors and victims alike could not have done other than what they did. Only after the trial did Hausner show empathy for the *she'er-it ha'pleta* (surviving remnant), warning others not to "find fault with those who did not revolt; [you can only] stand and wonder at the courageous spirit of those hundreds who resisted the enemy."[11]

The trial transformed the survivor from being "the other" to being "one of us" in Israeli society. Young Israelis interviewed after the Eichmann Trial felt that the trial enabled them to be less judgmental towards survivors and they acknowledged their important role in the War of Independence, since over half of the Israeli soldiers were Holocaust survivors.[12]

In America, however, some academics continued to charge that Jews had contributed to their own annihilation. Holocaust historian Raul Hilberg wrote in his introduction to *The Destruction of European Jewry (1961)*, "Insofar as we may examine Jewish institutions, we will do so primarily through the eyes of the Germans." After scrutinizing the Nazi machinery of destruction, he concluded that the *Judenräte* (Jewish Councils) caused mass killings by using "German euphemisms… to blot out visions of death." He accused Jewish victims of "plunging themselves physically and psychologically into catastrophe."[13]

Hannah Arendt, who covered the Eichmann Trial and subsequently published *Eichmann in Jerusalem,* also blamed European Jewish leaders for the demise of their Jewish communities and concluded that Jews had cooperated in their own destruction.[14]

Most scholars agree with historian Saul Friedlaender's more nuanced analysis of the role of Jewish leaders: "Objectively the *Judenrat* was probably an instrument in the destruction of European Jewry, but subjectively the actors were not aware of this function, and, even if they were aware, some of them—or even most of them—tried to do their best according to very limited strategic possibilities in order to stave off the destruction."[15]

A renewed fear of extermination in Israel during the two-week period prior to the 1967 Six Day War further broke down the "us" and "them" division between Holocaust survivors and *sabras* (native-born Israelis). Many Israelis, desperate to know how to cope with the fear of annihilation, asked survivors such questions as: What choices are possible under conditions of terror? How does one make life-affirming decisions in the face of terror and total destruction?

Israeli soldiers empathized with survivors as they compared their own plight with the desperate acts that many Jews performed during the Holocaust to survive. Faced with moral dilemmas during this terror-filled period, the Israelis realized that they too would have to do whatever was necessary in order to survive.[16]

Today, it is clear that resistance has to be understood in a broader context. As we have shown in the pages of this book, resistance could take many forms, only one of which was armed revolt. Indeed, in most instances armed revolt was suicidal and could lead to the death of other Jews. One must distinguish between a courageous act that could make a difference and a suicidal venture. One also has to understand the consequences of individual choices and their impact on the community. The real power of resistance is not only that it might succeed in defeating an oppressor, but that it can transform a nightmarish situation into one that has some semblance of meaning and hope.

Ghandi's voice of passive resistance empowered people in India to confront British colonialism and work towards independence. Will his voice be a moral authority for victims in this century? Or will resistance be futile? The real power of nonviolent resistance, whether it is cultural or religious or political, empowers the individual to live with hope instead of despair.

By blaming the victim, we lose any possibility of fathoming the psychological mindset of a person who lives under total terror. When we belabor victims with questions about why they didn't resist, we distance ourselves from them. After all, what choices are really possible in a genocidal state? Perhaps, instead, we should focus on the existential question of how one faces imminent death. How does one cope with everyday matters while living under constant threat? Blaming the victims not only distorts history; it also perpetuates their victimization.

Resisting an oppressive regime or an individual requires courage, the inner strength to withstand extreme anxiety, and the ability to imagine the possibility of survival. Many of us downplay resistance because we know we do not possess the abilities needed to resist, or we exaggerate the importance of resistance because we want to believe that we have the ability to control our own fate. Many Israeli historians have studied the dynamics of resistance because daily life in Israel is often filled with threatening situations. When American Jews in the 1940's felt insecure due to the persistence of anti-Semitism, they too exaggerated the degree of resistance during the *Shoah*. They did not want to feel helpless or show the world that they were weak victims.

The role of the Holocaust survivor in our society has been transformed from that of a person who was largely shunned to that of a person who often commands—indeed, demands—moral authority. But a dialectic continues to persist between the stereotype of victims and survivors who did not fight back and the examples of Elie Wiesel and other survivors who have become voices of moral conscience.

Our constant views of genocide and mass terror on television and computer screens may emotionally numb us from empathizing with the plight of the victims caught in these horrible situations. Too often we remain passive bystanders.

Although we may have limited options for combatting the oppression of others, we must mobilize our inner resources to do what we can and empathize with victims instead of either blaming them or ignoring them. Only by responding actively will we evolve from passive bystanders to resisters.

# GLOSSARY

**Aktion** (German: action) Roundups or violent attacks on Jews.

**Aliyah** (Hebrew: going up) Immigration to the Land of Israel. *Aliyah Bet* was the "illegal" immigration of Jews during and following World War II.

**Armée Juive** (French: Jewish Army) A Zionist resistance group in France that engaged in sabotage and armed resistance.

**Armija Krajowa** (Polish: Home Army, AK) Polish underground organization. Some AK partisan units were hostile to Jews and killed Jews they found in the forests. Most Jews who fought with AK units hid their Jewish identities.

**Armija Ludowa** (Polish: People's Army) Polish Communist underground organization that fought Nazis in Polish cities and forests. It provided some support for the Jewish underground in ghettos and included several Jewish partisan units.

**Betar** (Hebrew: initials of Brit Yosef Trumpeldor—Covenant of Joseph Trumpeldor) Youth movement of the Zionist Revisionist movement. Members fought with the FPO/UPO in Vilna and the Jewish Military Union (ZZW/JMU) in the Warsaw Ghetto uprising.

**Bund** (Yiddish: Union) Jewish socialist political party, very active in prewar Poland. Although anti-Zionist in its ideology, it cooperated with leftist Zionists in resistance activities during the Holocaust.

**FPO/UPO** (Yiddish: Fareynegte Partizaner Organizatsye/ United Partisan Organization) Jewish underground group established in the Vilna Ghetto in 1942. After trying unsuccessfully to mount an uprising in the ghetto, they fled to the forests and fought there as partisans.

**Generalgouvernement** (German: General Government) Area of Poland occupied by Germany but not incorporated into the Reich. It was organized into a separate administrative unit in October 1939 and included the Krakow, Warsaw, Radom, and Lublin districts and, after 1941, Galicia.

**Hachsharah** pl. Hachsharot (Hebrew: training, preparation) Agricultural training farms for young Zionists who planned to make *Aliyah*.

**Hashomer Hatza'ir** (Hebrew: Young Guard) Zionist Marxist youth movement whose members aspired to living in Israel. They stressed Socialism and the use of the Hebrew language; active in resistance activities.

*Hatikvah* (Hebrew: The Hope) The national anthem of Zionists that became the national anthem of Israel.

**Hechalutz** (Hebrew: The Pioneer) An umbrella organization of Zionist youth movements. All aspired to immigrate to Palestine and build kibbutzim; they were active in resistance activities. Hechalutz Hatza'ir (Young Pioneer) and Dror (Freedom), united in 1939 and often worked together.

**Judenrat** pl. Judenräte (German: Jewish Council) Jewish Councils were appointed by the Germans to administer ghettos and Jewish communities. Officials had to comply with German rules and risked death if they didn't carry out orders. They were responsible for the welfare of ghetto residents and, among other activities, they distributed food and shelter, created employment, supervised sanitation, maintained law and order, and set up schools and cultural events.

**Kibbutz** pl. Kibbutzim (Hebrew: Collective farm settlement in Palestine) Also a branch of youth movement members who planned to immigrate to the Land of Israel as a group to establish a settlement.

**Kiddush Hashem** (Hebrew: Sanctification of the Divine Name) Jewish martyrdom—dying because of your Jewish heritage—that originated with Rabbi Akiva and other Jews in the first century CE, who were killed because they would not abandon their Jewish faith.

**Kristallnacht** (German: Night of Broken Glass) Nazi attacks in Germany and Austria on November 9-10, 1938. Nazis burned, damaged, or destroyed about 1,400 synagogues, killed some 100 Jews, damaged thousands of Jewish shops, warehouses, and homes, and arrested more than 30,000 Jews, whom they sent to concentration camps.

**Maquis** (French) Resistance groups in France that included separate Jewish units; 15 to 20 percent of maquis were Jewish.

**Oyneg Shabbes/Oneg Shabbat** (Yiddish/Hebrew: Joy of Sabbath) Underground archives in the Warsaw Ghetto founded by the historian Emanuel Ringelblum. He recruited diverse writers to document Jewish life in Poland under the Nazis. The archives were hid before the ghetto was liquidated. Some material was retrieved after the war; parts were lost.

**Po'alei Zion** (Hebrew: Workers of Zion) Major Zionist movement of Jewish workers before 1939 that combined the principles of Jewish nationalism and socialism.

**PPR** (Polish: Polska Partia Robotnicza, Polish Workers' Party) Polish communist party 1942-1948.

**Reichsvertretung der Deutschen Juden** (German: Reich Representation of German Jews) Central Organization of German Jews, established in September 1933. It represented the full spectrum of German Jews to the Nazi authorities.

**Shema Yisrael** (Hebrew: Hear, O Israel) The basic affirmation of monotheistic Jewish belief in one god, recited in prayers three times daily. This prayer is also recited prior to death.

**Sonderkommando** (German: special unit) Groups of Jewish prisoners who were forced to work at the gas chambers and crematoria in the death camps.

**Tisha B'Av** (Hebrew) Ninth day of the Hebrew month of Av, a day of fasting and mourning commemorating the destruction of both Jewish Temples in Jerusalem as well as other catastrophes in Jewish history.

**Youth Aliyah** Zionist organization in Germany set up to help young adults and youth immigrate to the Land of Israel.

**ZOB/JFO** (Polish: Zydowska Organizacja Bojowa, Jewish Fighting Organization) Jewish underground armed group set up in the Warsaw Ghetto in 1942, with branches in other ghettos.

# ENDNOTES AND SOURCES

**DAVID ENGEL, pp. 10-16.**

1. Quoted in Karl A. Schleunes, *The Twisted Road to Auschwitz 1933-1939* (Chicago: Univ. of Illinois Press, 1970), 48.
2. Quoted in Eugen Hadamovsky, *Hitler kämpft um den Frieden Europas* (Munich: Zentralverlag der NSDAP, 1937), 166.
3. Heinz Kellermann, "Ende der Emanzipation?" *Der Morgen*: 9 (no. 3, August 1933), 174.
4. Quoted in Kellermann, 173.
5. Jacob R. Marcus, *The Rise and Destiny of the German Jew* (Cincinnati: Union of Am. Hebrew Congregations,1934), 2.
6. Kellermann, 174.
7. Heinrich Graetz, *Geschichte der Juden* (Leipzig: Verlag von Oskar Leiner, 1866), 4:1-3 passim.
8. "Martin Buber on Tasks of the Center for Jewish Adult Education," in Yitzhak Arad, Yisrael Gutman, and Avraham Margaliot, eds. *Documents on the Holocaust* (Yad Vashem, 1981), 51-52.
9. Quoted in Rivka Perlis, *Tenu'ot haNo'ar haHalutsiyot bePolin haKevushah* (Tel Aviv: Hakibbutz Hameuhad, 1987),140.
10. "Restauration oder Renaissance?" *Der Morgen*: 9 (no.7, 1934), 390-91.
11. In the first months of the Nazi occupation of Poland some non-Jewish Poles thought they were at a disadvantage because, unlike the Polish Jews, they did not have collective representation to plead their cause. See David Engel, *In the Shadow of Auschwitz: The Polish Government-in-Exile and the Jews, 1939-1942* (Chapel Hill: Univ. of North Carolina Press, 1987), 169.
12. For an account of how Jews in various countries came to experience the Nazi regime see David Engel "Holocaust," *YIVO Encyclopedia of Jews in Eastern Europe*, http://www.yivoinstute.org/publications/
13. For the text of Kovner's speech and a colleague's response see David Engel, *The Holocaust: The Third Reich and the Jews* (London: Longman, 2000),103. Also in Arad, *Documents on the Holocaust*, 433-438.
14. Quoted in Saul Friedländer, *Nazi Germany and the Jews* (New York: Harper Collins, 1997), 60.
15. Rózka Korczak, *Lehavot beEfer*(Merhavia: Moreshet,1965)50.
16. Quoted in Yael Peled (Margolin), *Krakov haYehudit 1939-1943* (Tel Aviv: Hakibbutz Hameuhad, 1993), 163.

**YITZCHAK MAIS, pp. 18-24.**

1. Michael Marrus, "Varieties of Jewish Resistance: Some Categories and Comparisons in Historiographical Perspective," in Yisrael Gutman, ed., *Major Changes Within the Jewish People in the Wake of the Holocaust: Ninth Yad Vashem Historical Conference, June 1993* (Jerusalem: Yad Vashem, 1996), 272-273. Regarding how Jewish Theology disregarded the Holocaust, see Emil L. Fackenheim, *God's Presence in History: Jewish Affirmations and Philosophical Reflections* (NY: Harper Torchbooks, 1972), 71. Regarding Sociology, see Zygmunt Bauman, *Modernity and the Holocaust* (London: Polity Press, 1989) ix, 10-11. For an opposing view see Hasia R. Diner, *Before The Holocaust: American Jews Confront Catastrophe 1945-1962* (Ann Arbor: Univ. of Michigan Press, 2004).
2. Regarding Jews as "...the perfect victims—weak, ineffectual, incapable of helping themselves," in Holocaust related films, including Steven Spielberg's *Schindler's List* see Judith E. Doneson, *The Holocaust in American Film*, (Syracuse: Syracuse Univ. Press, Second Ed. 2002), 203-215.
3. Marion A. Kaplan, *Between Dignity and Despair: Jewish Life in Nazi Germany* (New York: Oxford Univ. Press, 1998); see also Isaiah Trunk, *Jewish Responses to Nazi Persecution* (New York: Stein and Day, 1982), ix-xi, and Eva Fogelman, "On Blaming the Victim," this volume, 134.
4. Primo Levi, *The Drowned and the Saved* (London: Sphere Books, 1989), 122.

5. For a discussion of Holocaust museums and the issue of survivor culpability, see Yitzchak Mais, "Institutionalizing the Holocaust: Issues Related to the Establishment of Holocaust Memorial Centers," in *Remembering for the Future: Papers of the International Scholars' Conference* (Oxford: Pergamon Press: 2, 1988),1778-1789. A revised, popular version appeared as, "Institutionalizing the Holocaust" in *Midstream: 34* (no. 9, Dec. 1988), 16-20.
6. Werner Rings, *Life With the Enemy: Collaboration and Resistance in Hitler's Europe 1939-1945* (New York: Doubleday, 1982), 154, 162, 172, 189.
7. Yehuda Bauer, *They Chose Life: Jewish Resistance in the Holocaust* (New York: American Jewish Committee, 1973), 55-56.
8. The traditional perpetrator-driven periodization divides events as per the evolving anti-Jewish policies: 1933-39, legal exclusion; 1939-41, isolation and ghettoization; 1941-45, mass murder.
9. Marion Kaplan, *Between Dignity and Despair*, 33.
10. Avraham Barkai, *From Boycott to Annihilation: The Economic Struggle of German Jews, 1933-1943* (Hanover, NH: Univ. Press of New England, 1989), 98.
11. For a chronology of occupation, see David Engel, "Holocaust," *The YIVO Encyclopedia of Jews in Eastern Europe*, http://www.yivoinstitute.org/publications/
12. Lucy S. Dawidowicz, *The War Against the Jews, 1933-1945* (New York: Bantam Books, 1976), 327.
13. These earlier resettlements included: The forced relocation of Jews from smaller communities into larger ghettos, e.g., Lodz, Lublin, Warsaw, between 1939-1941; the July 1940 expulsion of 7,500 Jews from southern Germany to transit camps in France; the deportations of some 20,000 German and Austrian Jews to the Lodz Ghetto in November 1941, and over 35,000 Jews to the Minsk Ghetto from late 1941 onwards. In Czechoslovakia, the Nazis established "the model Jewish ghetto" at Terezin (Theresienstadt) in November 1941, to which almost all Jews from annexed Czech lands were deported.
14. Shalom Cholawsky notes that there were over sixty ghettos in the area of Belorussia with armed undergrounds, *Al Naharot Haniemen Vehadnieper* (Tel Aviv: Moreshet, 1982), 333-337; see also Shmuel Krakowski, *The War of the Doomed: Jewish Armed Resistance in Poland 1942-1944* (New York: Holmes and Meier, 1984), 161–234, and Dov Levin, *Fighting Back: Lithuanian Jewry's Armed Resistance to the Nazis, 1941-1945* (New York: Holmes and Meier, 1985).
15. See Filip Müller, *Eyewitness Auschwitz: Three Years in the Gas Chambers* (New York: Stein and Day, 1984), 70, 110-111.

**INTRODUCTION: SANCTIFYING LIFE AND GOD'S NAME, pp. 26-27.**

1. Ernst Simon, "Jewish Adult Education in Nazi Germany as Spiritual Resistance," *Leo Baeck Institute Yearbook*: 69 (1956).
2. Yisrael Gutman, "*Kiddush Ha-shem* and *Kiddush Ha-Hayim*," *Simon Wiesenthal Center Annual*: 1 (1977), 185-186.

**RABBI LEO BAECK, pp. 28-29.**
SOURCES
"Words of Consolation" in an attachment to a letter from the Association of Bavarian Jewish Communities (Verband Bayerischer Israelitischer Gemeinden), Munich, August 8, 1935. Central Archives for the History of the Jewish People (CAJHP) N 3/5. Translated from German by Ilona Moradof. English translation of "Yom Kippur prayer" in Michael Berenbaum, *A Promise to Remember: The Holocaust in the Words and Voices of Its Survivors* (Boston: Bullfinch Press, 2004), 9. German original in Leo Baeck Institute, New York.

JIZCHAK SCHWERSENZ, pp. 30-33.
SOURCE
Excerpts from Jizchak Schwersenz, *Machteret Chaluzim B'germania Hanazit* (Hakibutz Hameuchad Publishing House and Kibbutz Lohamei Hageta'ot, 1969), 55-57, 130-136. Translated from Hebrew by David Haber.

1. "The group viewed saving Jewish lives as a form of political resistance." Nathan Schwalb, Zionist emissary of the Hechalutz movement in Switzerland, is quoted as saying. "We're combating Hitler with every life we save!" in *Kaplan*, 212, 262 n. 28.

ADELA BAY, pp. 34-36.
SOURCE
Oral History of Adela Bay. Interview by Leonard Wacholder, 1977. Yaffa Eliach Collection donated by the Center for Holocaust Studies.

ZENIA MALECKI, p. 36.
SOURCE
Oral History of Zenia Malecki. Interview by Aviva Segall, March 14, 1986. Yaffa Eliach Collection donated by the Center for Holocaust Studies.

RABBI EPHRAIM OSHRY, p. 37.
SOURCE
Rabbi Ephraim Oshry, *Responsa from the Holocaust* (New York: Judaica Press, 1983), 19.

1. Rabbi Oshry (1914-2003) studied at the famed Slobodka Talmudic Academy in a suburb of Kovno. In New York he served as Rabbi of Beth Hamedrash Hagadol on the Lower East Side and Dean of Yeshiva Torah Ve-Emunah, a Jewish day school, in the Bronx.

MOSHE FLINKER, pp. 38-41.
SOURCE
Excerpts from *Young Moshe's Diary: The Spiritual Torment of A Jewish Boy in Nazi Europe* (Jerusalem: Yad Vashem, 1976). Reprinted with permission of the family of the late Moshe Flinker.

FRIEDL DICKER BRANDEIS, pp. 42-43.
SOURCE
Excerpts from Elena Makarova, *Friedl Dicker-Brandeis, Vienna 1898-Auschwitz 1944: The Artist Who Inspired the Children's Drawings of Terezin* (Los Angeles: Tallfellow/Every Picture Press in association with the Simon Wiesenthal Center/ Museum of Tolerance, 2001), 199-200, 211, 213. All quotes are from this source.

JANUSZ KORCZAK, pp. 44-45.
SOURCE
Excerpts from Janusz Korczak, *The Ghetto Years, 1939-1942.* (Ghetto Fighters' House and Hakibbutz Hameuchad Publishing House, 1980), 121, 122, 123, 138.
Oral History of Erwin Baum. Interview by Naomi Rappaport, January 18, 1994, for the Museum of Jewish Heritage – A Living Memorial to the Holocaust, and United States Holocaust Memorial Museum, Record Group 50, Oral History, Interview with Froim Erwin Baum, RG-50.030*0016.

RABBI LEIB GELIEBTER, pp. 46-48.
SOURCE
Excerpts from the ethical will and report on the destruction of the Jewish community of Czestochowa by Rabbi Leib

Geliebter, Czestochowa, Poland, March 28, 1943. Collection of Dr. Joseph Geliebter. Translated from Yiddish by Sara Silber.

1. The reference is to the Talmudic discussion in Bava Batra 15a, in which Rabbi Simon says that Moses cried when he wrote the final eight verses of the Torah that describe his death outside the Promised Land.

INTRODUCTION: RECORDING THE TRUTH, TELLING THE WORLD, pp. 50-51.
1. From the last will and testament of Dawid Graber, age 19, August 19, 1942, buried with Oyneg Shabbes archive in Warsaw. "I would love to live to see the moment in which the great treasure will be dug up and scream the truth at the world. So the world may know all." Exhibition catalog, *Scream the Truth at the World* (New York: Museum of Jewish-Heritage – A Living Memorial to the Holocaust, 2001), 77.

EMANUEL RINGELBLUM, pp. 52-55.
SOURCES
Excerpts from "E. Ringelblum, O.S. [Oneg Shabbath]," *To Live With Honor and Die With Honor! Selected Documents from the Warsaw Ghetto Underground Archives,* edited and annotated by Joseph Kermish (Jerusalem: Yad Vashem, 1986), 2-21.
Poem *Szwonki* (*Doorbells*) by Wladyslaw Szlengel, in Polish. Jewish Historical Institute, Warsaw (Varia Collection).

ART OF THE HOLOCAUST, pp. 56-61.
1. All quotes from Olomucki in *The Last Expression: Art & Auschwitz* Exhibition Catalog (Evanston: Block Museum of Art and Northwestern Univ. Press, 2002).
2. Leo Haas, "The Affair of the Painters of Terezin," Zdenek Ehrmann, *Terezin* (Prague: Council of Jewish Communities in the Czech Lands, 1965), 158.
3. Shachar Leven, "The Pen and the Sword: Jewish Artist and Partisan, Alexander Bogen," *Yad Vashem Magazine:* 30 (Spring 2003), 10-11.
4. Arnold Daghani, *The Grave Is in the Cherry Orchard* (London: Eden Press, 1961), 100.

UNDERGROUND NEWSPAPERS, pp. 62-65.
SOURCES
Excerpts from *Dos Fraye Vort*, May 23, 1942. Archives at YIVO Institute for Jewish Research, New York (RG 1400–P Series–Folder 6). Translated from Yiddish by Miriam Kreiter.
Excerpts from *Jeune Combat*, No. 5, September 4, 1943. Yad Vashem Archives (0.9/232). Translated from French by Gigi Aron, Nancy Fisher, and Renée Weiner.
Excerpts from *Hechalutz Halochem*, October 8, 1943. Yad Vashem Archives (0.6/711). Translated from Polish by Dr. Salomea Kape and Miriam Kreiter.
Excerpts from *Nitzotz*, Hanukkah 1944, Yad Vashem Archives (M.1P/24). Translated from Hebrew by Bonnie Gurewitsch.

1. Dawidowicz, 269-270.
2. Renée Poznanski, "The Geopolitics of Jewish Resistance in France," *Holocaust and Genocide Studies:* 15 (no. 2, Fall 2001), 245-259.
3. *Eclaireurs Israélites de France* (the Jewish Scouts): Some joined maquis forces as L'Armée Juive (the Jewish Army); others escaped over the Pyrenees to Spain, en route to Palestine [see Pyrenees essay p. 94].
4. Rabbis were allowed freedom of movement and entry to internment camps as chaplains. Rabbi Mendel Langer, who visited Les Milles and other camps, was guillotined by Vichy authorities on July 23, 1943, after he was caught with a

suitcase full of explosives. Renée Poznanski, *Jews in France During World War II* (Hanover, NH: Brandeis Univ. Press and US Holocaust Memorial Museum, 2001) 187, 419.

PHOTOGRAPHING THE HOLOCAUST, 66-73.
1. Quoted in Michael Berenbaum, *The World Must Know: The History of the Holocaust as told in the United States Holocaust Memorial Museum* (Boston: Little, Brown and Company, 1993), 92.

BRONIA K., 74-76.
SOURCE
Excerpts from the Oral History of Bronia K. Fortunoff Video Archive for Holocaust Testimonies. Yale Univ. Library.

INTRODUCTION: HELPING, HIDING, ESCAPING, pp. 78-79.
1. Leo Baeck, "A People Stands Before Its God," Eric H. Boehm, *We Survived: Fourteen Histories of the Hidden and Hunted of Nazi Germany* (Santa Barbara: ABC-Clio Information Services, 1985), 287.
2. "Pracovna Skupina (Working Group)," *Encyclopedia of the Holocaust* (New York: Macmillan, 1990), 1184.
3. Leni Yahil, *The Holocaust: The Fate of European Jewry* (New York: Oxford Univ. Press, 1990), 496.
4. Meir Michaelis, *Mussolini and the Jews* (Oxford: Clarendon Press, 1978), 364, 388.
5. Bob Moore, *Victims & Survivors: Nazi Persecution of the Jews in the Netherlands 1940-1945* (London: Arnold, 1997), 179.

MORDECHAI TENENBAUM, pp. 80-85.
SOURCE
Excerpts from a letter from Mordechai Tenenbaum to comrades in the Land of Israel, April 1943. Yad Vashem Archives (M.11/9). Translated from Hebrew by David Haber.

1. Slogan from Abba Kovner's manifesto, which he read at the Hechalutz meeting on December 31, 1941, calling for armed resistance in the Vilna Ghetto. See endnote 13 in David Engel's essay in this volume.
2. Wladyslaw Sikorski (1881-1943), a Polish general who became prime minister of the Polish government-in-exile, was commander in chief of the resistance movement in Poland and Polish forces that fought with the Allies.

TZIPPORA BIRMAN, pp. 86-88.
SOURCE
Excerpts from a letter written by Tzippora Birman. Appendix to Bronia Klibanski, "The Underground Archives of the Bialystok Ghetto (Founded by Mersik and Tenenbaum)," *Yad Vashem Studies: 2* (1975), 304-325.

1. Anton Schmid (1900-1942), a German soldier who worked with the Jewish underground, was arrested and executed by a military court in January 1942. Schmid was honored by Yad Vashem as a Righteous Among the Nations.

HENRYKA LAZOWERT, p. 89.
SOURCE
Henryka Lazowert, "The Little Smuggler," Emanuel Ringelblum, *Polish-Jewish Relations During the Second World War*, edited and annotated by Joseph Kermish and Shmuel Krakowski (New York: Howard Fertig, 1976), 148.

RABBI MICHAEL DOV WEISSMANDEL & GISI FLEISCHMANN
pp. 90-93.
SOURCES
Letter written by Michael Dov Weissmandel, January 15,

1945. Yad Vashem Archives (M.20/93). Translated from Hebrew by Bonnie Gurewitsch.
Excerpts from a letter written by Gisi Fleischmann, October 17, 1943. Moreshet – The Anielevich Memorial Holocaust Study and Research Center, Israel (D.1.1263). Translated from German by Ilona Moradof.

1. Yehuda Bauer, *History of the Holocaust* (New York: Franklin Watts, 1982), 310-312.
2. A transport to Auschwitz was sent from Slovakia on Yom Kippur, October, 1942, in spite of negotiations and bribery.
3. Reference to Zivia Lubetkin, resistance leader and a founder of the JFO in the Warsaw Ghetto.

YITZCHAK ZAKKAI, pp. 94-97.
SOURCE
Excerpts from Yitzchak Zakkai, *Ma'avar Hapyrenayim* (Crossing the Pyrenees) (Israel: Kvutzat Be'erot Yitzchak, 1976). Translated from Hebrew by David Haber.

ELLEN LEWINSKY ARNDT & RUTH ARNDT GUMPEL, pp. 98-101.
SOURCES
Interviews with Ellen Lewinsky Arndt by Barbara Lovenheim, 1998-2001, Rochester, NY, as research for *Survival in the Shadows: Seven Jews Hidden in Hitler's Berlin* (Rochester, NY: Center for Holocaust Awareness and Information, 2002). Unpublished manuscript by Ruth Arndt Gumpel, 1992. Collection of Ruth Arndt Gumpel.

1. The Factory *Aktion* occurred on February 28, 1943. The Nazis rounded up 7,000 Jewish workers and their families in Berlin; 4,000 escaped the raid. An estimated 1,200 to 1,400 survived in hiding. See Lovenheim, 68-70, 224; and Kaplan, 202.
2. The Baum Group, an underground anti-Nazi organization led by Herbert and Marianne Baum, was the largest German-Jewish resistance group. Formed in Berlin in 1936, members were primarily young Jewish Communists and Zionists. In May 1942 they blew up an anti-Communist exhibition. Most were hunted down and executed, including Ellen's friend Heinz Birnbaum; 500 other German Jews were shot and deported in reprisal. Only a few members survived the war. Kaplan, 214-15; Eric Brothers, "On the Anti-Fascist Resistance of German Jews," *Leo Baeck Institute Yearbook* (1987), 369-382.

SHULAMIT LACK, pp. 102-104.
SOURCE
Oral History of Shulamit Lack. Interview by Aviva Segall, July 9, 1984. Yaffa Eliach Collection donated by the Center for Holocaust Studies.

1. An underground workshop established and run by Zionist youth movements in Budapest forged a variety of 85 different documents, using 150 different stamps. They were produced singly, in the dozens, hundreds, or thousands, as needed. The workshop was moved at least 16 times in 1944, before it was demolished by the Hungarian Arrow Cross just prior to the Soviet occupation of Budapest. The documents were used by tens of thousands of people. Yahil, 644.

INTRODUCTION: "TO GET KILLED OR TO KILL," pp. 106-107.
1. Cited in Joseph Walk, "Jewish Education Under the Nazis," *Jewish Resistance During the Holocaust: Proceedings of the Conference on Manifestations of Jewish Resistance, Jerusalem, April 7-11, 1968* (Jerusalem: Yad Vashem, 1971), 129.
2. Isaiah Trunk, *Judenrat: The Jewish Councils in Eastern Europe Under Nazi Occupation* (NY: Macmillan, 1972), 465-466.

3. Yisrael Gutman, *Anashim v'Efer b'Auschwitz (Smoke and Ashes: The Story of Auschwitz-Birkenau)* (Sifri'at Po'alim, 1957), 153-154; Oral History of Henry Fuchs. Interview by Aviva Segall, 1986. Yaffa Eliach Collection donated by the Center for Holocaust Studies, and Jean Claude Pressac, *Auschwitz: Technique and Operation of the Gas Chambers* (New York: Beate Klarsfeld Foundation, 1989), 498.

4. Shalom Yoran, *The Defiant: A Triumphant Tale of Vengeance and Survival* (New York: St. Martin's Press, 1986), 81.

ABBA KOVNER, pp. 108-113.
SOURCE
Excerpts from Abba Kovner, *A Missive to Hashomer-Hatza'ir Partisans* (Tel Aviv: Moreshet, 2002). Translated by Abba Kovner into Hebrew from the Yiddish original. Translated from Hebrew by Ariel Hurwitz.

1. Quoted in Bauer, *History of the Holocaust*, 250.
2. Jurgis was the underground name of Yisrael Zieman (Heinrich Ziemanas), the Party Commissar & First Secretary of the Communist Party in the Vilna district. He was also the Commander of the Soviet-Lithuanian undergrounds in the city and forests of southern Lithuania. Before the war, he was a teacher in the Shalom Aleichem High School in Kovno. He concealed his Jewish identity in the forest.
3. The first group of Jews to leave Vilna with Josef Glazman was based in the Narocz forest. They were unable to sustain themselves as independent, Jewish units. All but one were killed in battle with the Germans.
4. It is interesting that Kovner's estimate of the number of Jewish dead is so accurate, prior to any official statistical tabulation. The larger number refers to other groups murdered directly by the Nazis, including Roma and Slavs.

TUVIA BIELSKI, pp. 114-119.
SOURCE
Excerpts from Tuvia Bielski, *"Yehudei Ya'ar," Sefer Milchamot Hageta'ot* edited by Yitzchak Zuckerman and Moshe Basuk (Hakibutz Hameuchad Publishing House Ltd. and Kibbutz Lohamei Hagetaot, 1954), 637-648. Translated from Hebrew by David Haber.

1. See Joshua 6:18 and chapter 7. The Biblical Achan looted the destroyed city of Jericho. The entire people of Israel were punished for his action; Achan was stoned to death.

CHAYA PALEVSKY, pp. 120-123.
SOURCE
Oral History of Chaya Palevsky. Interview by Bonnie Gurewitsch, May 3, 2000, for the Museum of Jewish Heritage – A Living Memorial to the Holocaust.

JACOB GUTFREUND, pp. 124-125.
SOURCE
Excerpts from Jacob Gutfreind (Gutfreund), "Jewish Resistance in Belgium," *They Fought Back: The Story of the Jewish Resistance in Nazi Europe*, edited by Yuri Suhl (New York: Crown Publishers, Inc., 1967), 304-311. Reprinted with permission of Beverly Spector.

1. Leni Yahil notes that altogether about 4,000 Jewish children were saved by CDJ and other groups. Yahil, 496.

REBELLION IN THE GHETTOS, pp.126-129.
SOURCES
Letter from Mordechai Anielewicz edited by Yitzchak Zuckerman ("Antek"), *A Surplus of Memory: Chronicle of the Warsaw Ghetto Uprising*. Translated and edited by Barbara Harshav (Berkeley: Univ. of Calif. Press, 1993), 357.
Aaron Brandes, *"Hamachteret B'Bendin"* (The Underground in Bedzin), and Liber Brenner, *"Im Neshek Bayad"* (With Arms in Hand), *Sefer Milchamot Hageta'ot*, 338-342; 333-337. Translated from Hebrew by Bonnie Gurewitsch.

DEATH CAMP UPRISINGS, pp. 130-133.
SOURCES
Excerpts from "Testimony of Alexander Pechersky," Miriam Novitch, *Sobibor: Martyrdom and Revolt* (New York: Holocaust Library, 1980), 89-99.
Oral History of Richard Glazar. Interview by Bonnie Gurewitsch, October 26, 1981. Yaffa Eliach Collection donated by the Center for Holocaust Studies.
Oral History of Noach Zabludovits. USC Shoah Foundation Institute for Visual History and Education, Interview Code 26035, January 12, 1997. Translated from Hebrew by Bonnie Gurewitsch.

1. Yitzhak Arad, *Belzec, Sobibor, Treblinka: The Operation Reinhard Death Camps* (Bloomington: Univ. of Indiana Press, 1987), 299.
2. See endnote number 3, "To Get Killed or To Kill."

EVA FOGELMAN pp. 134-137.
1. Susan Sontag, *On Photography* (New York: Farrar, Straus, and Giroux, 1973), 20.
2. Bruno Bettelheim, "The Ignored Lesson of Anne Frank," *Harper's Magazine* (November 1960), 45-50.
3. Bettelheim, "Individual and Mass Behavior in Extreme Situations," *Journal of Abnormal and Social Psychology*: 38 (October 1943), 417-452.
4. Bettelheim, *Individual and Mass Behavior*, 452.
5. Judith E. Doneson, *The Holocaust in American Film* (Philadelphia: The Jewish Publication Society, 1987), 79.
6. Menachem Friedman, "The Haredim and the Holocaust," *Jerusalem Quarterly*: 53 (1987), 86-114; see also Dina Porat, "Amalek's Accomplices: Blaming Zionism for the Holocaust —Anti-Zionist Ultra-Orthodoxy in Israel During the 1980s," *Journal of Contemporary History*: 27 (1992), 695-729.
7. Hanna Yablonka, *Survivors of the Holocaust: Israel After the War* (New York: New York Univ. Press, 1992), 60.
8. Arnold Foster, *Square One* (NY: Donald I. Fine, 1992), 228.
9. Abba Kovner video testimony (New York: National Jewish Archive of Broadcasting of the Jewish Museum: NJAB E28, May 4, 1961). This testimony is also available at the United States Holocaust Memorial Museum, Washington, D.C. and the Israel State Archive, Jerusalem.
10. Hanna Yablonka, *The State of Israel vs. Adolph Eichmann* (New York: Schocken Books, 2004), 223-224.
11. Yablonka, *The State of Israel*, 226.
12. Yablonka, *The State of Israel*, 211.
13. Raul Hilberg, *The Destruction of European Jews* (Chicago: Quadrangle Books, 1961), V, 668-669.
14. Hanna Arendt, *Eichmann in Jerusalem: A Report on the Banality of Evil* (New York: Viking Press, 1963).
15. Saul Friedländer, "On the Possibility of the Holocaust: An approach to an Historical Synthesis" in Yehuda Bauer and Nathan Rotenstreich, eds. *The Holocaust as Historical Experience* (New York, Holmes and Meier, 1981), 1-21; see also Aharon Weiss, "Jewish Leadership in Occupied Poland—Postures and Attitudes," *Yad Vashem Studies*: 12 (1977), 355-365.
16. Shapira Avraham (Ed.) *The Seventh Day: Soldier's Talk About Six Day War* (NY: Charles Scribner's and Son, 1970), 181.

# INDEX

# CREDITS

Cover: Archives of the YIVO Institute for Jewish Research, New York; p. 3: USHMM, courtesy of Shulamith Posner-Mansbach; p. 6: USHMM, gift of Eliezer Zilber; p. 17: German Historical Museum, Berlin (© 2006 Artists Rights Society (ARS), New York/VG Bild-Kunst, Bonn); p. 21: Copyright ©1933 by The New York Times Co. Reprinted with permission; p. 25: Ghetto Fighters' House, Israel; p. 29: Bildarchiv Abraham Pisarek, Berlin; p. 31: USHMM, courtesy of Jizchak Schwersenz; p. 32: Jewish Museum Berlin, gift of Jizchak Schwersenz; p. 35: Collection of Rebecca Wacholder; p. 36: Gift of Henny Durmashkin Gurko; p. 37 (top): Photographer: Zvi Kadushin, ©Beth Hatefutsoth, Photo Archive, Tel Aviv; (center): Collection of the Oshry family, photography by Alana Cole-Faber; p. 39 (left and right): Collection of the Family of the Late Moshe Flinker; p. 43 (left): Jewish Museum in Prague (©Lily Edna Amit); p. 43 (right): Jewish Museum in Prague; p. 45: Ghetto Fighters' House, Israel; pp. 47-48: Rabbi Leib Geliebter Memorial Foundation; p. 49: Gift of Herman and Gerda Korngold; pp. 53-55: Ringelblum Archive, Jewish Historical Institute, Warsaw, Poland; p. 57: Musée d'Histoire Contemporaine – BDIC, Paris; pp. 58-59: Leo Baeck Institute, New York (©2006 Artists Rights Society (ARS), New York/VG Bild-Kunst, Bonn); p. 60 (top): Archives of the YIVO Institute for Jewish Research, New York (©Arnold Daghani Estate); p. 60 (bottom): USHMM, The Abraham and Ruth Goldfarb Family Acquisition Fund; p. 61 (top): Permanent Loan from Thomas Fritta-Haas to the Jewish Museum Berlin (©Thomas Fritta-Haas); p. 61 (bottom): Gift of Herman and Gerda Korngold; p. 62: Archives of the YIVO Institute for Jewish Research, New York; pp. 63-65: Yad Vashem Photo Archives; p. 67 (top): USHMM, gift of George Kadish; p. 67 (bottom): ©Archive of Modern Conflict/ Chris Boot; p. 68 (top and bottom): Ghetto Fighters' House, Israel; p. 69: ©Archive of Modern Conflict/ Chris Boot; p. 70 (top): USHMM, gift of Eliezer Zilber; p. 70 (bottom): Photographer: Zvi Kadushin, ©Beth Hatefutsoth, Photo Archive, Tel Aviv; p. 71: USHMM, gift of George Kadish; p. 72: Collection of Faye Schulman; p. 73: State Museum of Auschwitz – Birkenau; p. 75: Ghetto Fighters' House, Israel; p. 76: Ghetto Fighters' House, Israel; p. 77: Ringelblum Archive, Jewish Historical Institute, Warsaw, Poland; pp. 81, 82, 85, 87, 88: Ghetto Fighters' House, Israel; p. 89: Ringelblum Archive, Jewish Historical Institute, Warsaw, Poland; p. 91: Yad Vashem Photo Archives; p. 93: Yad Vashem Photo Archives; p. 95: Collection of Felix Stahl; p. 96: Ghetto Fighters' House, Israel; p. 97: Collection of Felix Stahl; pp. 99-100: Collection of Ellen and Erich Arndt; p. 101: Collection of Ruth Gumpel; p. 103: Collection of Shulamit Lack; p. 105: USHMM, The Abraham and Ruth Goldfarb Family Acquisition Fund; pp. 109-110: Moreshet – The Mordechai Anielevich Memorial Holocaust Study and Research Center; p. 113: Ghetto Fighters' House, Israel; p. 115 (three photos on the left): Ghetto Fighters' House, Israel; p. 115 (photo on the right): Collection of the Aron Bell Family; p. 116: Ghetto Fighters' House, Israel; p. 121 (left and right): Collection of Chaya Palevsky; p. 122: Ghetto Fighters' House, Israel; p. 125: Jewish Museum of Belgium; p. 127 (lower left): Ghetto Fighters' House, Israel; p. 127 (upper right): USHMM, courtesy of Benjamin & Hanka Schlesinger; p. 129: USHMM, courtesy of Leah Hammerstein Silverstein; p. 131: Ghetto Fighters' House, Israel; p. 132: National Archives Prague, Richard Glazar Collection, Inventory number 12, Box 1; p. 133: USHMM, courtesy of Yad Vashem; Back cover: Photographer: Zvi Kadushin, ©Beth Hatefutsoth, Photo Archive, Tel Aviv.

# ACKNOWLEDGEMENTS

The following institutions have lent artifacts and other materials for the exhibition and films: American Jewish Joint Distribution Committee Photo Archives, New York; Anne Frank Fonds, Switzerland; Anne Frank Stichting, Amsterdam, Holland; Archives at Kibbutz Hazorea, Israel; Beth Hatefutsoth, Tel Aviv, Israel; Beit Theresienstadt Museum, Israel; Belarusian State Museum of the History of the Great Patriotic War; Bildarchiv Abraham Pisarek, Berlin, Germany; Bundesarchiv, Germany; Central Zionist Archives, Israel; Fortunoff Video Archive for Holocaust Testimonies, Yale University; Franklin D. Roosevelt Presidential Library; German National Library, Frankfurt, Germany; German Resistance Memorial Center, Berlin, Germany; Getty Images; Ghetto Fighters' House, Israel; Great Projects Film Co., Inc.; Historical Institute of the Resistance and Contemporary History, Savona, Italy; Historical Museum of Warsaw, Poland; Holocaust Museum Houston; Institut für Zeitungsforschung, Dortmund, Germany; Jasenovac Memorial Site, Croatia; Jewish Historical Institute, Warsaw, Poland; Jewish Historical Museum, Belgrade, Serbia; Jewish History and Culture Museum of Belarus; Jewish Museum Berlin, Germany; Jewish Museum in Prague, Czech Republic; Jewish Museum of Belgium; Jewish Museum of Deportation and Resistance – Mechelen, Belgium; Jewish Museum of Greece; Jewish Partisan Educational Foundation; League of Nations Archives, UNOG Library, Geneva, Switzerland; Leo Baeck Institute, New York; Los Angeles Museum of the Holocaust; Maria Austria Institute, Holland; Mémorial de la Shoah/CDJC, France; Moreshet – The Mordechai Anielevich Memorial Holocaust Study and Research Center, Israel; National Archives Prague, Czech Republic; National Council of Jewish Film; Nederlands Fotomuseum, Holland; Nederlands Instituut voor Oorlogsdocumentatie, Holland; Russian Jewish Congress, Museum of the Holocaust; Russian Research and Educational Holocaust Center; State Museum of Auschwitz – Birkenau, Poland; The Montreal Holocaust Memorial Centre, Canada; The Warsaw Rising Museum, Poland; United States Holocaust Memorial Museum; University of Minnesota Archives; University of Southern California Shoah Foundation Institute for Visual History and Education; U.S. National Archives and Records Administration; Vancouver Holocaust Education Centre, Canada; Yad Vashem Archives and Museum, Israel; YIVO Institute for Jewish Research, New York.